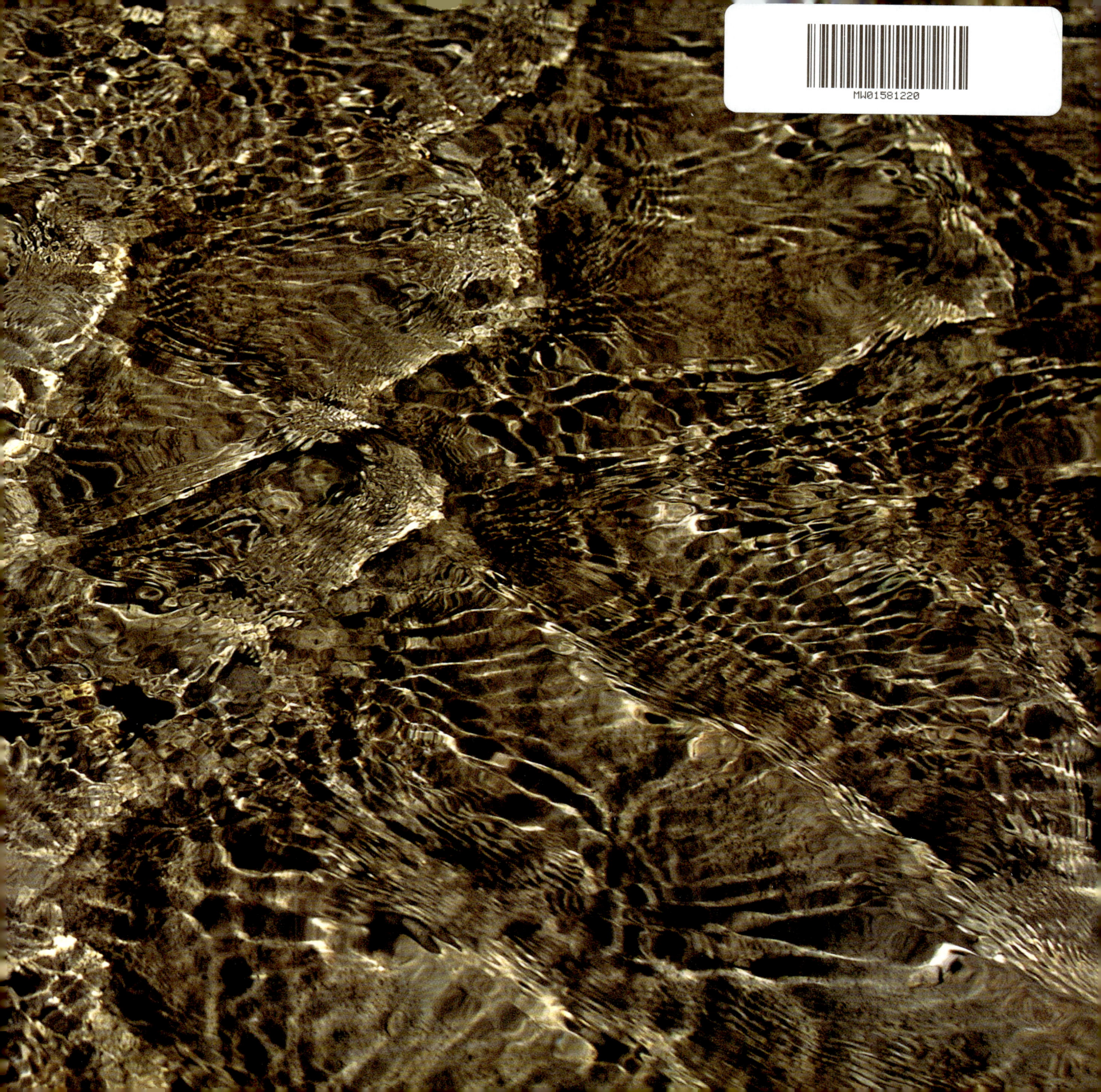

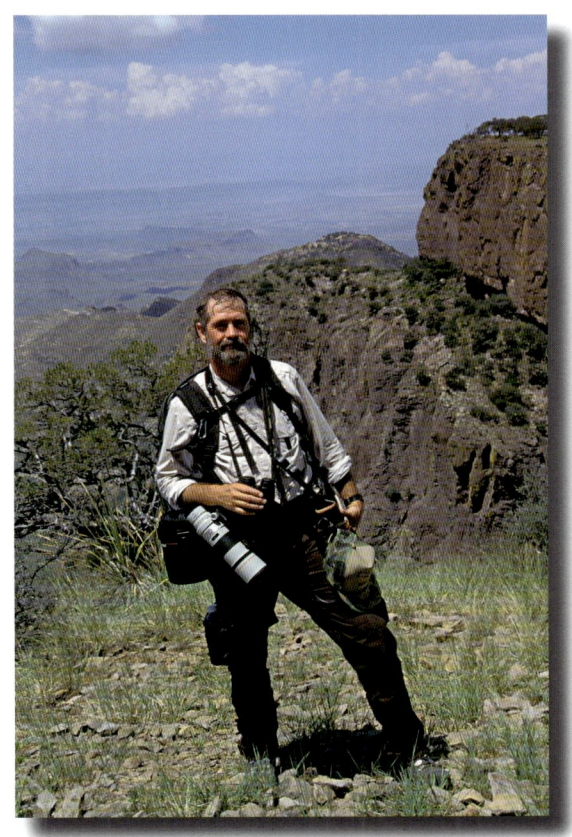

Greg Lasley in Big Bend, 1998

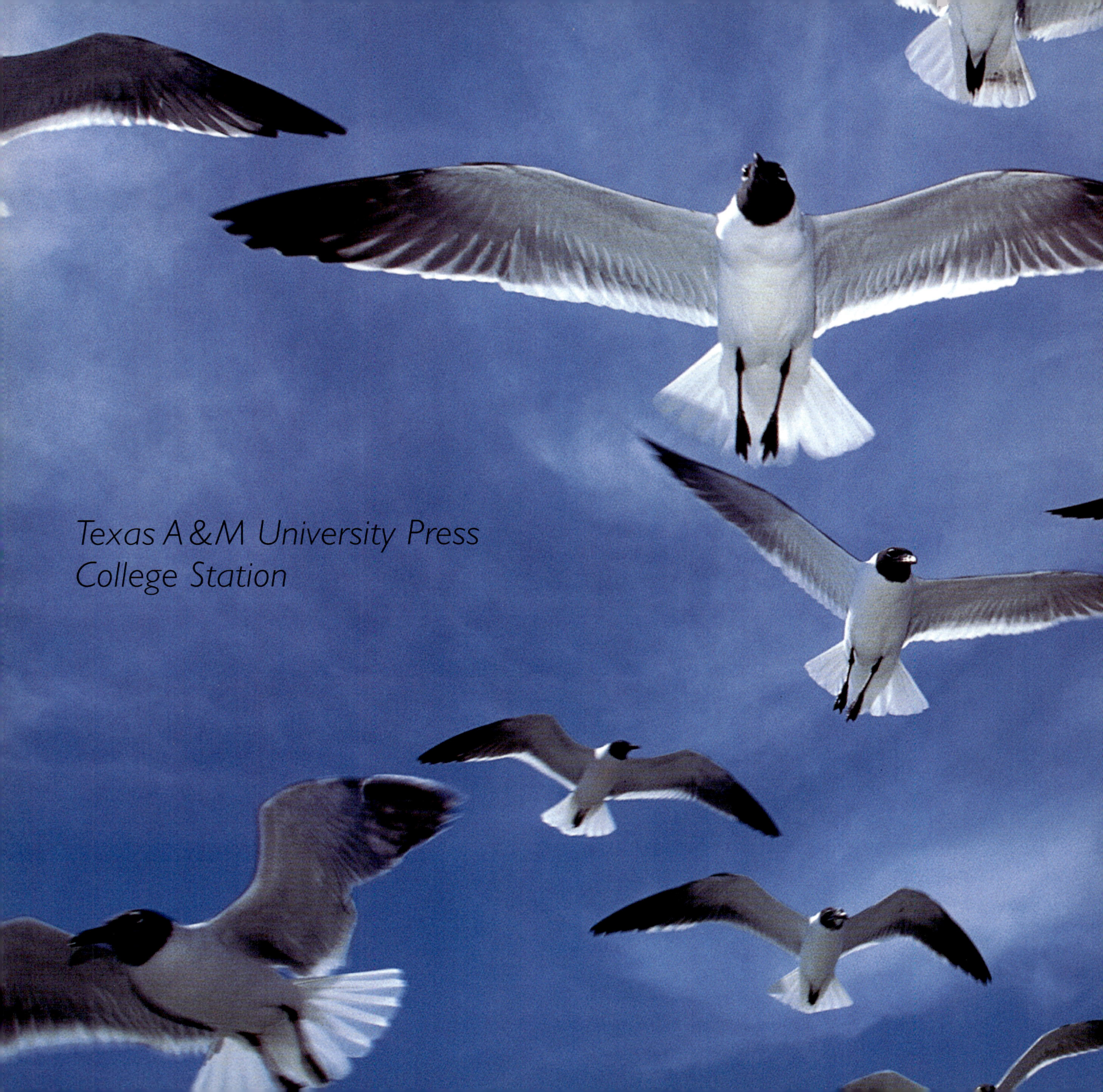

Texas A&M University Press
College Station

Greg Lasley's Texas Wildlife Portraits

Introduction by John and Gloria Tveten

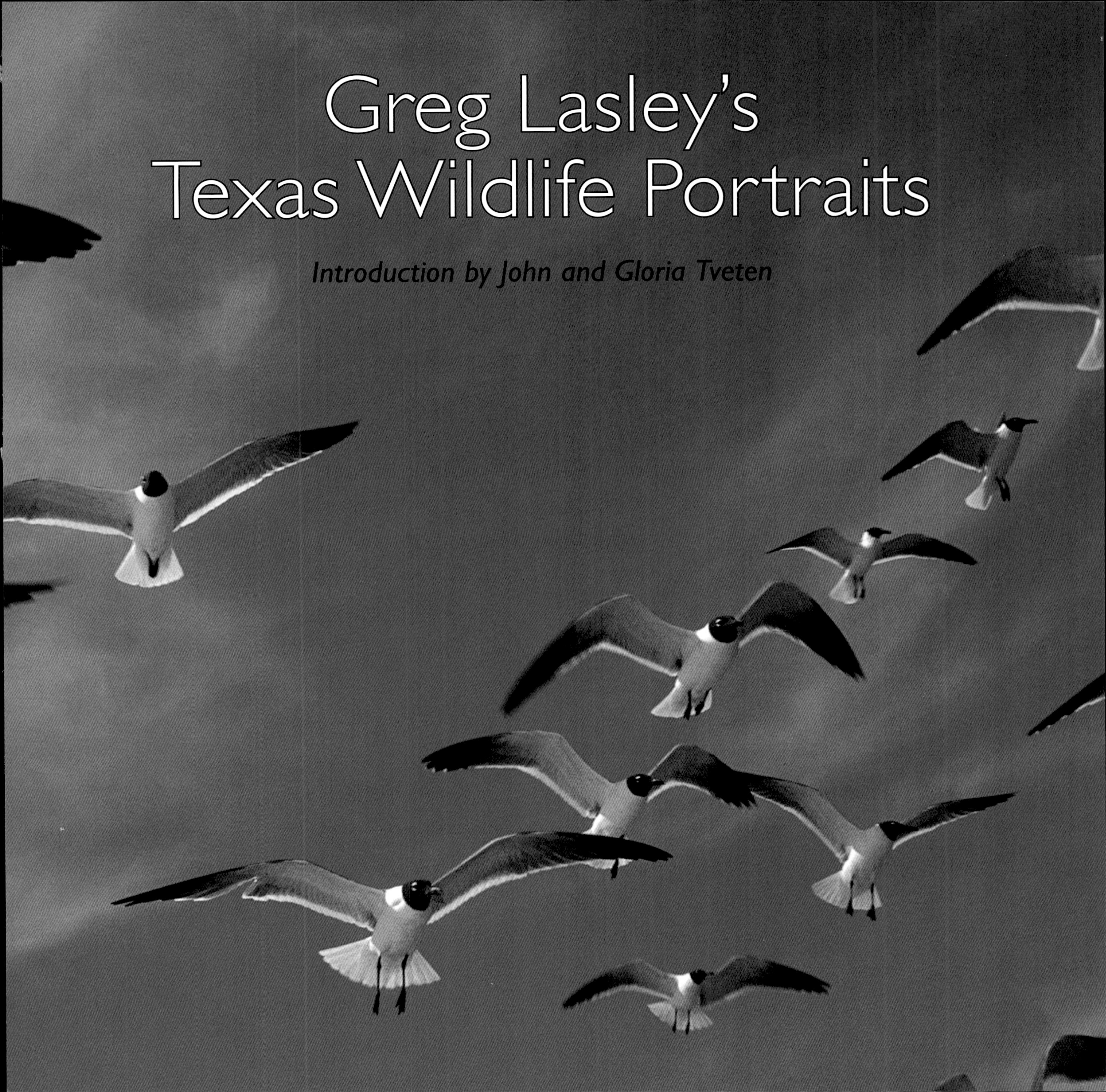

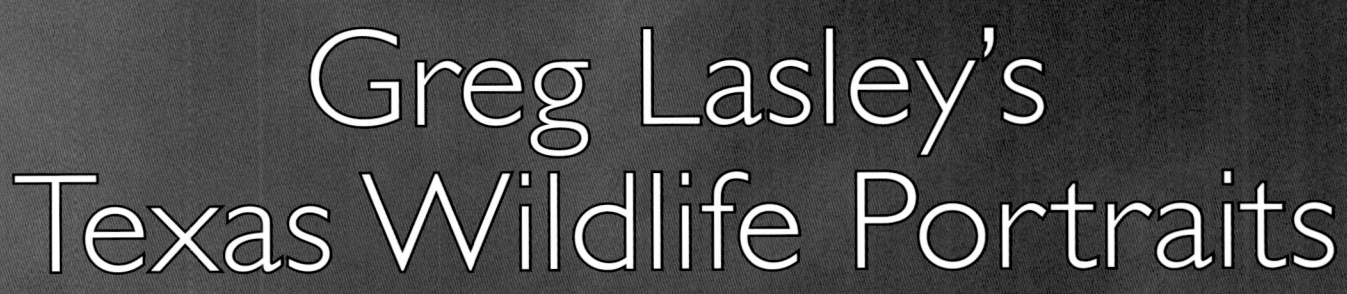

*Endpapers: Water flowing over limestone in a shallow **Hill Country** stream at Lost Maples State Natural Area, Bandera County.*

Page 1: Greg Lasley at the South Rim, Big Bend National Park, Texas, in August 1998. Photo by Steve Bentsen.

*Title page: The most common gull species along the Texas coast is the **Laughing Gull**, so called because its vocalizations are somewhat suggestive of human laughter. This gull stays in Texas all year and is hard to miss at any coastal location. The group of Laughing Gulls in this image was following the ferry between Galveston and Port Bolivar in Galveston County on a spring day.*

*Right: A wide variety of rodents may be found across Texas. One of the most common throughout the state is the **Hispid Cotton Rat**. It occurs in many habitats such as overgrown pastures and fence rows, abandoned farm buildings, and old woodpiles. This rat was munching on some sunflower seeds that had spilled from a bird feeder in Starr County in far South Texas.*

NUMBER FORTY-TWO:
LOUISE LINDSEY MERRICK
NATURAL ENVIRONMENT SERIES

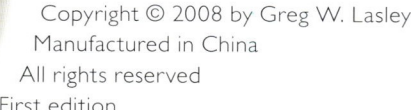

Copyright © 2008 by Greg W. Lasley
Manufactured in China
All rights reserved
First edition

This paper meets the requirements of ANSI/NISO Z39.48-1992 (Permanence of Paper). Binding materials have been chosen for durability.
∞

Library of Congress
Cataloging-in-Publication Data

Lasley, Greg.
Greg Lasley's Texas wildlife portraits / By Greg Lasley.
   p. cm. — (Louise Lindsey Merrick natural environment series ; no. 42)
Includes index.
ISBN-13: 978-1-60344-057-8 (cloth : alk. paper)
ISBN-10: 1-60344-057-7 (cloth : alk. paper)
1. Wildlife photography—Texas.
2. Zoology—Texas. I. Title.
TR729.W54L37 2008
779'.3209764—dc22
                2007049872

This book is lovingly dedicated to my wife, Cheryl Ann Johnson.
Her love, companionship, and positive support of my photography continue to sustain me in more ways than I can possibly describe.

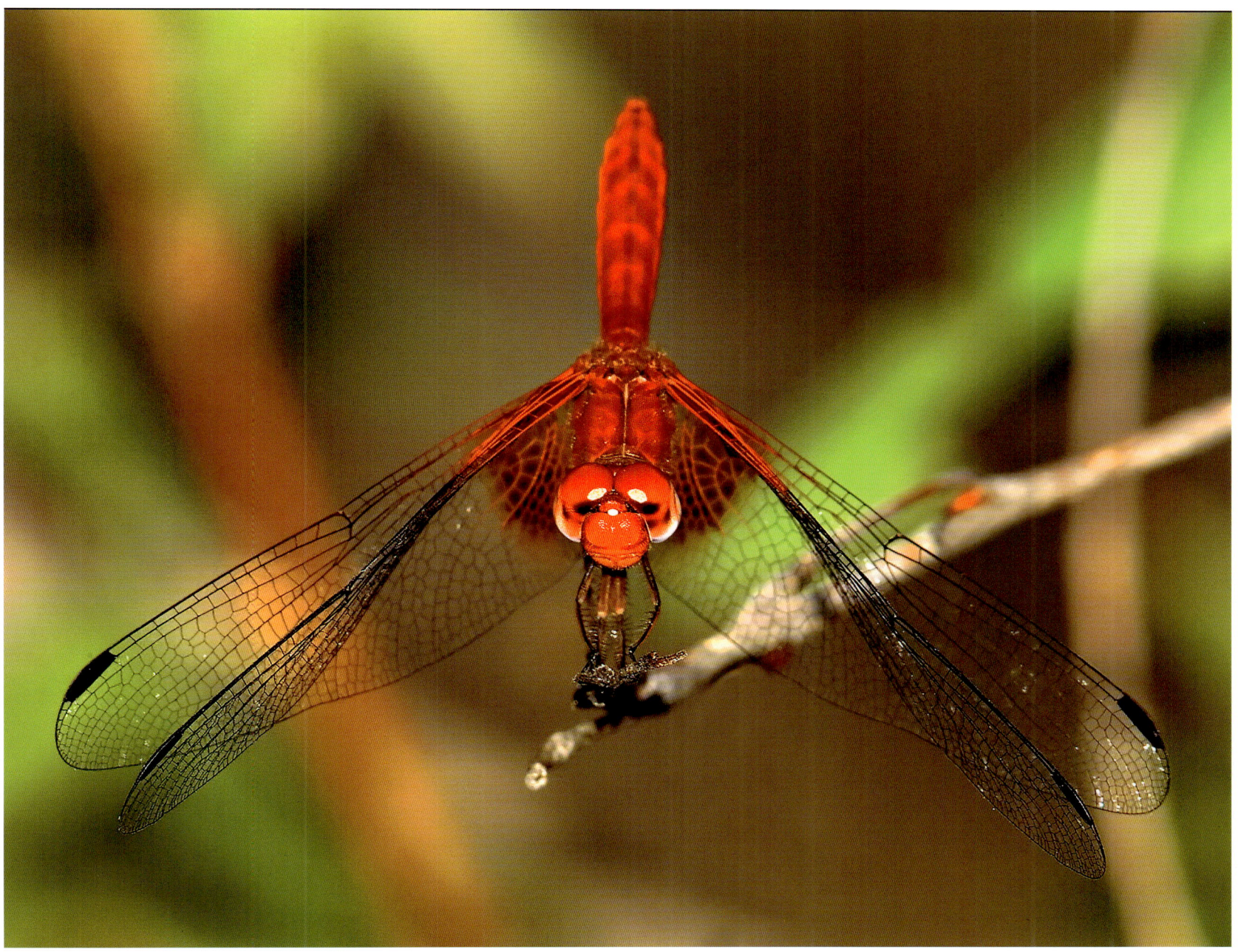

The **Mayan Setwing** is only known from a few spots within the United States, but it may also be found in parts of Central America. There are several species of red dragonflies in Texas and the United States, but the Mayan Setwing is the rarest. This brilliant male was perched on the edge of a small stream in a canyon on Big Bend Ranch State Park in Presidio County as it guarded its area against intrusions by other male setwings.

Contents

Introduction, by John and Gloria Tveten 7

Photographer's Comments 27

Acknowledgments 123

Wildlife Photo Index 124

Index 128

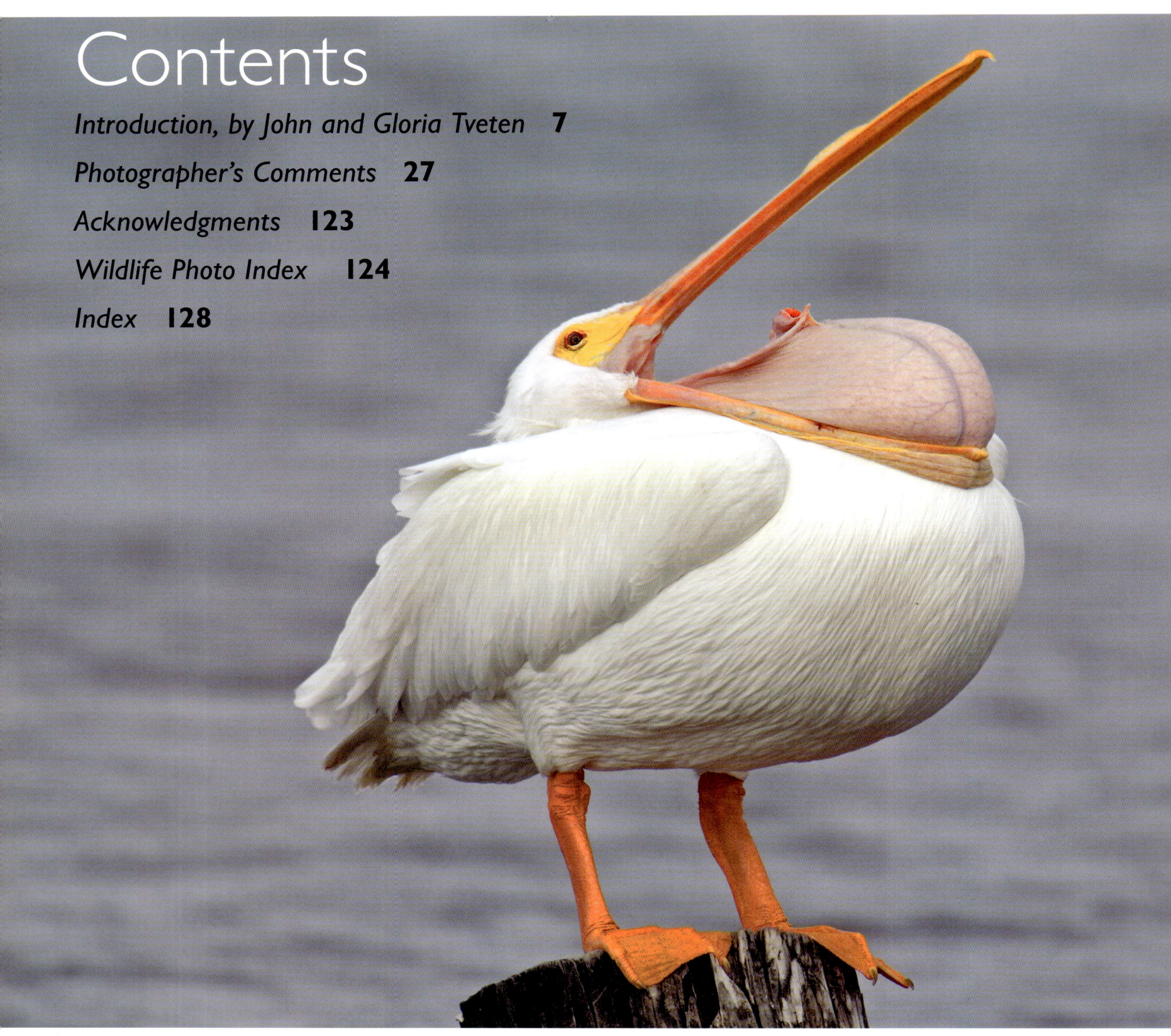

Introduction

BY JOHN & GLORIA TVETEN
with captions by Greg Lasley

American White Pelicans *are common winter residents of the Texas coast, and a number of them remain to breed in the summer as well. This bird was resting on a pier along the Texas City Dike in Galveston County. While I was watching, the pelican yawned and, in doing so, turned its pouch inside out against its chest to give me a rather unusual photo opportunity.*

SEVERAL YEARS AGO, after six months of intensive photography in the Valley Land Fund Wildlife Photo Contest, a few of the contestants gathered at Greg Lasley's home in Austin, Texas, to renew old friendships and review each other's prize-winning color slides. It proved to be a wonderful evening filled with camaraderie born of common interests and exhausting days afield, but it was extremely educational as well. As we sat on the deck in the cool of the evening and listened to Greg describe his techniques and the effort that went into each and every image, we wished that every budding nature photographer could share in the experience. Now, through the images and photographer's captions in this book, Greg provides just such an opportunity on an even broader stage.

Texas harbors an astonishing array of wildlife. Often called a "biological crossroads," the state blends eastern flora and fauna with representatives from the West. Northern species reach the southern limits of their range in Texas, while many others inhabit South Texas and the Rio Grande Valley, venturing no farther north. The Piney Woods of East Texas, the grasslands of the Panhandle, the scenic Hill Country of Central Texas, the mountains and deserts of the Trans-Pecos, the coastal prairie, and the remaining thorn-scrub forest tracts along the Rio Grande all contain their own complement of wildlife, some found nowhere else in North America.

One might thus suspect that Texas claims an ample supply of avid naturalists who study and revel in these treasures, and that certainly proves to be the case. Local birders search the fields and forests year-round for resident species and the occasional vagrants that add excitement to their quest. Countless others venture out in ever increasing numbers in search of butterflies, dragonflies and damselflies, mammals, or reptiles and amphibians. Many carry cameras and document their discoveries, particularly in this new digital age. More and more naturalists have now become ardent photographers as well. Most see photography as a welcome addition to their amateur pursuits; others seek to join the ranks of widely published professionals.

In our minds, one Texan best personifies the combination of expert naturalist and consummate wildlife photographer. That person is Greg Lasley. Indeed, Greg is widely known for his numerous photographs in regional and national publications and for his encyclopedic knowledge of birds. We feel privileged to have counted him as a friend and fellow birder for some thirty years. It has been less a privilege to compete with him in photo contests, however, for we have never managed to match his photographic skills or his numerous awards! In his own words, Greg first began to photograph birds in 1977 "as a novice, but enthusiastic bird-watcher." His interest lay in documenting appearances of rare birds through photographs and sound recordings, a discipline sadly lacking at that

Top left: The **Masked Tityra** *is a Mexican species of flycatcher found in many locations in that country. It was big news, however, when one showed up near the Rio Grande in Bentsen Rio Grande State Park in Hidalgo County in 1990. This particular bird was the first one ever recorded within the United States, and, as of this writing, remains the only record in this country.*

Top right: The **Tufted Flycatcher** *is a small, cinnamon colored, crested flycatcher of Mexico and Central America. In 1991 one showed up at Big Bend National Park in Brewster County, Texas. This shot was part of the documentation that confirmed this first record for the United States.*

Bottom left: Documenting a rarity with photographs can often mean getting images that are not particularly scenic, interesting, or beautiful to look at. The point is to get images that show identifying characteristics of the particular species. In 1999 the first **Black-tailed Gull** *ever found in Texas was located at the Brownsville landfill. This shot shows the adult Black-tailed Gull (the large, dark bird more or less in the center with the black tail with a white tip on it) as it flew away with several Ring-billed and Laughing Gulls.*

Bottom right: The **Masked Duck** *is a tropical species that sometimes may be found in Texas. It is an invasive species, which means that occasionally several of these birds will show up in Texas at different locations at about the same time. The adult Masked Duck in this photo was at Brazos Bend State Park in Fort Bend County in 1996. Several others were scattered around other parts of Texas at that time.*

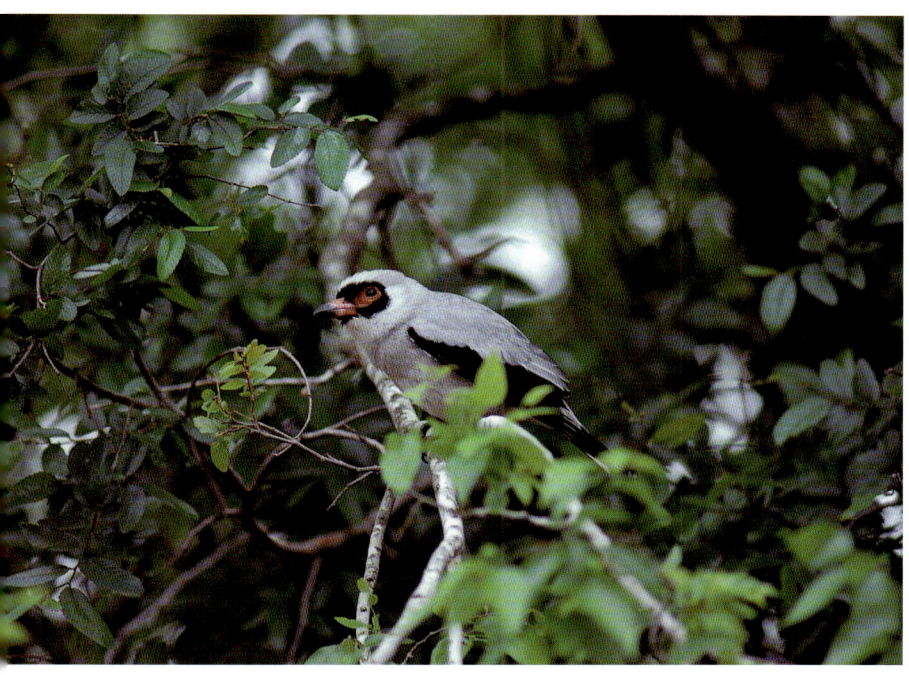
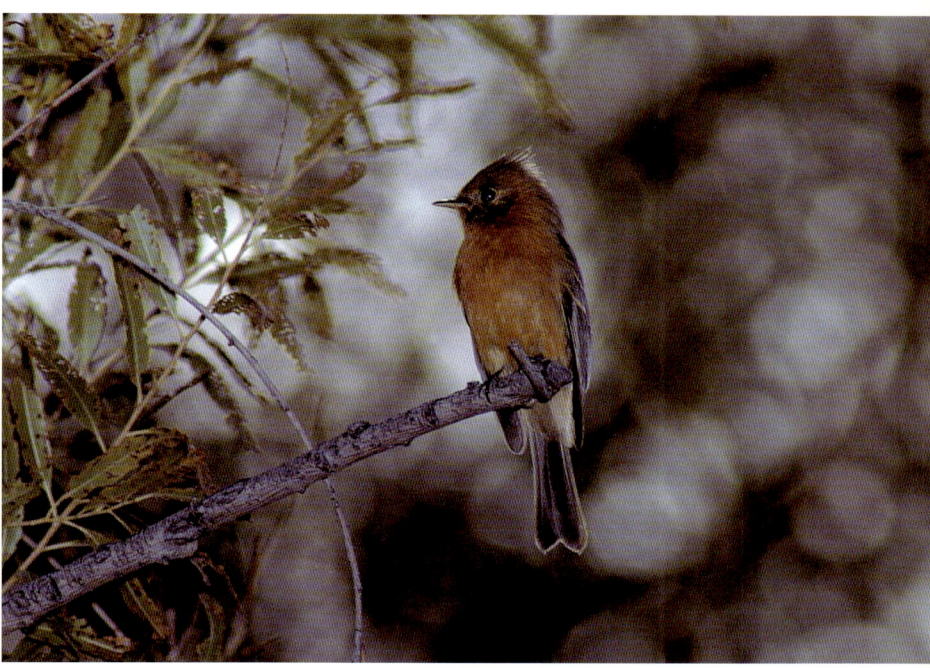
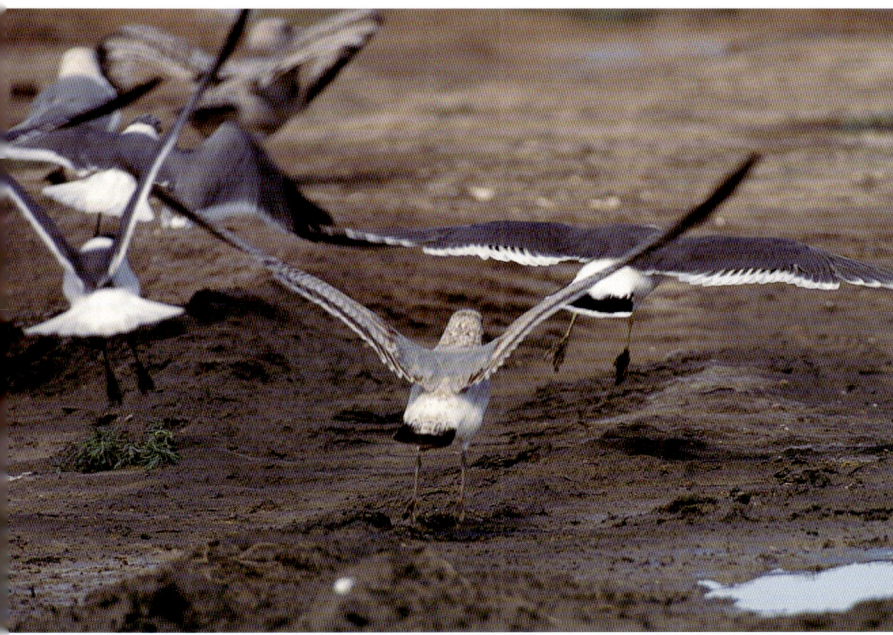
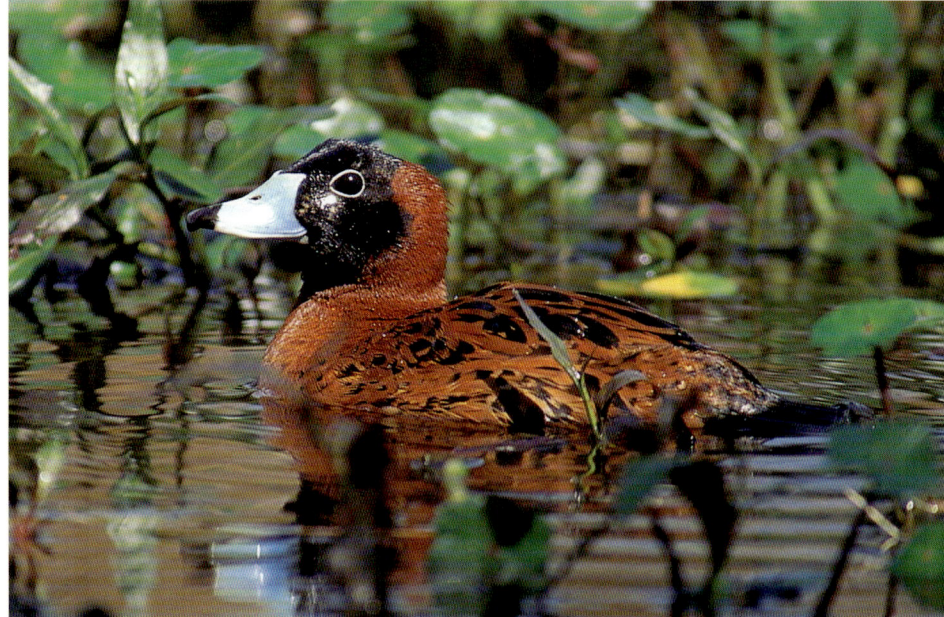

time. When our paths crossed through the years—at High Island on the upper Texas coast in spring, along some clear stream in the Hill Country, or at a refuge in the Rio Grande Valley—a camera and long telephoto lens always hung from Greg's shoulder. They were as much a part of his persona as the ever-present binoculars. If an unprecedented bird species wandered across the Rio Grande or appeared in the Davis Mountains, Greg was there to document it as a new state record. Some of us occasionally decided to leave our heavy camera gear at home, preferring to simply watch birds and not be burdened with the mechanics of photography. Not so Greg Lasley. He shared our love of watching birds, but he also approached his quarry from a scientific perspective.

Greg used his photographs in countless programs for Audubon societies and other nature groups throughout the state, teaching others about bird identification and the thrill of birding, always encouraging his audience to document their finds, if not with a camera, at least with detailed notes and sketches. On this point, he proved relentless, and Texas ornithology is the richer for it. Before his effort, most rare birds were either accepted or rejected for the state list by reason of brief and often vague descriptions. Greg insisted on credible documentation, a worthy goal indeed.

From 1983 through 2000, Greg and fellow ornithologist Chuck Sexton served as coeditors of the Texas Region for *American Birds*, a publication that was retitled *Field Notes* and then *North American Birds*. Greg also served as secretary of the Texas Bird Records Committee of the Texas Ornithological Society for fourteen years and was on the Bird Records Committee of

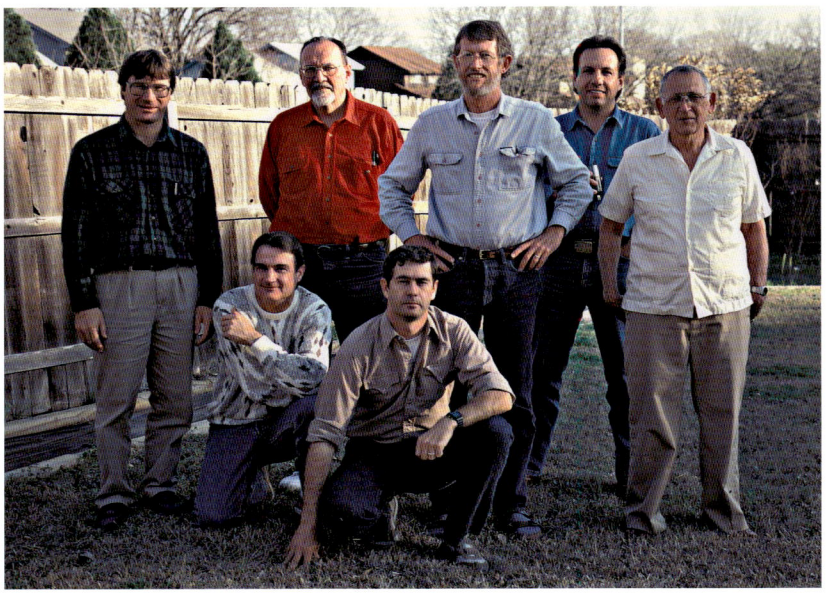

This shot was taken in my backyard in Austin, Texas, in March 1990 at an annual meeting of the Texas Bird Records Committee of the Texas Ornithological Society. Standing, left to right: Chuck Sexton, Keith Arnold, John Arvin, Ted Eubanks, and Warren Pulich. Kneeling, left to right: Jim Morgan and Greg Lasley. Photo by Cheryl Johnson.

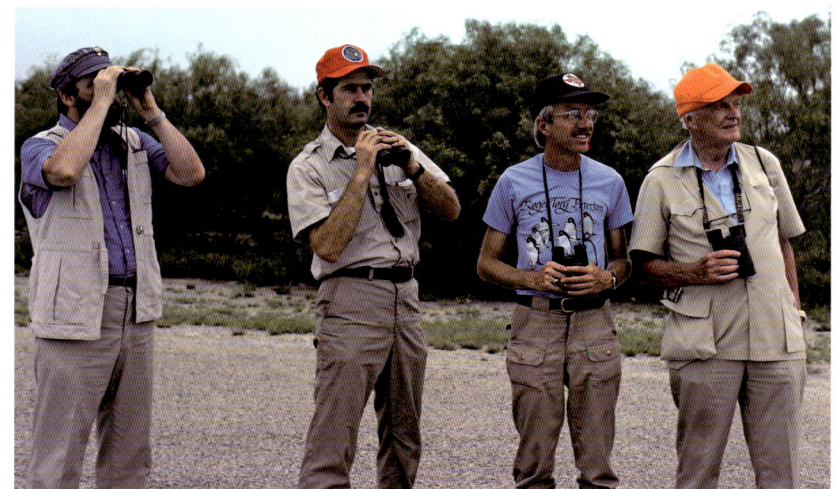

This shot was taken on May 1, 1985, at Falcon State Park, Starr County, Texas. Left to right: Jim Tucker, Greg Lasley, Victor Emanuel, Roger Tory Peterson. We were participating in a "Big Day," which is an effort to see as many species as possible within one calendar day. On this date, we set a new Texas and American Birding Association (A.B.A) area Big Day record with 244 species. That record stood for many years.

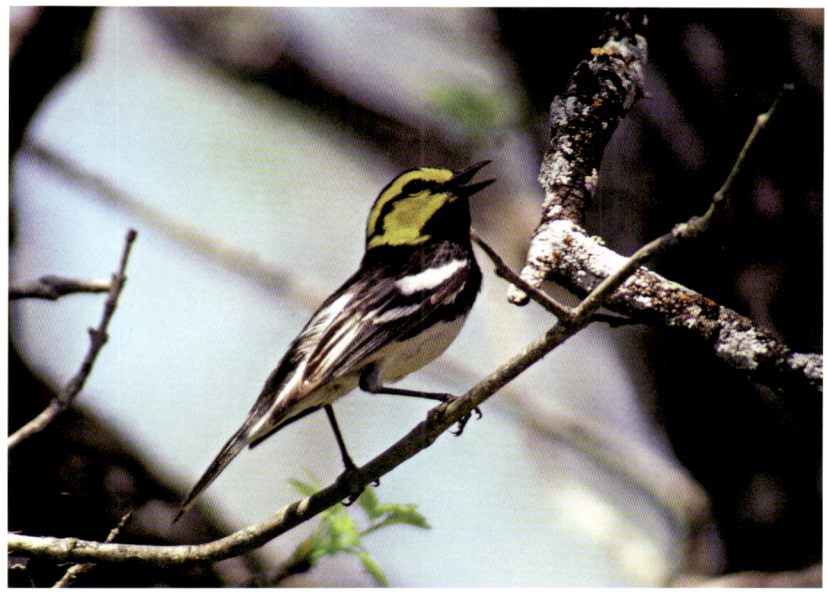

On an early April day in 1988, I was near the edge of Lake Travis near Mansfield Dam when I heard a singing **Golden-cheeked Warbler**. *Carefully slipping through the thick tangle of understory in the juniper woodland, I stood near the base of a small oak for quite some time. Then, suddenly the male golden-cheek came hopping along through some small twigs very near to me. The bird stopped, cranked back his head, and began to sing. I was using a fairly grainy 200-speed slide film, a handheld Minolta camera body, and a Vivitar 400mm lens, but I was able to take several shots of this bird. Although I had taken photos of this species in the past, this particular shot was certainly the best. Ed Kutac was just finishing a book called* Birder's Guide to Texas, *and he wanted a Golden-cheeked Warbler to be on the cover. The publisher paid me three hundred dollars, as I recall, to use the image on the cover of Ed's book. This was about the time that Golden-cheeked Warbler was being declared an endangered species, and others were also interested in photos of the bird to illustrate various articles about its endangered status. This shot was published in at least a dozen magazines and books between 1989 and 1992 and is the one most responsible for my becoming more serious about photography. This particular image is still the most published single image I have ever taken.*

the American Birding Association for two terms. In these capacities, he was heavily involved with bird records in Texas and throughout North America, earning a reputation as one of the country's leading bird experts.

During this time, Greg worked in law enforcement with the Austin Police Department, retiring as a lieutenant in 1997 after twenty-five years. From 1985 through 1997, he led birding tours part-time for Victor Emanuel Nature Tours, one of the most prestigious of the many tour companies, and upon his retirement from police work, he divided his efforts between wildlife photography and the birding tours. In that capacity he covered much of the Western Hemisphere, from Hudson Bay through Central and South America to Antarctica. He visited the latter icebound continent an amazing twelve times, always accompanied, of course, by his trusty cameras. However, we hasten to add that he never let his personal photographic or birding goals get in the way of his duties as a leader. Dedicated to his charges, Greg is above all a respected teacher and interpreter of natural history.

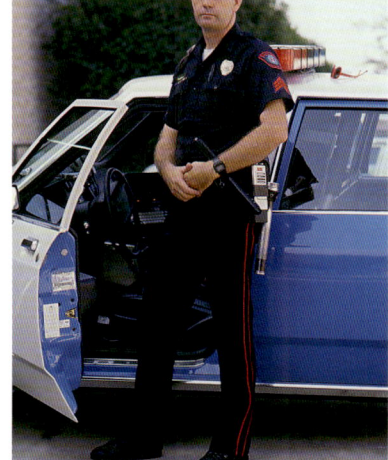

Greg Lasley as a sergeant with the Austin Police Department, September 1990. Photo by Andrew W. Haynes Sr.

In spite of extensive international travel, Greg's work remains rooted in Texas, and he has visited every county in the state in pursuit of wildlife. A lightened tour load now leaves him free to concentrate on his photography.

In 1988, Greg notes, he photographed a Golden-cheeked Warbler, an endangered species that nests only in Texas. Some of those images were published in books and magazines, and his new career was off to a flying start. Continually upgrading his equipment and perfecting his skills, he quickly moved into the forefront among bird photographers.

Then, in 2000, Greg entered the Valley Land Fund (VLF) photo contest, a six-month event held in the Rio Grande Valley every other year and billed as "the richest photo contest in the world." There Greg and contest partner Larry Ditto competed with other professional and advanced amateur photographers from across the country and won first place in the grueling marathon. In 2002, they finished a creditable third.

Greg's birding skills served him well in the VLF contest. In the book of winning images, *Focus on the Wild,* he wrote in the section reserved for the two "VLF Wildlife Photographers of the Year" that one of his many highlights was "discovering a sizable population of Botteri's Sparrows scattered through the ranch's grasslands. The species occurs nowhere else in Texas except in the southernmost counties and rarely at that." Few of the other contestants would have been able to recognize a Botteri's Sparrow; fewer still would have known its habits well enough to locate and photograph the rare avian prize.

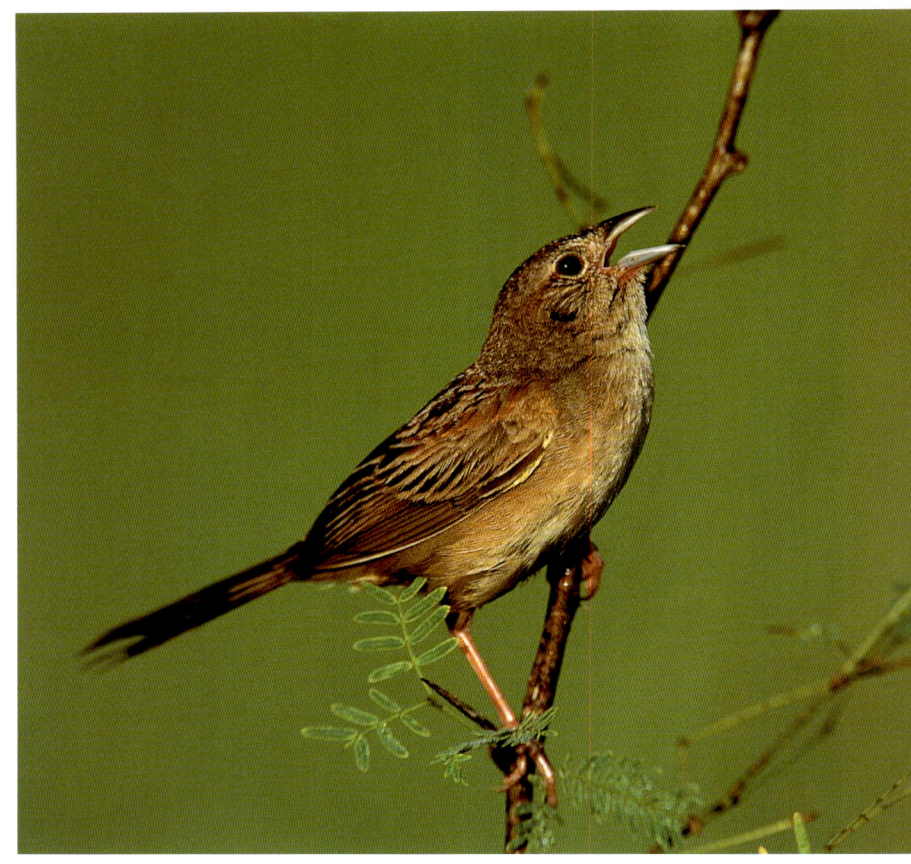

Within Texas, the **Botteri's Sparrow** *is an uncommon bird that nests in the coastal grasslands of the extreme southern areas of our state. It is a very specialized species and may be found only in certain types of healthy grasslands. This singing male was perched on a mesquite limb on a ranch in Kenedy County as it proclaimed its presence to the world. To the casual observer, this small brown bird might not even be seen, yet its distinctive song and subtle, yet attractive coloration, will draw the attention of bird-watchers and other interested students of Texas wildlife.*

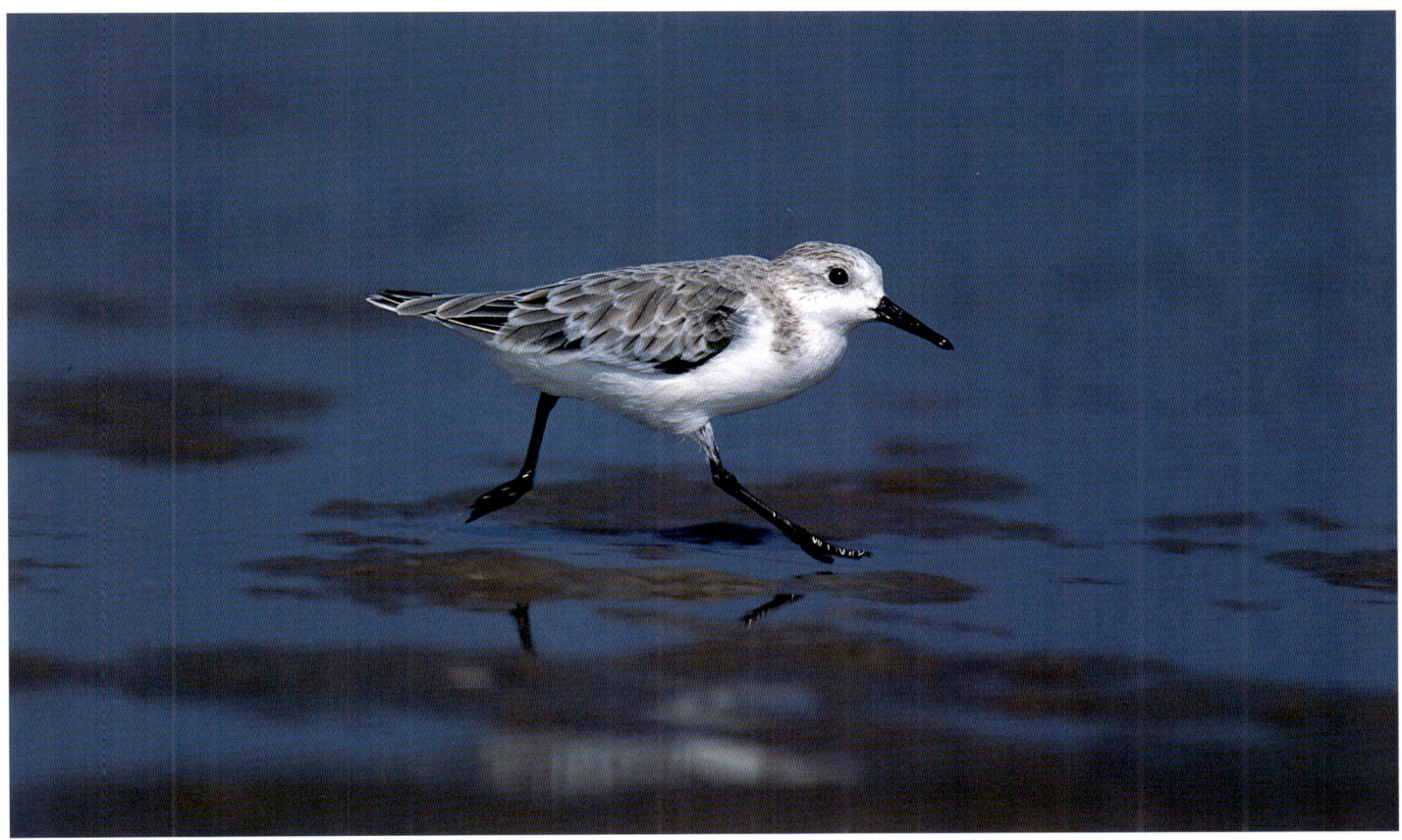

Anyone who has visited a Texas beach has probably seen little gray birds running up and down the shoreline with each passing wave. They were probably **Sanderlings.** *This species breeds on the Canadian tundra but may be found in Texas about ten months of the year. This Sanderling was running along the beach at Bolivar Flats in Galveston County. Notice that I was able to capture both feet in midair!*

Photographs of birds were no more vital in the contest, however, than were those of mammals, snakes, butterflies, or spiders. Images could be entered in fifty different categories, and all provided essential points toward the winning total. By necessity, Greg had to photograph a wide variety of wildlife, and he quickly adapted to the challenge. In 2000, we were fortunate to take home several awards in insect and reptile categories, although we could not challenge Greg and Larry or several others among the top prize winners in the overall competition. By the 2002 contest, however, we could no longer match Greg's close-up photography, to say nothing of his skill in photographing birds.

It was a learning experience for all of us, one that brought us closer together through shared trials and tribulations and through the shared goal of protecting Texas wildlife and educating people about the need for conserving its essential habitat. Quoting Greg and Larry in *Focus on the Wild*: "This was truly 'Iron Man' photography. We got in shape, got a tan, picked up a few ticks, lost a little weight, lost a lot of sleep . . . all for that great shot no one else would get. But it was fun!"

Fun, indeed. But Greg's photos reveal much more than that. He possesses a deep understanding of his subjects and the ability to portray them at their best. His bird images are not only portraits; they show each species in its native habitat, going about its daily routine. His hawks are often captured in flight, primaries spread and fingering the air, piercing eyes shining brightly and intent on prey below. A photo of a Sanderling dashing down the beach catches the little bird in full stride, with both feet suspended above the wave-washed sand.

Similarly, Greg snapped the shutter just as an American Oystercatcher flicked its wings open to reveal the flashing pattern normally hidden as it feeds. We see an American White Pelican "yawning" widely, its pouch inverted like a pink balloon; a graceful Barn Swallow feeding its young while on the wing; and a Crested Caracara daintily preening a single tail feather with its massive beak.

Many of the songbirds have been photographed as they sing, beaks open and throats swelling in hormonal ardor. One can almost hear the avian music pouring forth from the superbly framed and tack-sharp images. As Kathy Adams Clark, our

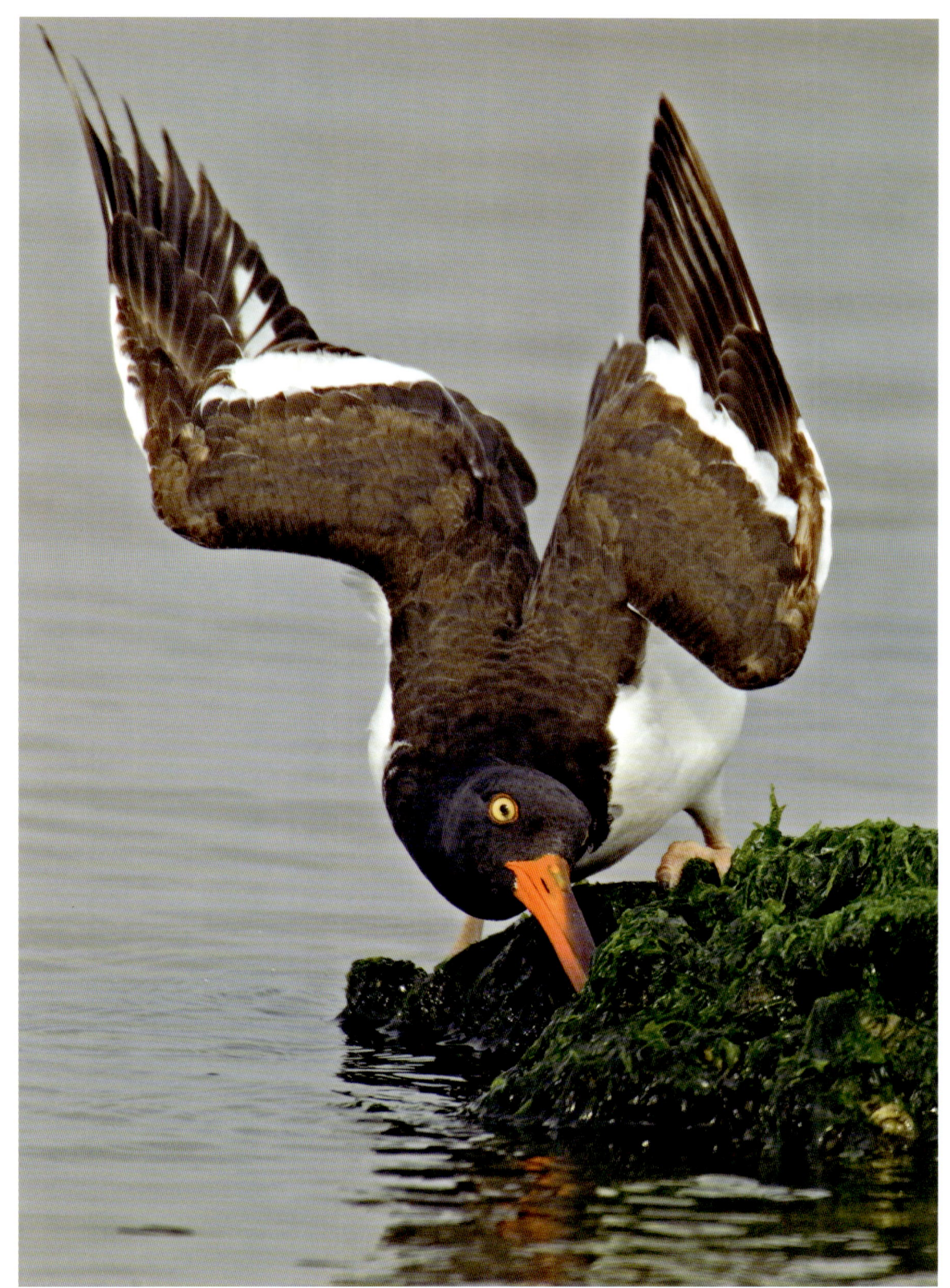

American Oystercatchers *are fairly common residents of the Texas Gulf Coast. Oystercatchers are large, relatively powerful shorebirds, and they use their stout bills to open oyster shells and other prey items. This individual was struggling to remove some tasty treat wedged in a rock along the Texas City Dike in Galveston County.*

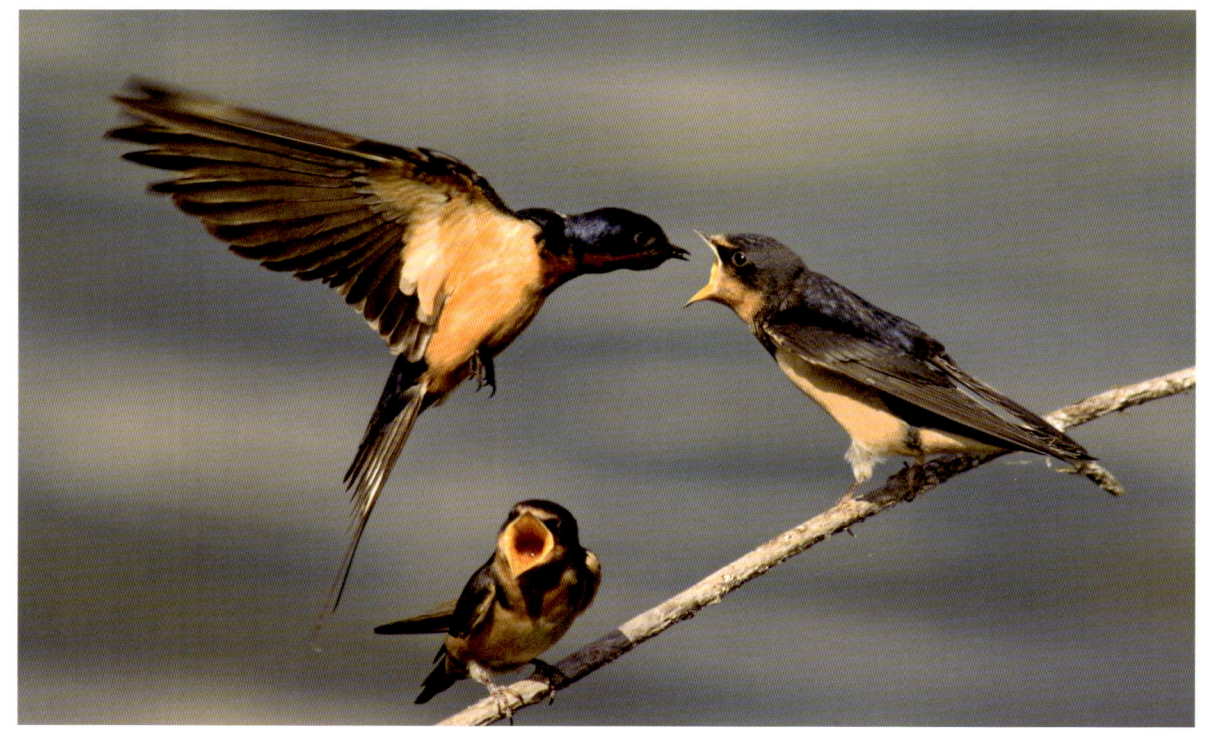

*I was driving along the edge of a pond in Austin, Travis County, in May when I saw two young **Barn Swallows** perched on a stick over the water. In a few moments, one of the parents swooped in to feed the young. By slowly positioning my truck at a good vantage point, I was able to get a few shots of the adult feeding one of the young birds, while the second youngster waited in eager anticipation.*

mutual friend and photo agent as owner of KAC Productions, once told us after spending time with Greg in the field: "His reflexes are SO good!"

It takes all of that to be a great bird photographer: intimate knowledge of the subject, an artistic sense, quick reflexes, and enormous patience and persistence. Few do it better than Greg Lasley.

After knowing Greg as a birder for so many years, we delight in seeing the new direction his photography has taken him. We chuckle at a photo of an armadillo drinking at a pond, its long pink tongue extended and reflected in the quiet water. We learn about odonate behavior from photos of dragonflies perched in the "obelisk position," bodies pointed at the sun to reduce the heat of a hot Texas summer. Other dragonflies

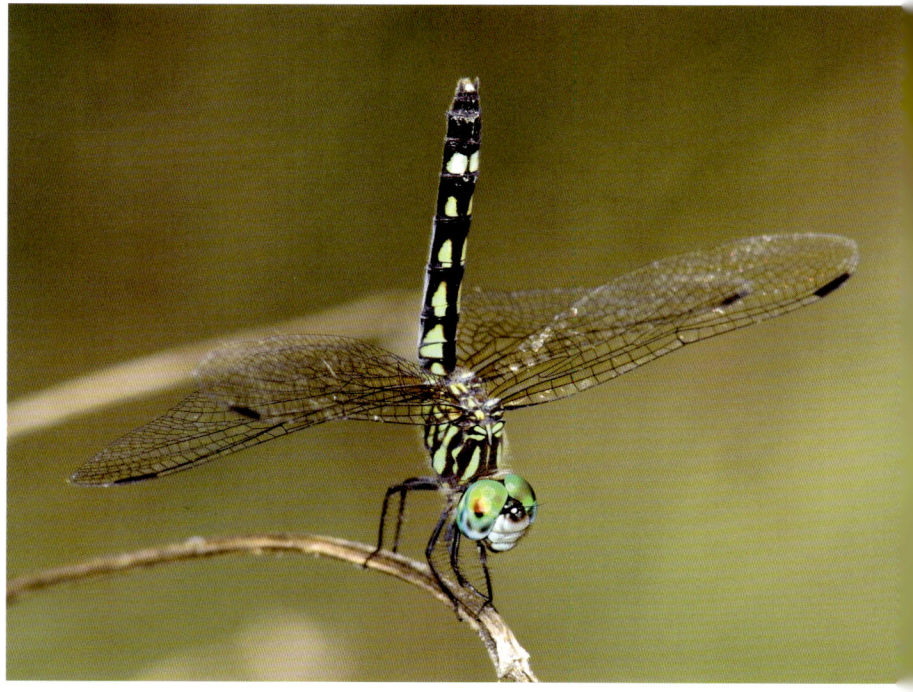

Many species of damselflies gather in groups to mate or deposit eggs. This small concentration of **Springwater Dancers** *was on the edge of an eight-inch-high waterfall along a West Texas stream in the Davis Mountains, Jeff Davis County. The blue males are clasping the brown females while the females deposit eggs into the wet moss and algae just under the water's surface.*

Opposite: In parts of Central and South Texas, the **Thornbush Dasher** *may be one of the most commonly seen small dragonflies. It is often found in scrubby brushlands near ponds. To stay cooler on a very hot day, many dragonflies assume an obelisk position. In this position, the insect points the tip of its abdomen directly at the sun, thereby reducing the area of the body exposed to direct sunlight. This Thornbush Dasher, in an obelisk posture, was in Travis County near Austin on a hot summer day.*

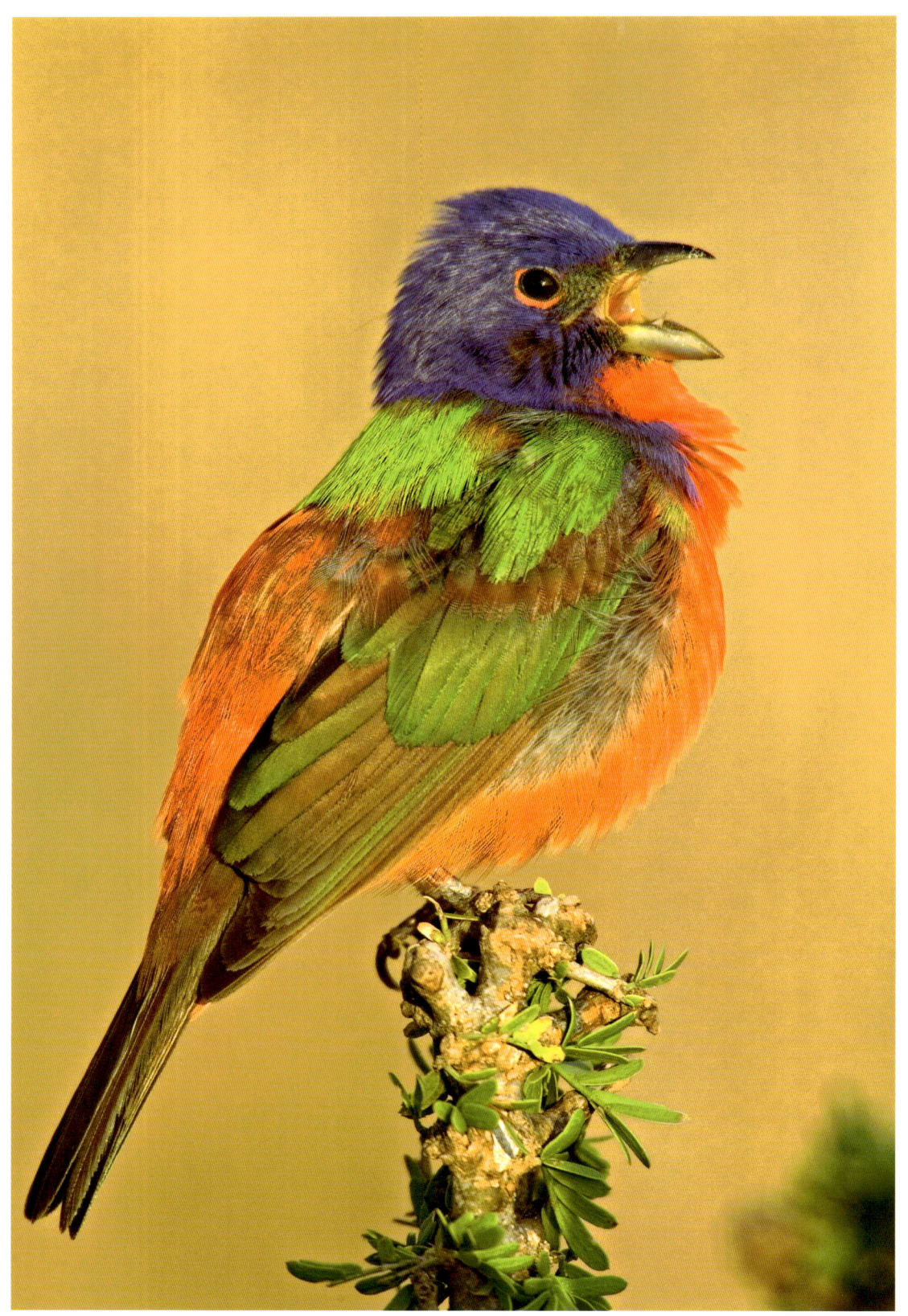

The **Painted Bunting** is quite common in late spring and early summer across much of Texas. But, due to the bird's small size, it often remains unseen by the general public. It is truly an unbelievably beautiful songster. I noticed a Painted Bunting one afternoon in Hidalgo County in early May. The bird seemed to have a favorite song perch, so I thought I'd try to get some shots of it the next morning if the light was right. Early the next morning, I parked my vehicle close enough to the perch to get some nice shots with a big lens and waited. Before the sun was up, the bird came to his perch and began singing. I sat there for many long minutes with the bird in my viewfinder, but without any decent light. I was afraid the bird would leave before the sun broke the horizon. Finally, sunrise! As the first rich streaks of sunlight bathed the bunting in the warm glow, I got a number of shots as he loudly defended his territory. The yellow-brown background is simply drought-stressed grassland that is out of focus.

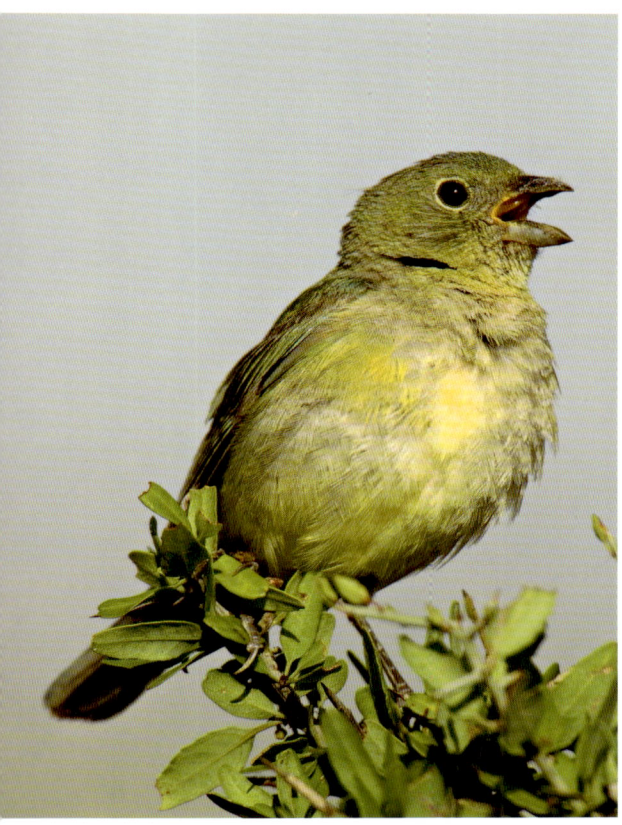

*Male **Painted Buntings** are among the most colorful of the breeding birds of Texas, but many people do not realize that it takes two full years for a male Painted Bunting to get its gaudy plumage. The singing bird in this shot was a one-year-old male that successfully defended a territory all spring and summer near McCook in Hidalgo County.*

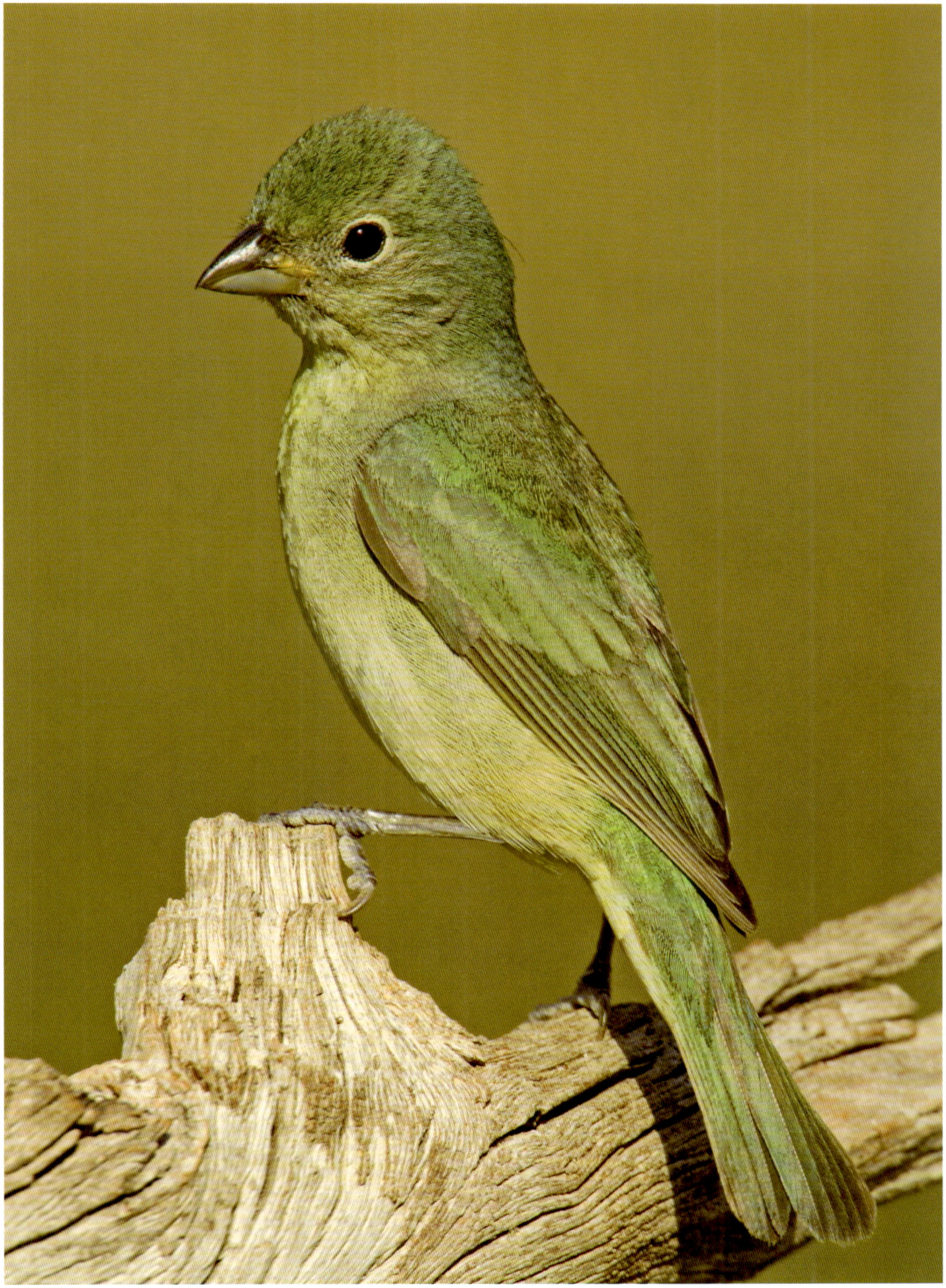

*Female **Painted Buntings** are a lovely green color, unique among North American birds. Though far more subtle in appearance than the colorful adult males, the females are quite attractive in their own right. This female Painted Bunting was perched on a mesquite stump near a South Texas water hole in Hidalgo County.*

and damselflies reveal spectacular colors and delicate patterns before Greg's lens, intricacies almost impossible to see without the magnification the portraits provide. Indeed, in recent years, Greg has become an exceptional photographer of these odonates, an authority in a rapidly expanding field of interest. We may never see a Mayan Setwing or mating pairs of Springwater Dancers except in his impeccable photos.

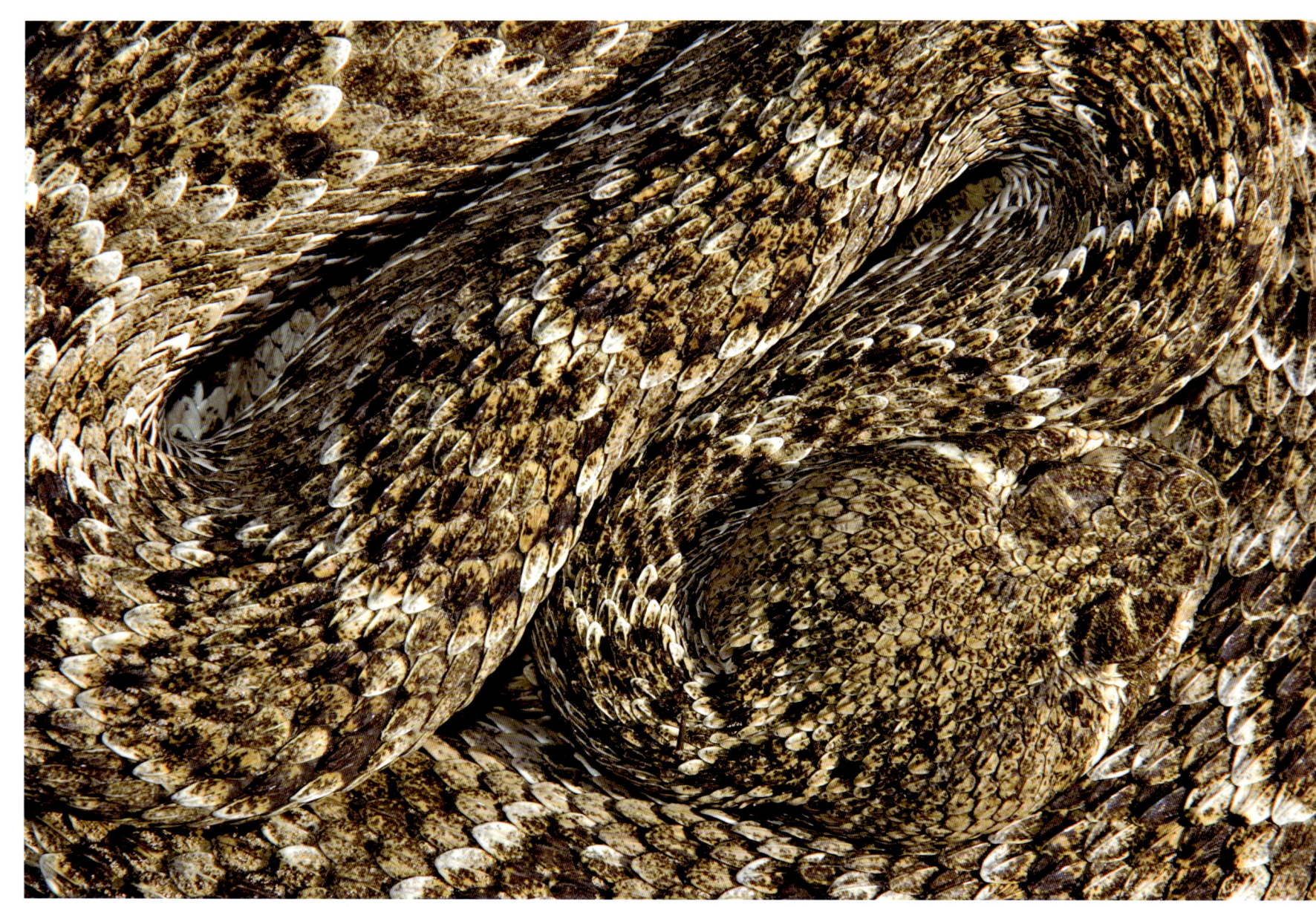

Opposite:
The **Western Diamond-backed Rattlesnake** certainly commands caution and respect since a bite from this animal can be very dangerous. Still, this snake is a native Texan, and it is my feeling that it performs an important role in the web of life. I am always aware that I am in rattlesnake country when I tramp through the wilds of Texas, but rather than fear an encounter with the snake, I actually look forward to my next one. This individual, about four feet long, was resting under a mesquite tree on a ranch in Hidalgo County near Edinburg. The shot, from directly above, created an interesting pattern of textures and earth colors.

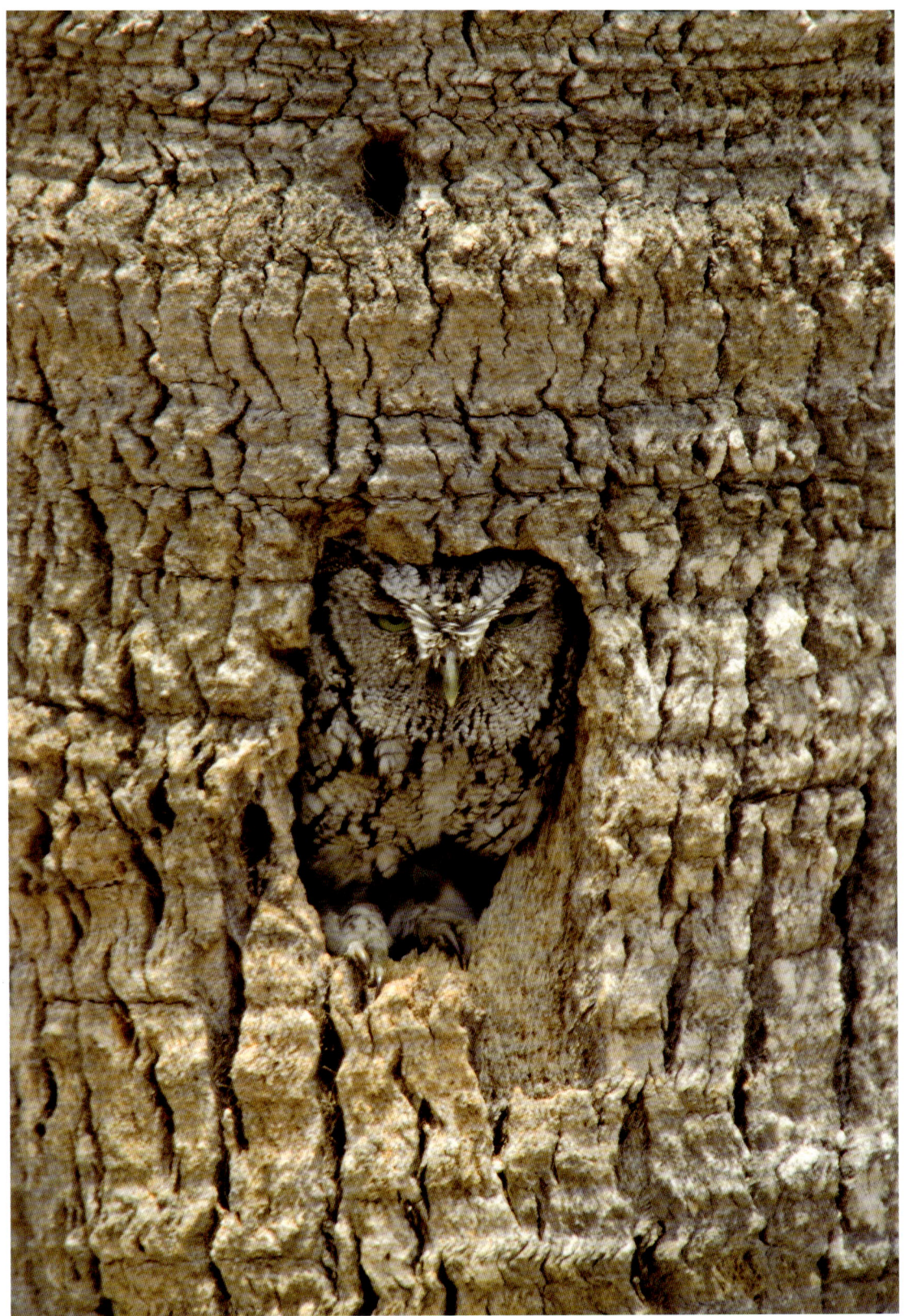

Eastern Screech-Owls are fairly common and widespread over the eastern half of Texas and may be found in a variety of habitats. The species is a cavity nester and may take advantage of any hole in a tree large enough to accommodate it. This owl glared at me from its nest hole in a dead palm trunk in South Texas in Hidalgo County.

The same could be said for fierce looking robber flies, colorful beetles, or a spider on a dew-covered web. All prove to be interesting subjects, as do the snakes that Greg delights in finding and photographing. His intimate portraits of rattlesnakes may seem just a little too intimate for some, perhaps, but as Kathy Clark phrased it recently, "Give Greg a camera, a big snake, and a little stick to nudge it into a good position and he's in heaven."

When we were working on our own book of the birds of Texas several years ago, we turned to Greg for many of those hard-to-get photographs we did not have. We also consulted him on his specialties, the state bird list and Texas rarities, as well as on other aspects of bird distribution. There was no better authority. We would do the same for almost any facet of natural history today, for Greg has traveled widely to observe and photograph the state's resources, and he shares his knowledge willingly with all who ask.

In recent years, as he notes in the Photographer's Comments, Greg has turned from color film to digital photography, as have most other professionals and amateurs alike. Images from both methods are included here, and the Wildlife Photo Index at the back of this book provides data on the equipment used for each image. The medium may be different now, but the skills and techniques remain much the same. Knowledge of the subject proves invaluable, and in that, Greg has few equals. Here he exposes his audience to wildlife large and small, from every corner of the state. As readers, we need only sit back and enjoy the view.

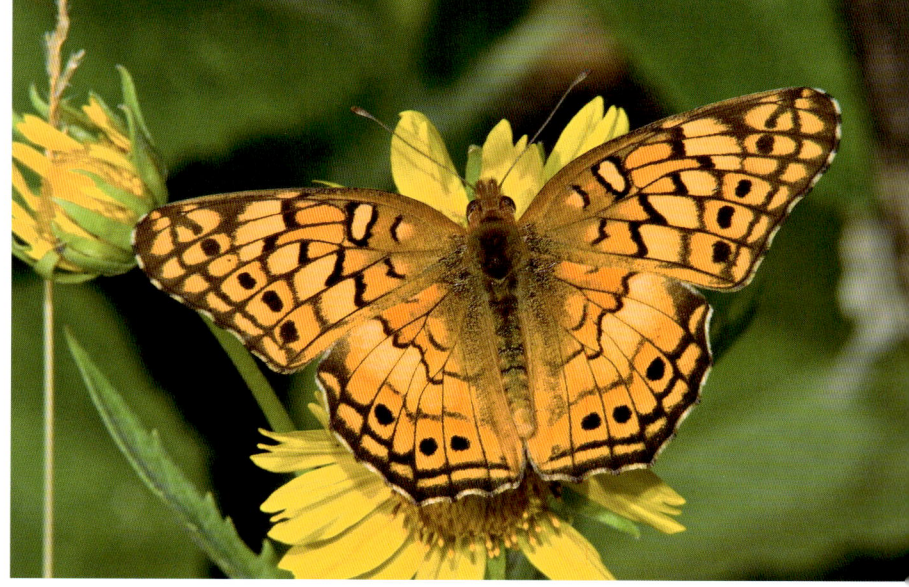

The **Variegated Fritillary** *is a conspicuous and fairly common butterfly across parts of Texas at certain times of the year. Sometimes it seems as if entire fields may be covered with these colorful butterflies as they probe flowers for nectar. This one was feeding on the nectar of some flowers along the Nueces River in Real County. The intricate pattern of the spread wings can only be appreciated with a close look such as this.*

I have heard it said, in jest, that "Armadillos are born dead on the side of the road," a comment aimed at the fact that most of us usually see this animal in that condition: dead along the side of the road. But, the animals do thrive in many areas of Texas, where they are sometimes regarded as pests because they will readily dig up home gardens in search of grubs and other insects. I had never actually seen an armadillo's tongue before this **Nine-banded Armadillo** *came down to the edge of a small pond in Hidalgo County to get a drink.*

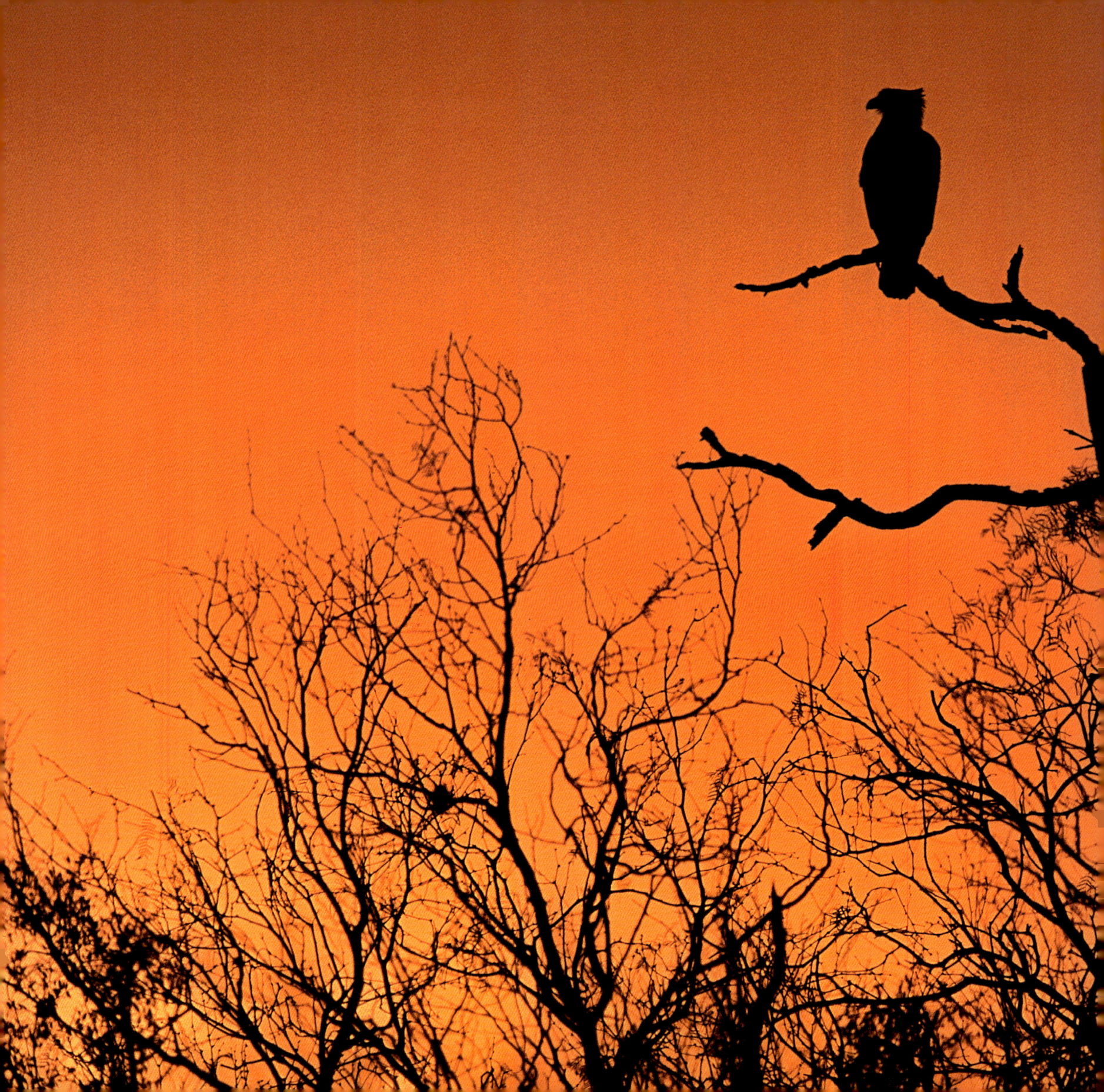

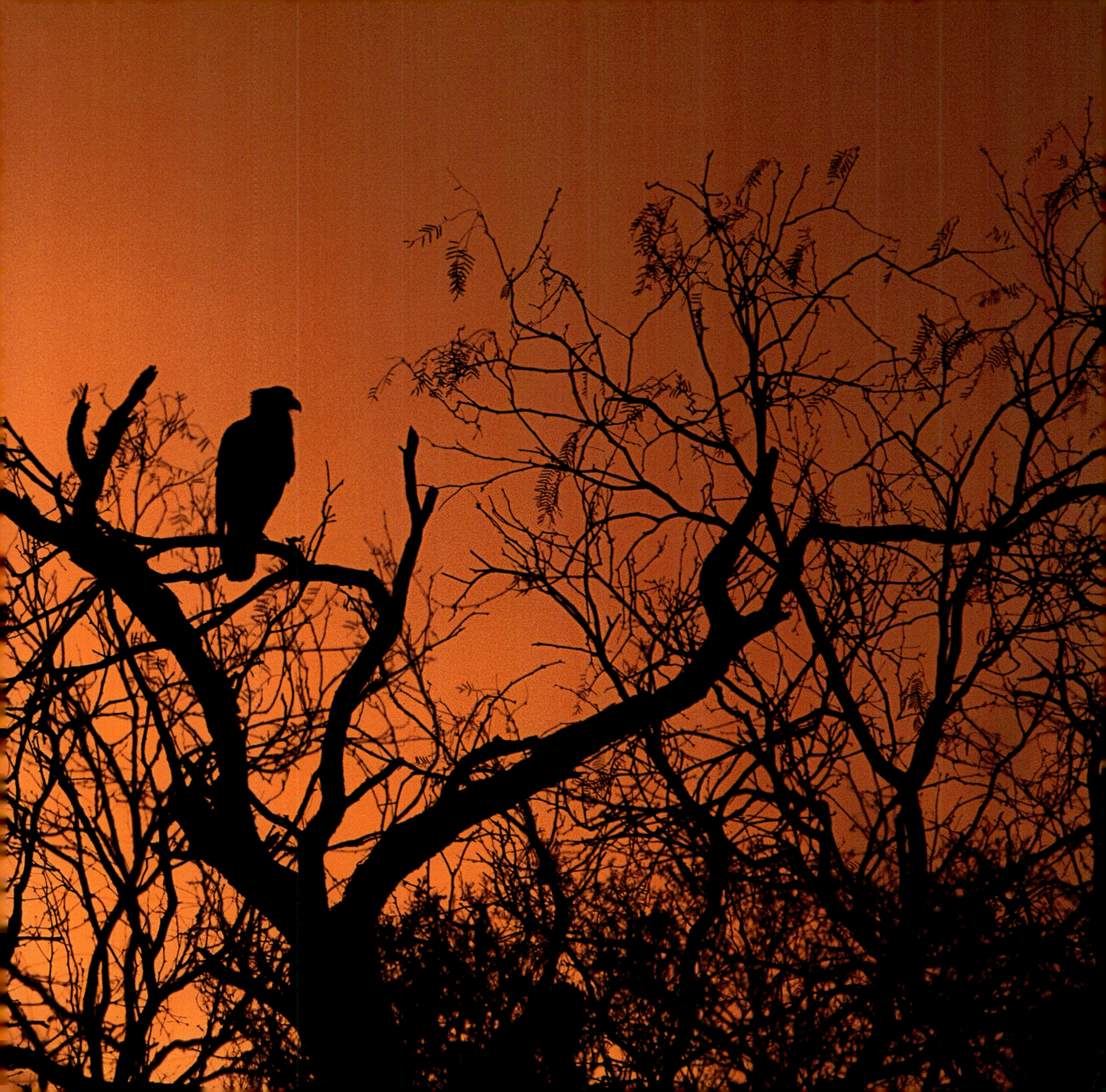

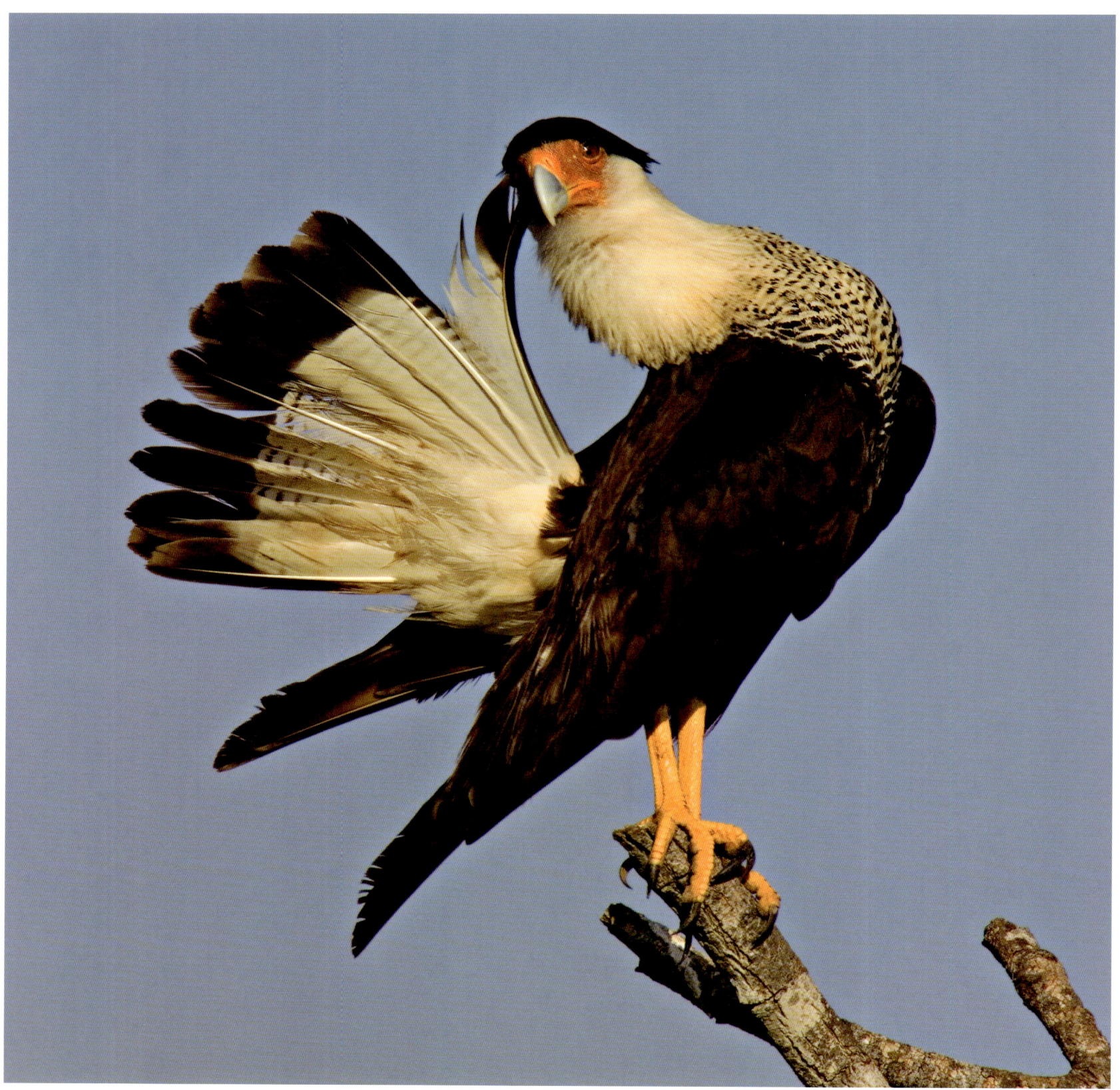

Photographer's Comments

BY GREG LASLEY

Pages 24/25 and opposite:
Sometimes the South Texas sky at sunset can turn completely orange. On a winter evening in Kenedy County, such was the case while two **Crested Caracaras** *rested on a mesquite limb, providing a beautiful South Texas sunset scene. For at least a week while I was on a ranch in Hidalgo County near McCook, I saw a Crested Caracara each morning at 8:00 a.m. sharp as it landed on a the same limb to preen in the morning sun. I slowly approached the bird in my truck several times until it finally allowed me to sit there and take photographs on several occasions. The bird would pull its tail feathers through its bill one at a time while cleaning and straightening them. This image shows the caracara working on one of the outer tail feathers at the conclusion of its daily ritual.*

PICK OUT ONE HUNDRED of your best images of Texas wildlife. This was the request from Texas A&M University Press. Where would I start? With perhaps twenty thousand slides and a similar number of digital images, how would I narrow it down to one hundred that show some of my best work of Texas wildlife?

My interest in nature began in childhood. I studied various aspects of it as I made my way through the Boy Scout ranks to Eagle Scout. In the late 1960s during high school, I worked part-time in the reptile house at the Atlanta, Georgia, zoo. I also kept dozens of snakes, some venomous, in cages in my home's basement. My mother was very tolerant, bless her heart, and probably did not appreciate the potential problems that I created by keeping such dangerous captive animals, but somehow we all got through it unscathed. I even took a girl on what I called a "date" to hunt Canebrake Rattlesnakes near the Okefenokee Swamp in south Georgia. Two summers working as a ranger at Philmont Scout Ranch in northern New Mexico fueled an interest in birds, and I learned the basics of falconry from another ranger.

After high school, my attention turned to things other than nature. I ended up in Austin in 1973, after a stint in the U.S. Air Force and soon found myself an officer for the Austin Police Department. I became interested in birds in a fairly serious way in the mid-1970s, and I was soon chasing rare birds when I wasn't chasing felons. Occasionally, I found on my own what appeared to be a rare bird and needed a way as a novice but enthusiastic bird-watcher to prove (or disprove) that the bird was what I thought it was. Thus, in 1977, my photographic adventures began. From the late 1970s until the late 1980s, most of my photography was focused on documenting unusual bird sightings. In 1988, I took some photos of the Golden-cheeked Warbler, an endangered bird that nests only in the Hill Country of Texas. The publication of one of these photos on the cover of a birding guidebook led to other requests for my bird photos. In the next year or two, a number of them were published in *Texas Highways Magazine, Texas Parks and Wildlife Magazine, American Birds, Wildlife Conservation,* and several other publications. After these initial publication successes, I became more serious about photography. Over the next few years, I slowly upgraded my camera equipment (always an ongoing process), developed more of the skills necessary to become a good wildlife photographer, and traveled the state of Texas and much of the United States photographing birds. Throughout the 1990s, hundreds of my photos found their way into various publications.

I began to take cameras with me whenever I traveled. By the mid-1980s, my birding skills were sufficiently developed that Victor Emanuel asked me to lead occasional birding trips for his company, Victor Emanuel Nature Tours (VENT). On my

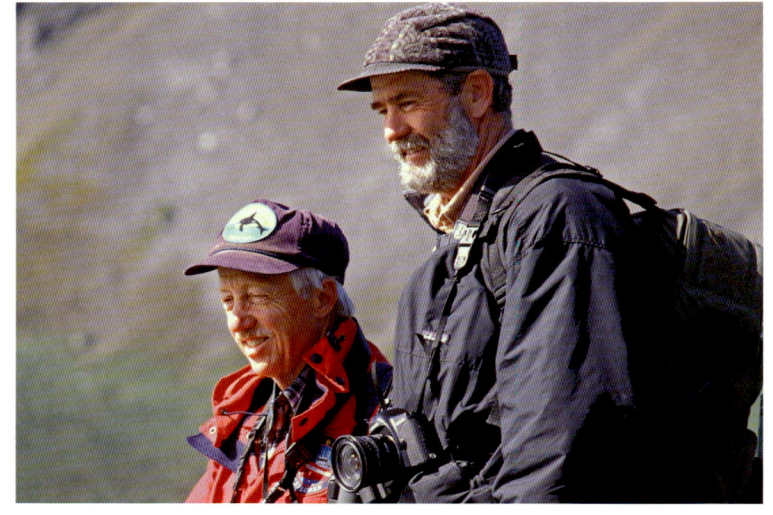

Victor Emanuel and Greg Lasley on the island of South Georgia in the south Atlantic in January 2000. Unknown photographer.

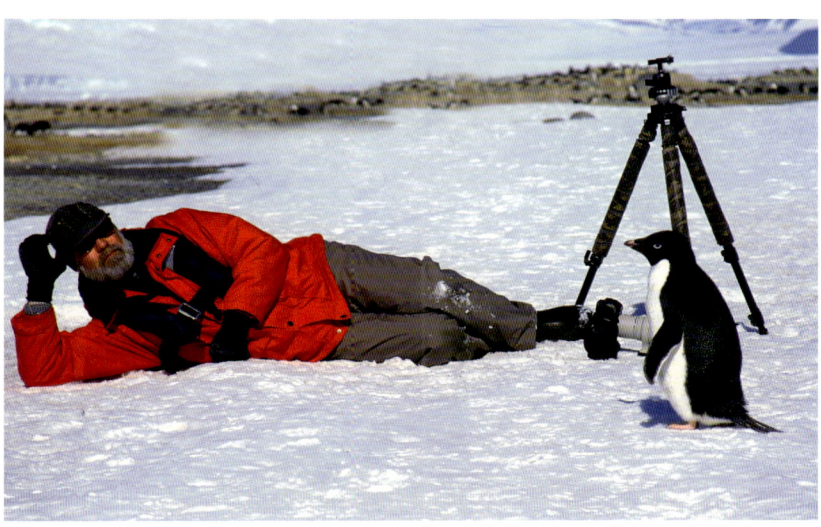

Greg Lasley in Antarctica, December 2001. While I was photographing a group of Adelie Penguins, one of them decided to investigate the situation. I placed the camera on the ground and lay back to watch the bird, which simply walked over and had a good look, then walked away. Photo by Birgit Freybe Bateman.

days off from my police work as well as on vacation time, I traveled extensively, both as a tour leader for VENT and on my own. There were pelagic trips off of Long Island, Cape Hatteras, Monterey, and the Texas Gulf Coast, and birding expeditions to the Chiricahua Mountains of southeast Arizona, the Chisos Mountains of Big Bend, and the American and Canadian Rockies. I photographed on the Texas coast in the spring, on the northern plains in summer, in New Hampshire and Maine in the fall, and in Florida in the winter. I also began to photograph birds outside of the United States, beginning while leading some of those trips for Victor Emanuel, first in Mexico and continuing into Canada, Venezuela, Guatemala, Panama, Argentina, Chile, Ecuador and the Galapagos Islands, Australia, and Antarctica. Traveling with my wife or others, I photographed birds in South Africa, Botswana, Namibia, Belize, Costa Rica, Puerto Rico, U.S. Virgin Islands, Saba, the Leeward Islands, the Bahamas, Peru, and Spain. Over many years, I learned about the vicissitudes of air travel while transporting many pounds of optical glass, tripods, and sometimes hundreds of rolls of film in lead-lined bags. Air travel is easier with digital cameras because you do not have to be concerned with film, but the equipment weighs just as much. Yet, even with these exotic locations and all the memories I have of them, Texas has been, and always will be, my primary photographic destination.

In 2000, I entered the Valley Land Fund Wildlife Photo Contest, a six-month-long photo competition in far South Texas—along with Larry Ditto of McAllen, Texas, a fellow photographer and friend. More than a hundred other accomplished photographers from around Texas and other parts of the country participated. We spent long hours on a single ranch, working to capture wildlife images in fifty different categories. This contest forced me out of my "comfort zone" of bird photography and into the world of photographing spiders, dragonflies, mammals, snakes, and other types of wildlife.

In late 2002, I took my first digital image, and I have never looked back. I still enjoy looking through my thousands of slides, but I must confess that I really enjoy looking at digital images on my large computer monitor.

Still, I wondered, how would I select one hundred shots? Should I concentrate on birds? Should I concentrate on colorful species that might grab the eye of a casual reader, or would it be better to concentrate on Texas specialties, even though some of them might not be very colorful? I looked through thousands of slides and thousands of digital images. Each brought back memories. There is that slide of the American Bittern peering through the dead reeds at Anahuac National Wildlife Refuge. The bittern was completely motionless, apparently thinking I could not see it. What about the Black-tailed Jackrabbit on a Kenedy County ranch, leisurely munching on grass with its ears folded back along the top of its head, seemingly without a care in the world? As I looked through images, memories of my many years in the wilds of Texas came flooding over me. For some of these memories I had film or digital images of the scene, yet for others the image remains only in my mind—although just as vivid. I remembered the cacophony of a chachalaca dawn chorus, the honking of a skein of geese, a coyote howling, the distinctive calls of many species of owls, the identifying beats of a woodpecker's hammering,

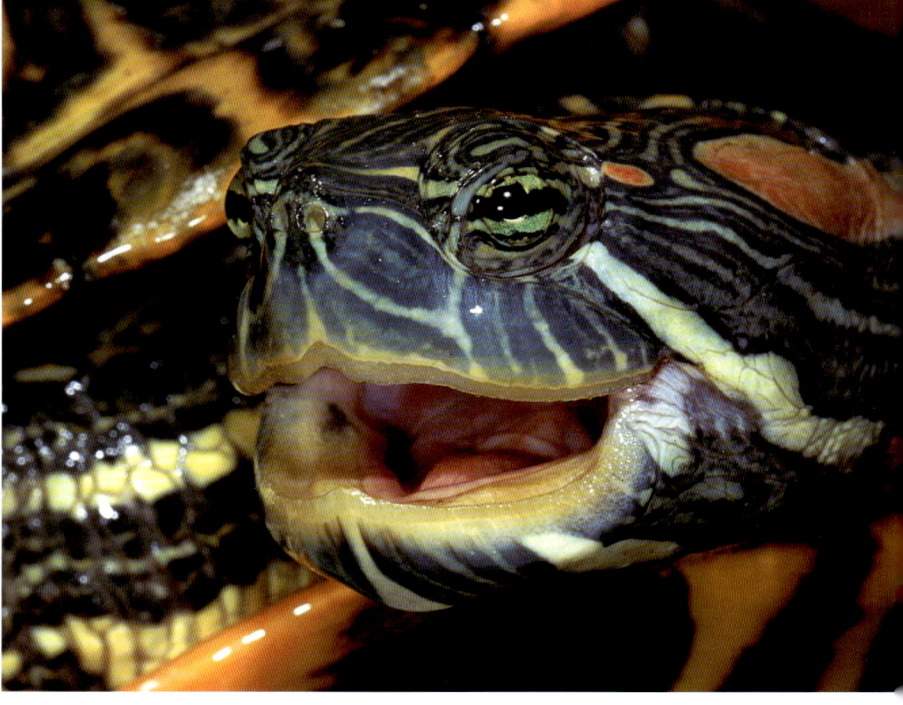

The **Red-eared Slider** *is one of the most common and often-seen aquatic turtles across much of Texas. There are some farm ponds in South Texas that seem to be teeming with this species. Red-eared Sliders eat a wide variety of food including fish, frogs, and almost anything they can catch. The turtle gets its common name from the reddish colored patch of skin on the side of its head. This one was making its way across a ranch road in Kenedy County and registered its displeasure at me when I got too close.*

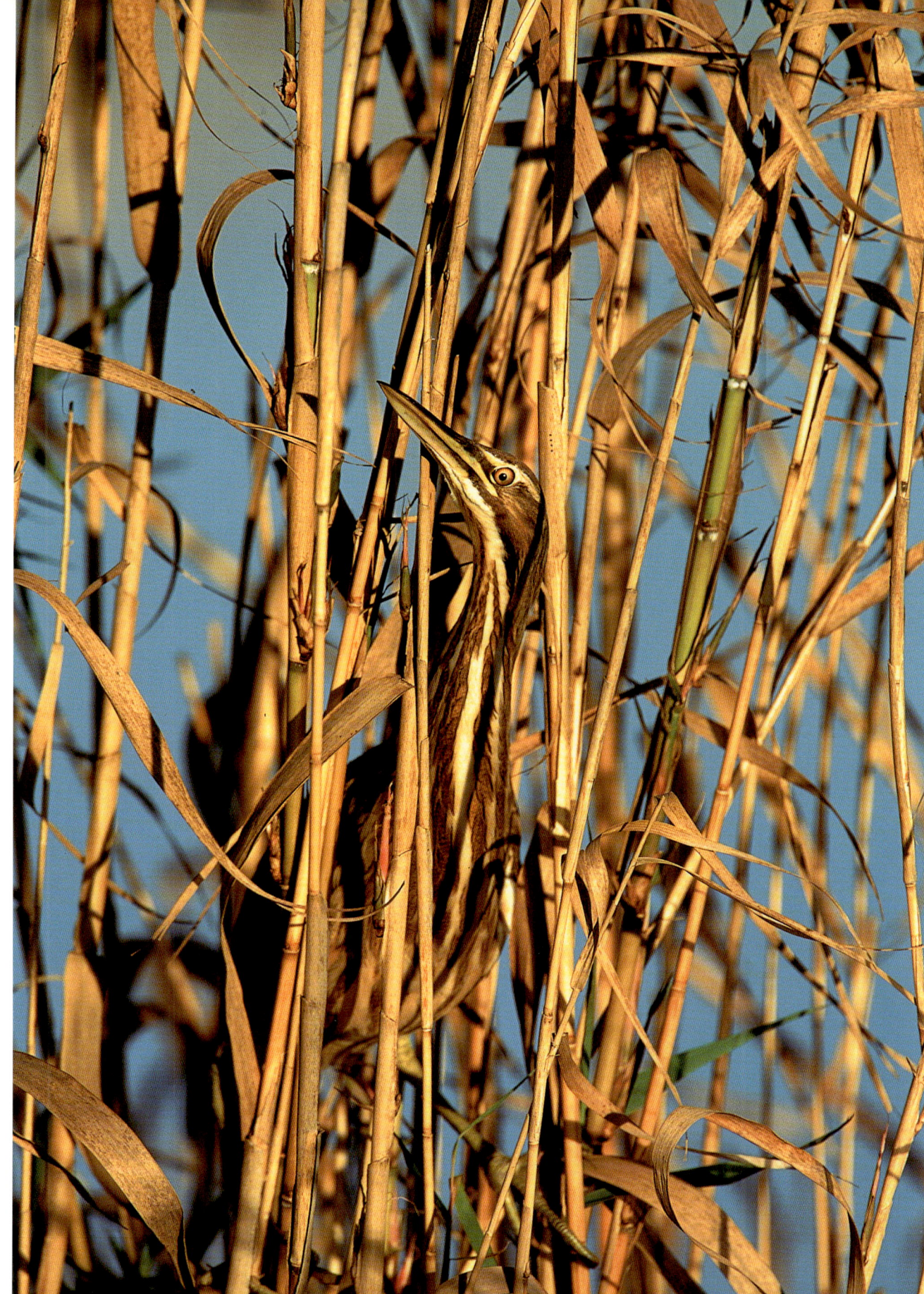

American Bitterns *are known for their ability to "freeze" when they perceive a threat. While driving along the edge of Shoveler Pond at Anahuac National Wildlife Refuge in Chambers County early one morning in March, I spied this bittern hiding in some cane stalks. The bird stayed in this position without moving for several minutes in an attempt to convince me it was not there at all.*

the cries of soaring hawks, the gabbling of quail, the rattle of grasshoppers in the heat of the day, the night chorus of frogs, the buzzy song of Golden-cheeked Warblers, the throbbing sounds of cicadas, the wind in the trees, the light and deafening noise of a bolt of lightning that struck too close, the dancing feet of a prairie-chicken on the roof of a photo blind at its lek, and silence. I remembered dew on a spider's web at dawn, baby ducks and ancient tortoises, a roadrunner dueling with a snake, rays of light through a pine forest, lizards basking in the sun, a bear strolling along a trail in Big Bend, iridescent damselflies in the thousands flitting over the surface of a pond in the late evening sun, and really dark darkness with no light pollution. I remembered an April snowstorm in the Panhandle, 103°F in South Texas in February, and rainstorms in the Hill Country so intense that previously dry stream beds turned into rushing torrents in mere minutes. Truly, I am a part of Texas, and Texas is a part of me.

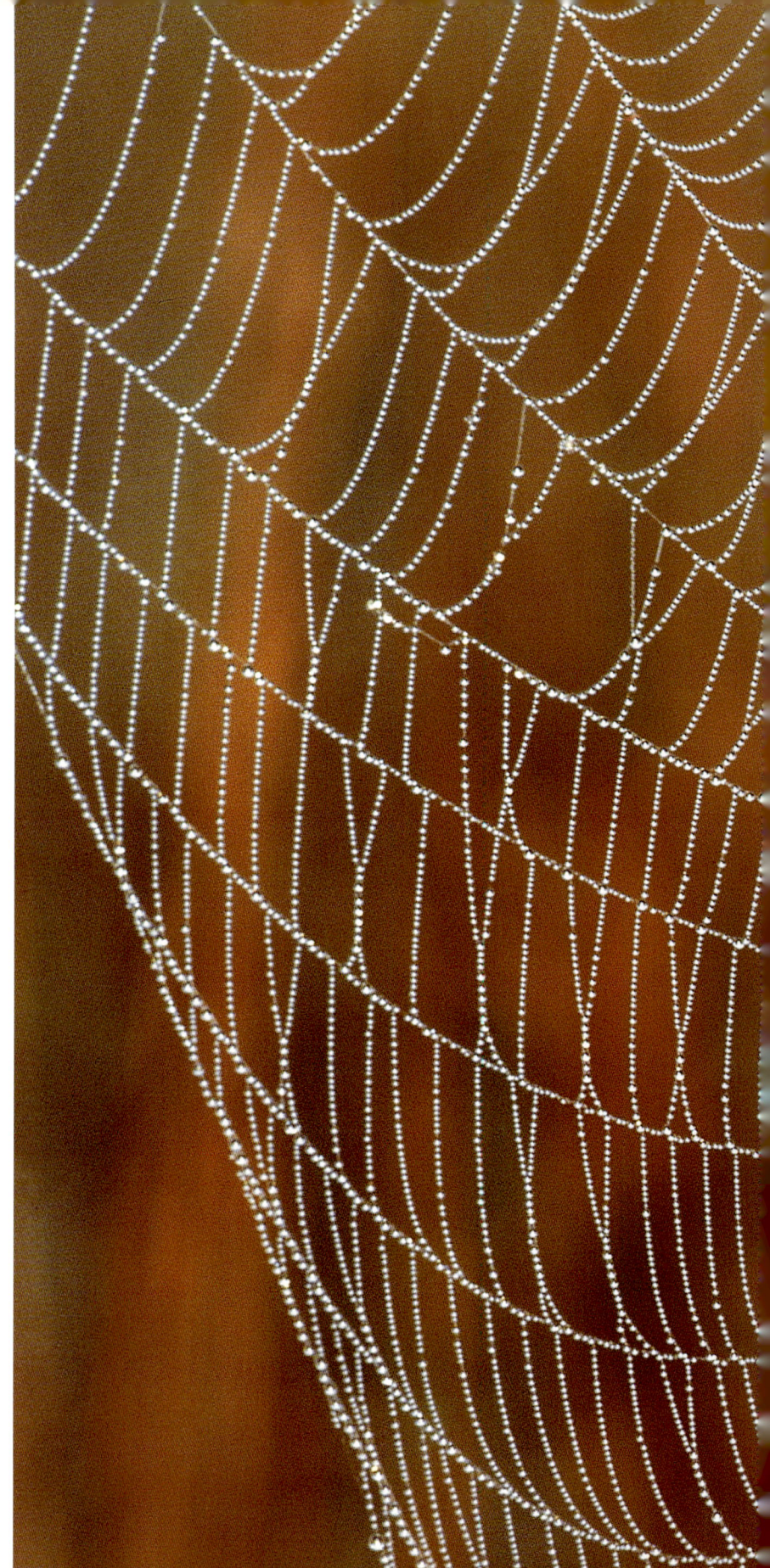

At sunrise after a night of heavy dew on a Kenedy County ranch, I came across this **spider web** *heavily laden with dewdrops. The web's owner still guarded its wet home. As the sun sparkled off the water drops on the web and illuminated the golden grass stalks in the background, I was able to get a few shots before the morning breeze picked up and ended the entrancing scene.*

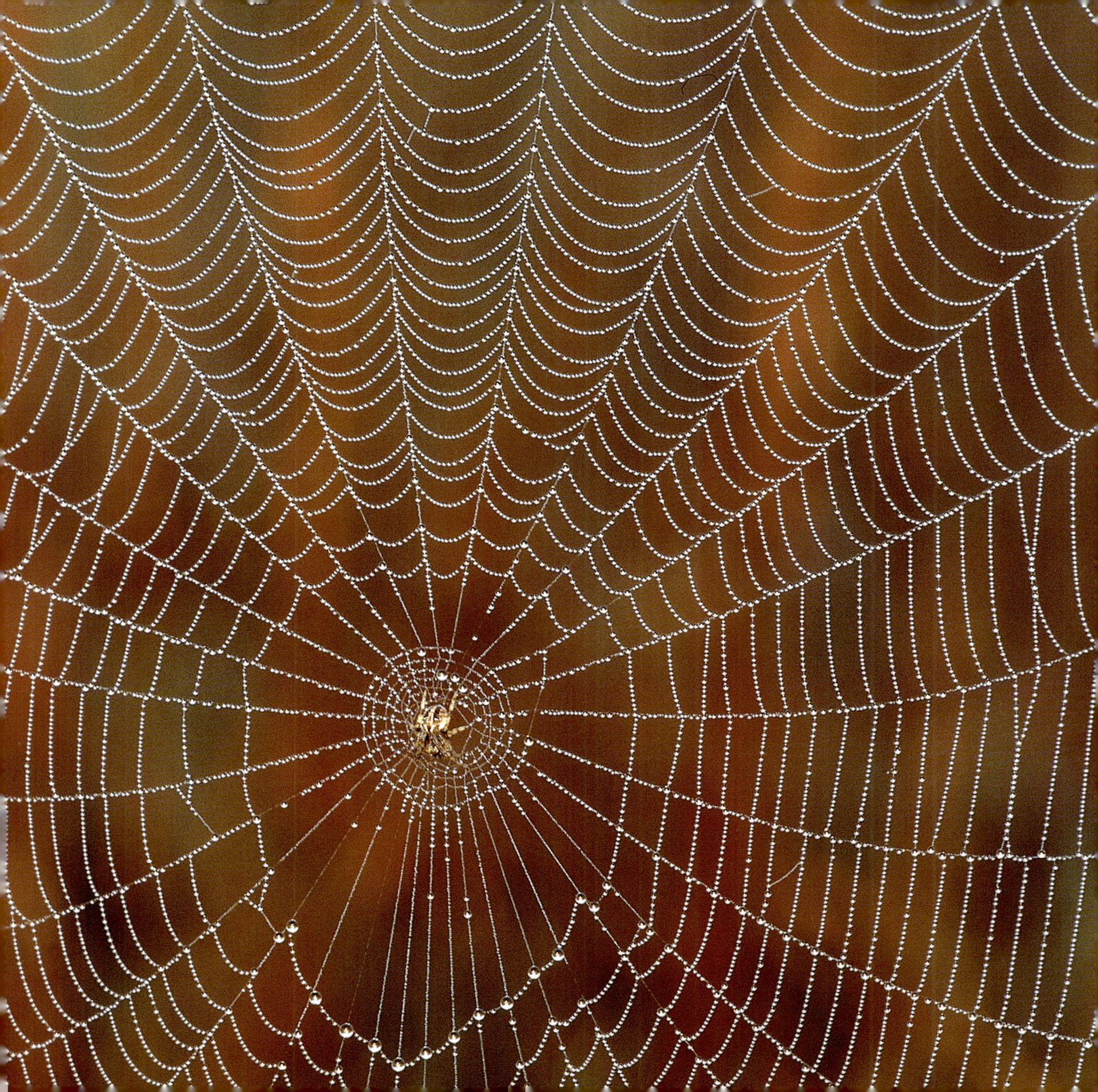

Looking at each image, I could usually remember what the weather was like when the photograph was taken, and I remembered the color of the sky and the angle of the light and who was with me. It was like reliving each experience. With the bittern, I remembered moving slightly to get the light at a better angle before finally capturing a moment in time in the life of this particular creature. I well recalled the absolutely massive American Alligator, covered with duckweed, as it stared at me in a coastal Texas marsh. I remembered the look in the eye of the coyote as he watched me and licked his chops while I waited, concealed in a photo blind. The coyote knew I was there, and I knew that the coyote knew I was there, yet we still had this incredible moment of eye contact.

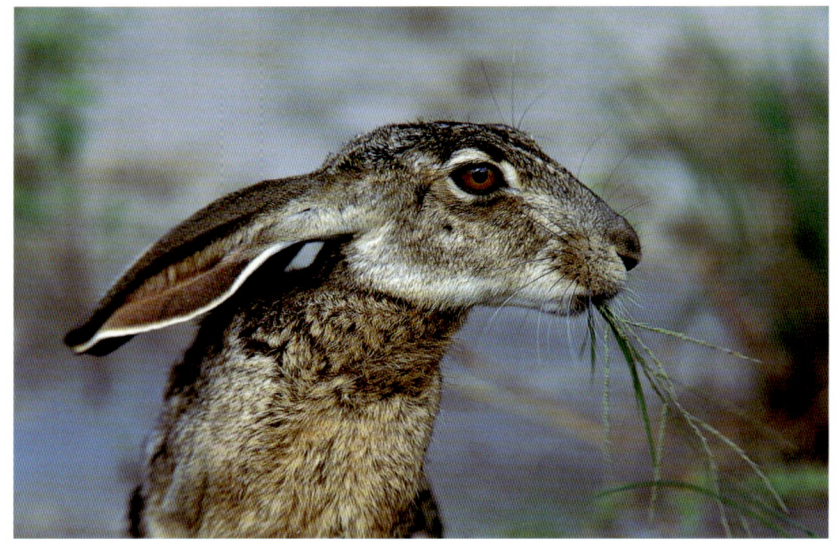

Black-tailed Jackrabbits *range widely across much of South and West Texas. Most of the time, we see these fleet-footed animals streaking across the desert flats as we pass by in an automobile, but on occasion one will allow closer observation. I spent a fair amount of time with a group of these critters on a Kenedy County ranch, and they often allowed me to sit quite close to them as they foraged and went about their daily activities. This one seemed totally relaxed as it enjoyed a grassy treat.*

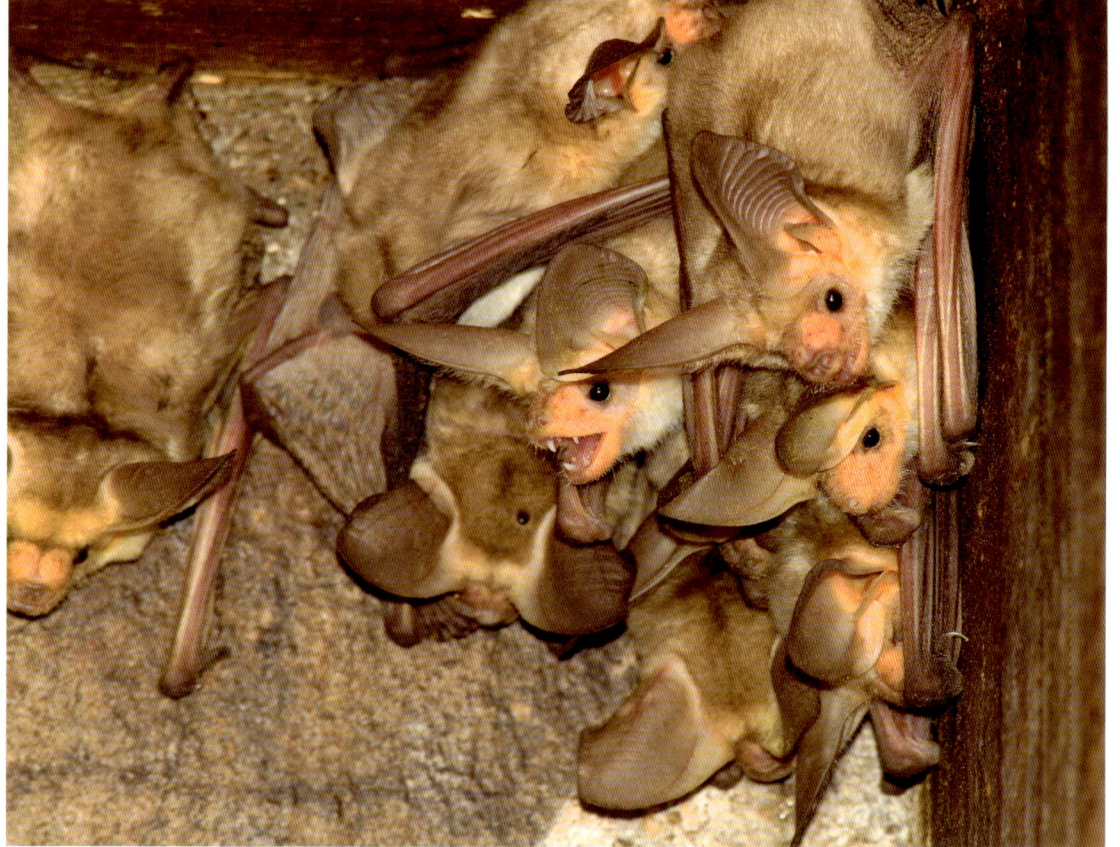

Pallid Bats *occur over a wide area of the American west including parts of West Texas. The species likes desert areas, especially near rocky outcroppings. Pallid Bats eat scorpions and centipedes but are known to take a wide variety of insects as well. This group of Pallid Bats was roosting under the eaves of a ranch house in the Chinati Mountains of Presidio County.*

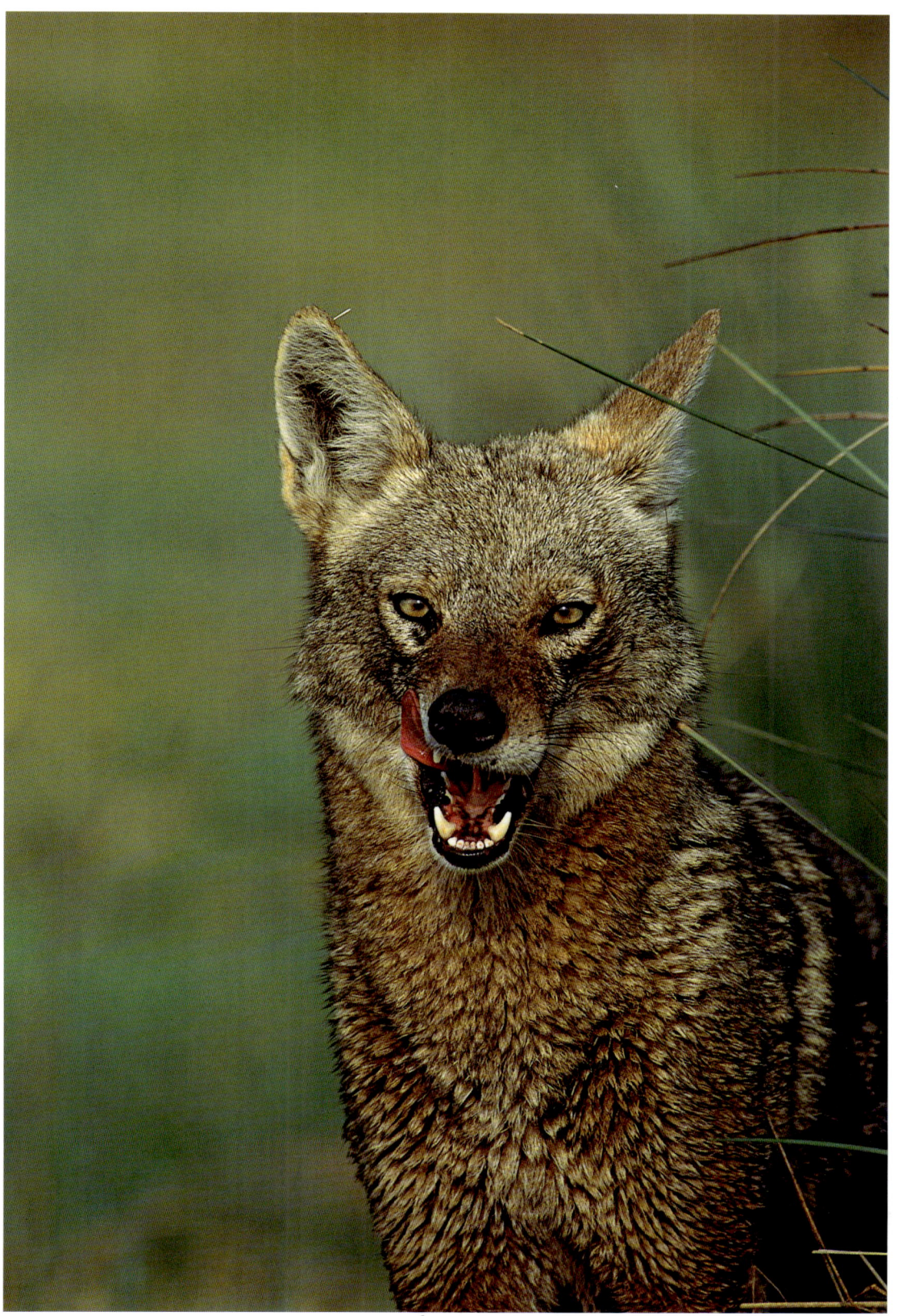

*I spent several mornings sitting in a blind on a Kenedy County ranch photographing vultures as they fed upon the carcass of a feral hog. On my second morning, a pair of **Coyotes** cautiously approached, but they seemed a little too shy to approach the hog. After more than an hour, one of the animals felt comfortable enough with the situation to come in to feed. I got several shots of him as he fed, but my favorite was this image as he licked his chops. The small cactus thorn in his right ear added an interesting touch. Coyotes are really beautiful animals, and despite their reputation as a nuisance, they are an important part of our wild heritage.*

I remembered working hard to get flight shots of Harris's Hawks in South Texas, hiking to a small desert spring in West Texas to photograph a rare dragonfly called Mayan Setwing, and staying up all night on many occasions to get shots of dragonflies emerging from their exuvia at a South Texas cattle tank or shots of Pallid Bats roosting on the eaves of a cabin in the Chinati Mountains of West Texas.

Still, my task remained—pick one hundred shots of Texas wildlife. I decided I wanted to have a variety of wildlife species, from bugs to mammals. Perhaps I could come up with a thousand photos that would show the diversity of Texas wildlife; perhaps, just maybe, I could narrow it down to five hundred and still have a decent collection that would be representative of what I have photographed in Texas. Only a hundred shots, the Press said, so I went back to work. The Rock Rattlesnake on the Miller Ranch in West Texas would have to be included, but which of the sixty-five shots of that particular snake would I choose? Certainly I must include the flying Harris's Hawk from the Las Colmenas Ranch in Hidalgo County, but again, which of the more than two hundred shots of that bird would I pick? It was a difficult task. After more difficult editing, I ended up with about 250 shots, each representing something special about Texas wildlife, at least to me. More editing, more culling, and finally I was able to call the Press and say that I had it down to about 125 images and that they could select the final shots.

The portraits of wildlife in this book, all of which were taken in the wild in Texas, represent a very eclectic collection of species. The focus is not on birds, insects, or mammals, but

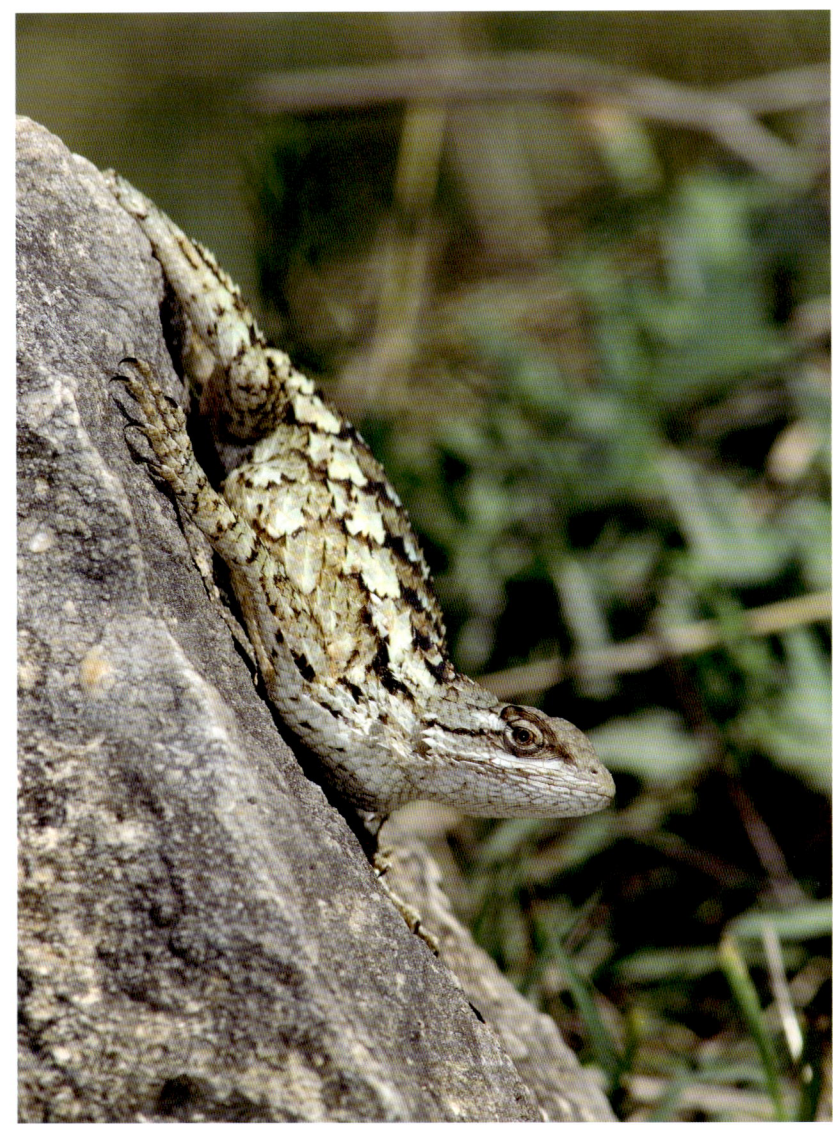

Texas Spiny Lizards *are quite common across much of Texas. They can grow to a fairly large size and occasionally may be a foot long. Sometimes they may be found sunning on a rock or a fence post while keeping a reptilian eye on the human observer. This one was on a rock near Vanderpool in Bandera County. The lizard remained motionless while I took a number of images, but it eventually scampered away when I pressed my luck and got too close.*

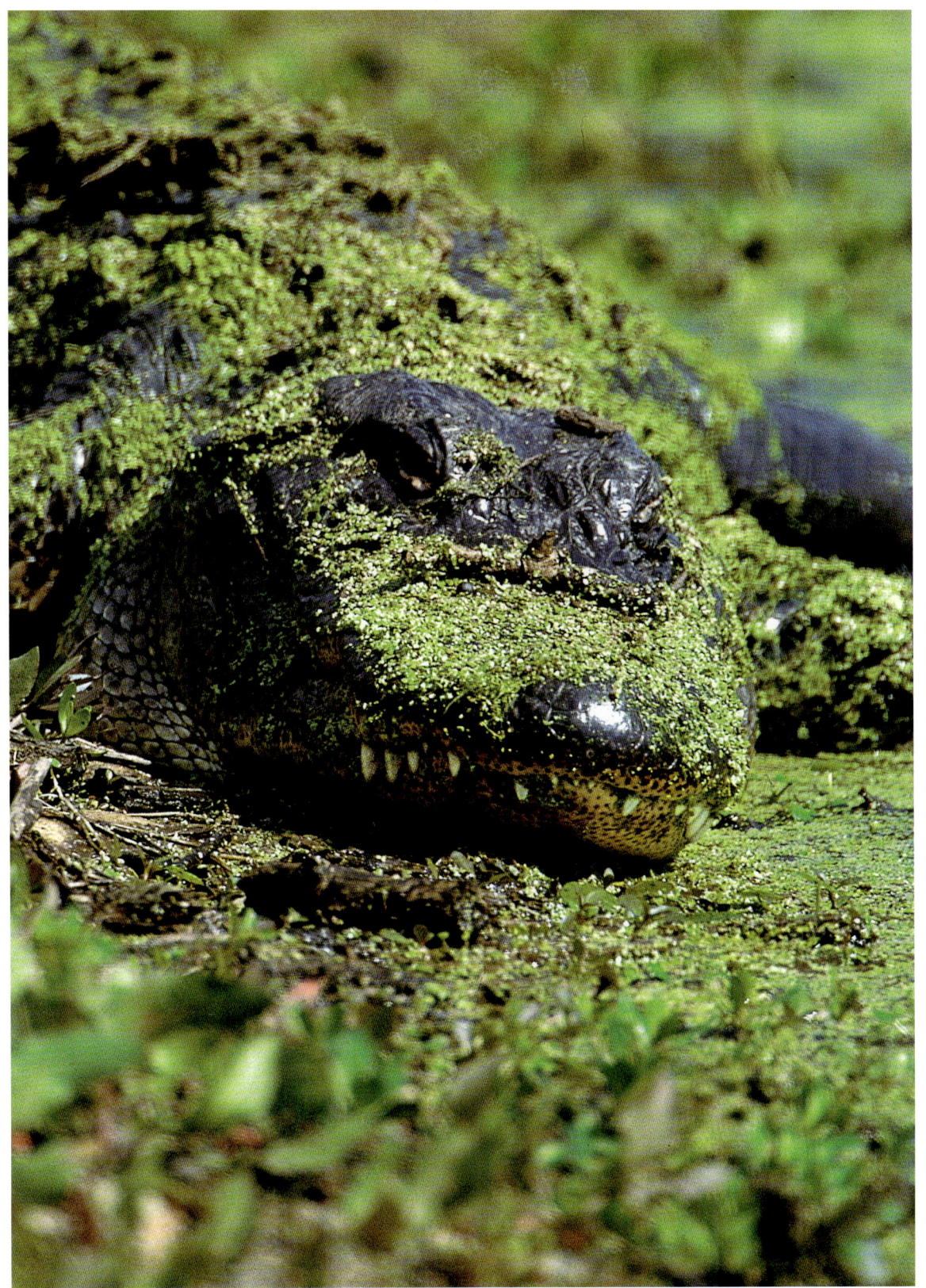

American Alligators *are quite common in parts of coastal Texas. This monster was at Brazos Bend State Park in Fort Bend County a few years ago. With the duckweed over its head and body, it blended in with its surroundings rather well. Though usually not aggressive if left alone, these reptiles certainly deserve our greatest respect when we are treading within their range and habitat.*

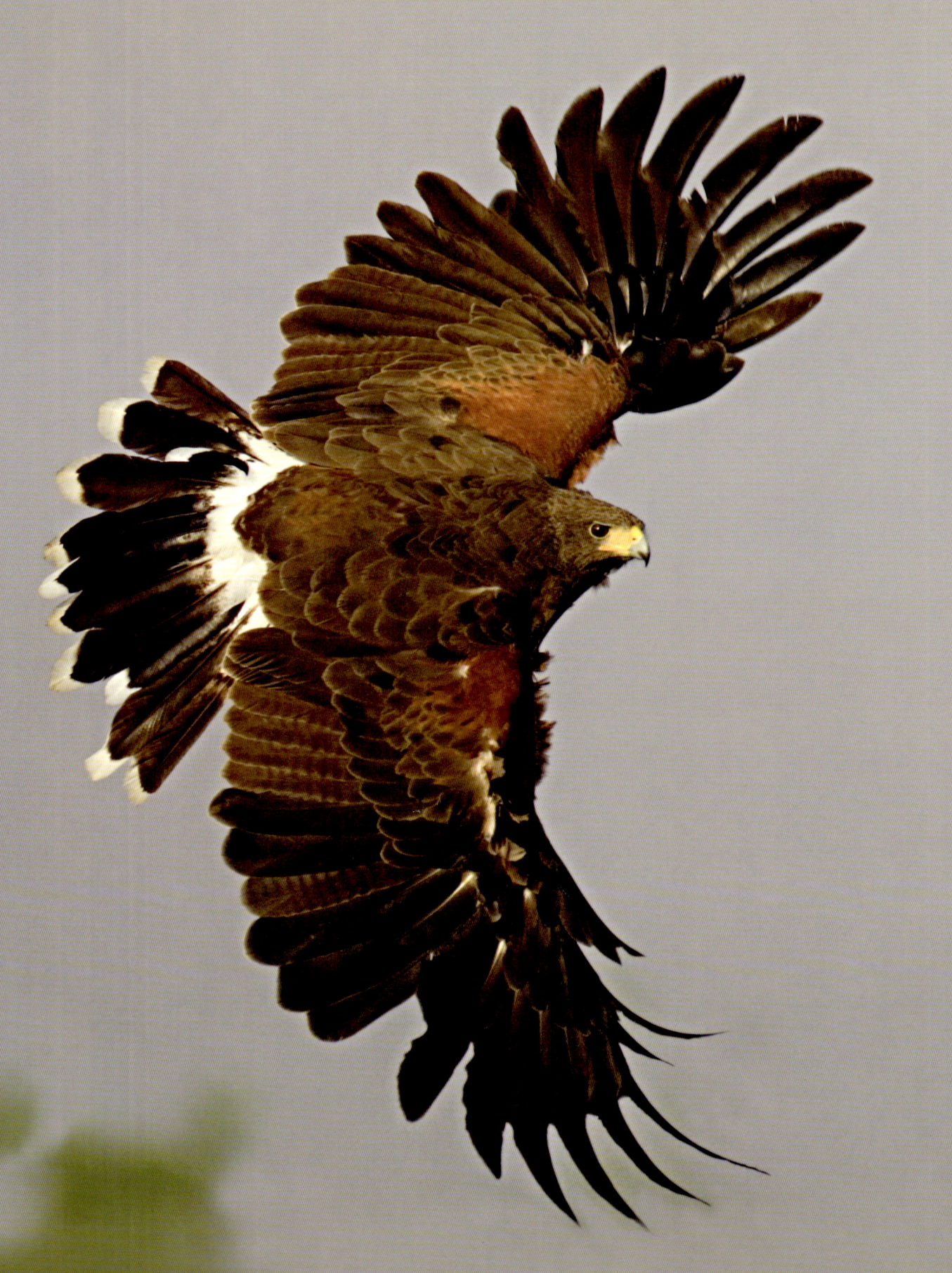

rather on Texas and the diversity of wildlife one photographer has been able to capture with a camera. I have tried to select images that show something interesting about the habits, behavior, or appearance of each species. The species shown in this book represent just a very small percentage of the wildlife in Texas, but I hope the selection gives a little of the flavor of this great state and its natural history. In this modern world of cities and highways, burgeoning populations, high-speed Internet, instant everything, and continuing loss of wildlife habitat, I am happy to report that Texas still hosts wild areas and wild creatures if you will only go out and look. Take advantage of our wonderful state. Our parks and other natural areas await you! I hope to see you out there.

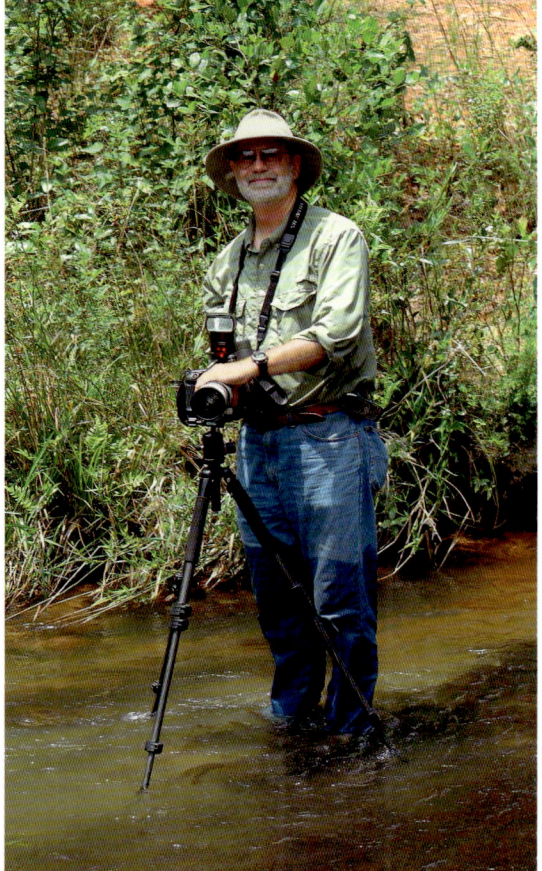

Greg Lasley wading in a stream in the mountains of north Georgia to photograph dragonflies in July 2005. Photo by Giff Beaton.

The **Harris's Hawk** *is an aerial predator of South and West Texas. The species is known to hunt in family groups, whereby several individuals will cooperate to flush quarry from a thicket so other members of the group can capture it. The Harris's is one of our most beautiful hawks, distinctly colored with its rusty shoulders, chocolate brown breast, back, and wings, and black and white tail. This subadult Harris's Hawk was making a banking turn at the edge of mesquite woodland in Hidalgo County near Edinburg.*

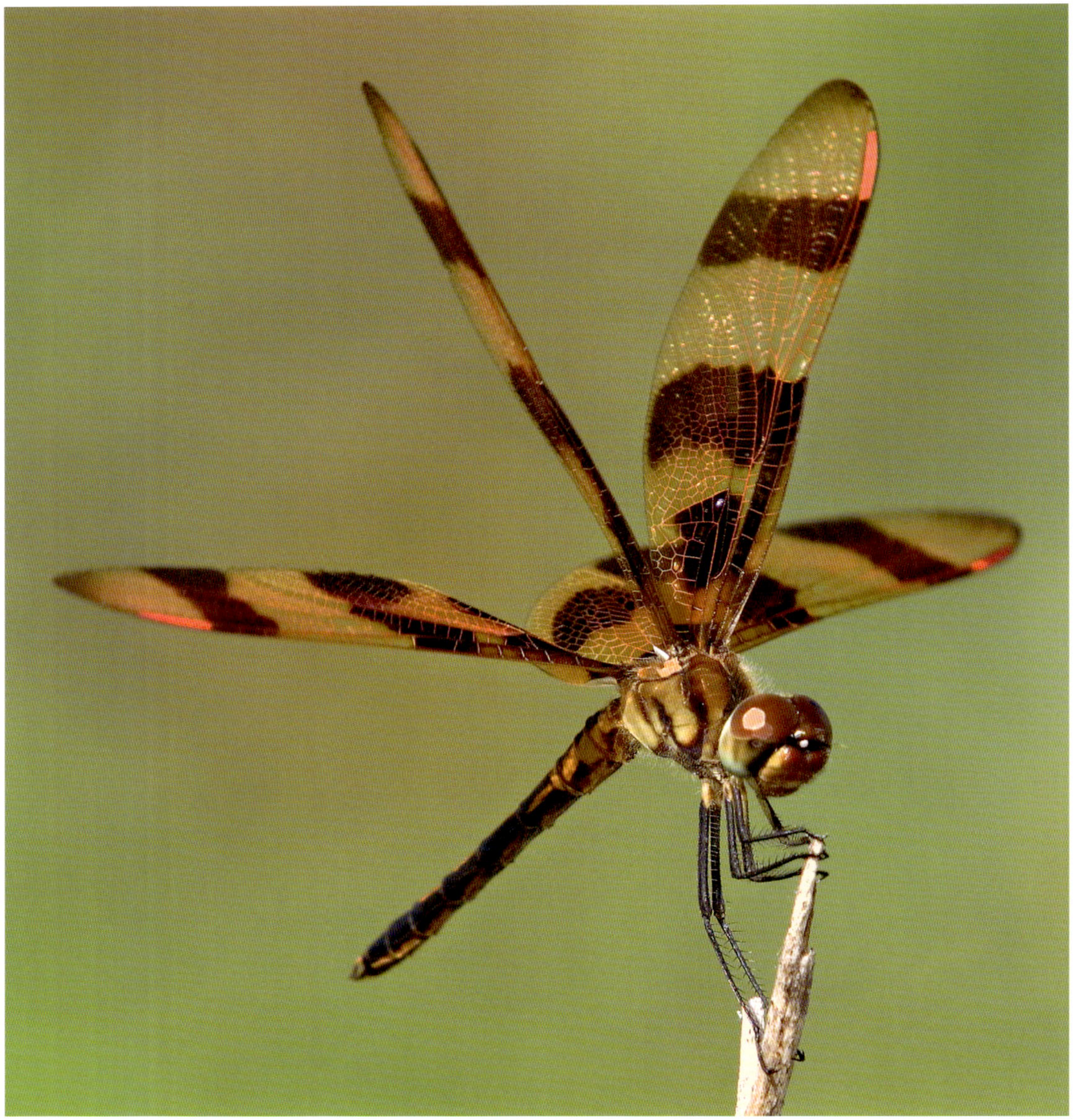

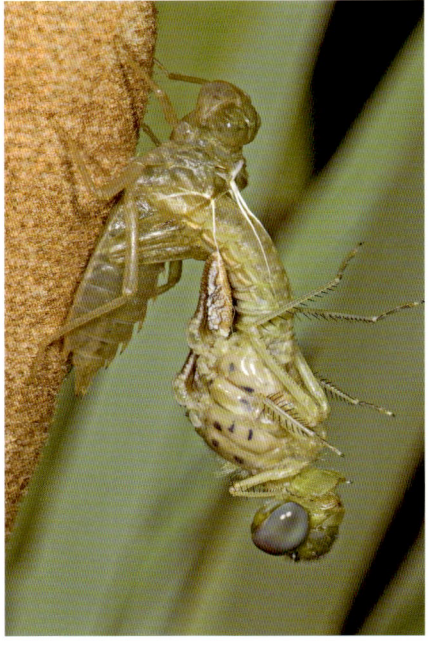

The **Halloween Pennant**, so called because of its black and orange coloration, is a showy dragonfly species found across much of Texas. One will sometimes perch on a weed tip with its rear wings held out and front wings held upward, perhaps to help balance in the wind. This male Halloween Pennant was in Travis County near Austin on a hot August afternoon.

We usually see dragonflies as they fly around a lake or pond. Many people do not know dragonflies actually spend their first year or so as an aquatic insect, a larva, living underwater. When the time is right, the larva climbs out of the water onto a stick or weed stalk, and over a period of several hours, the adult form of the dragonfly emerges. This transition usually takes place at night because the insect is very vulnerable to predation during this stage and would be easy prey for a flycatcher during daylight hours. I spent a number of nights on a Hidalgo County ranch, sitting alongside a cattle tank and trying to obtain images of this emergence process. The shot here, of a **Red-tailed Pennant** emerging from its larval shell on a cattail, was taken at about 3:00 a.m. one June morning.

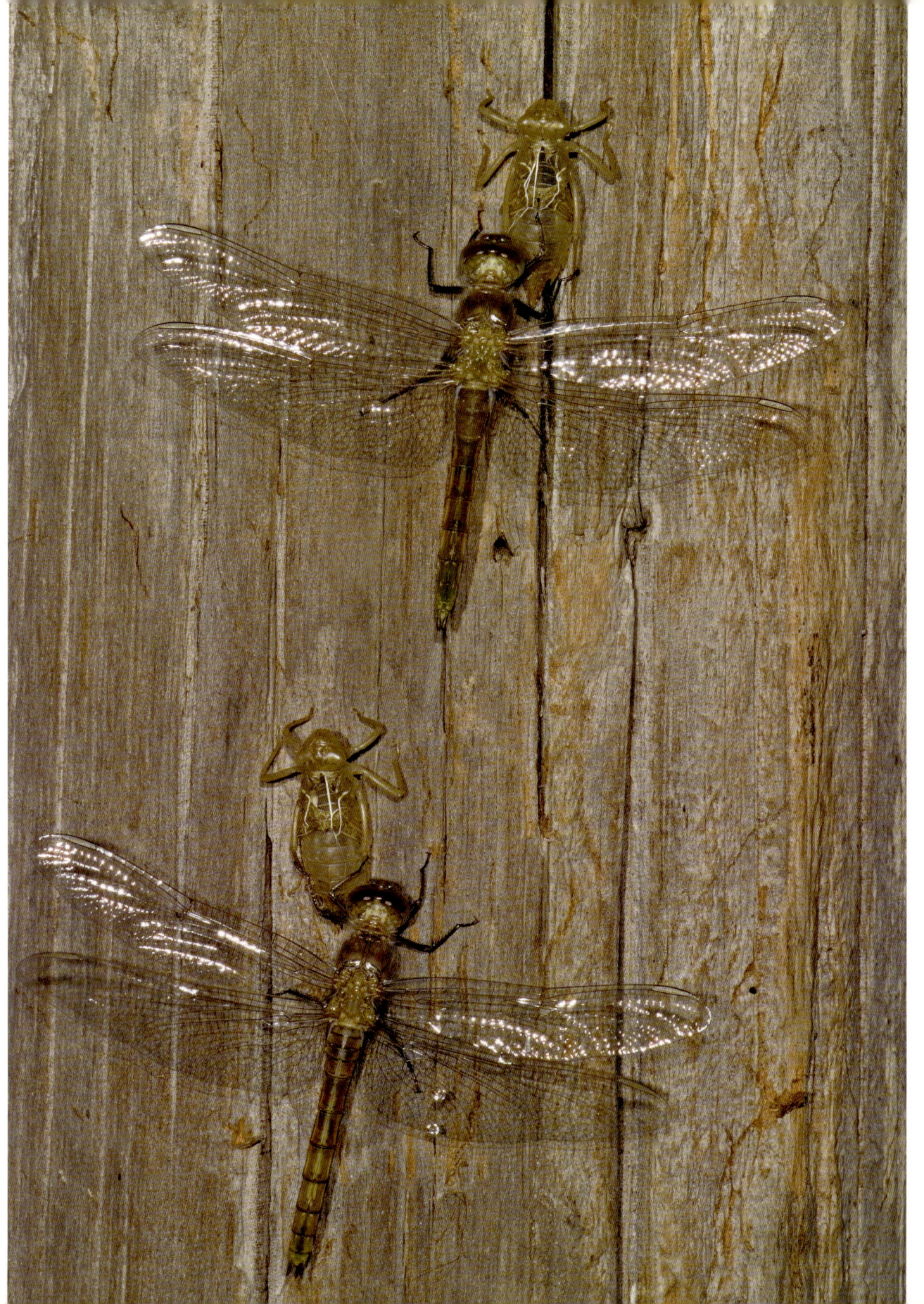

*These two **Red-tailed Pennants** had just recently emerged from their larval shells. A dragonfly will sit quietly for a period of time, allowing its wings to dry, then fly off to spend its first few days hiding in trees or brush until its body hardens and it is better able to escape predators. This image was taken on a Hidalgo County ranch.*

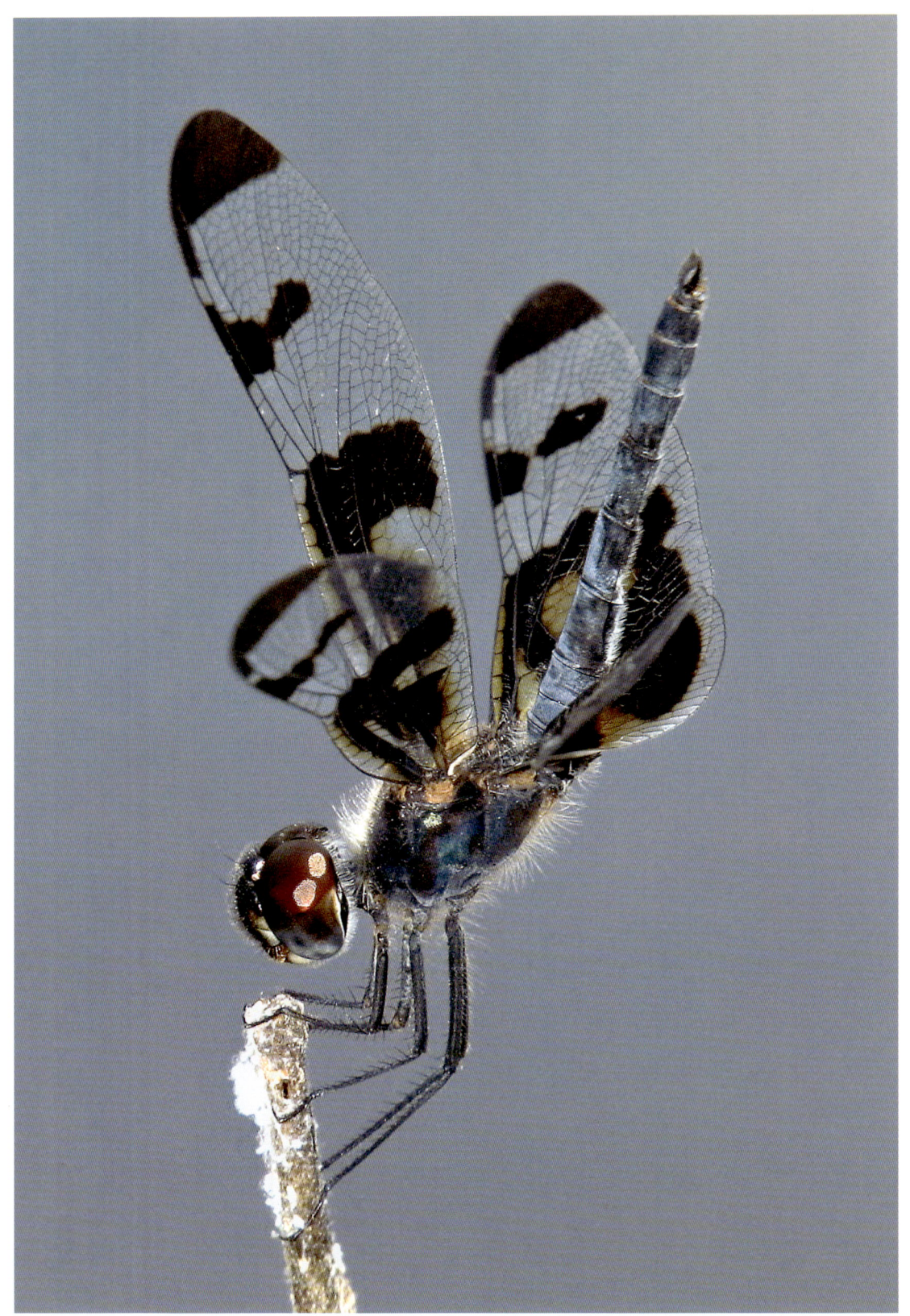

Left: **Banded Pennants** *are dragonflies that may be commonly found over a large area of Texas. This male is in an obelisk position, whereby a dragonfly points its abdomen toward the sun in order to minimize the area of the insect that receives direct sunlight. This is one method dragonflies use to perch in the hot sun on a summer day without becoming overheated. This image was taken in the Angelina National Forest near Zavalla in Angelina County.*

Opposite: If you walk slowly along a forested stream in East Texas, you may see an iridescent blue-black form dancing in the air around you. **Ebony Jewelwings** *are beautiful damselflies of East Texas and prefer shaded, forested streams with beams of sunlight filtering through the canopy. Watching this delicate damselfly in a dark forest as it flits through beams of light like twinkling tiny blue light bulbs is a magical experience. This one was near Zavalla in Angelina County.*

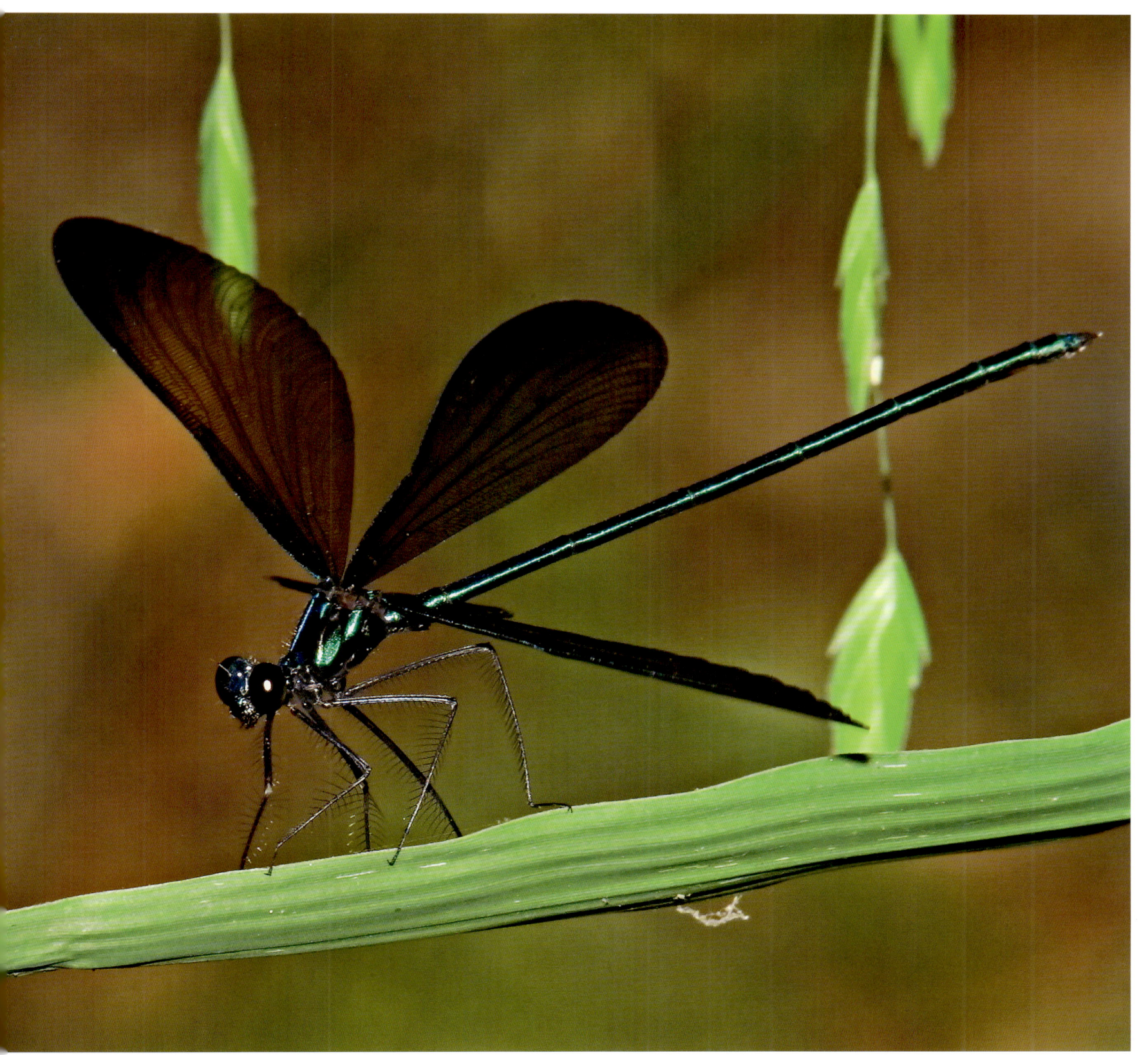

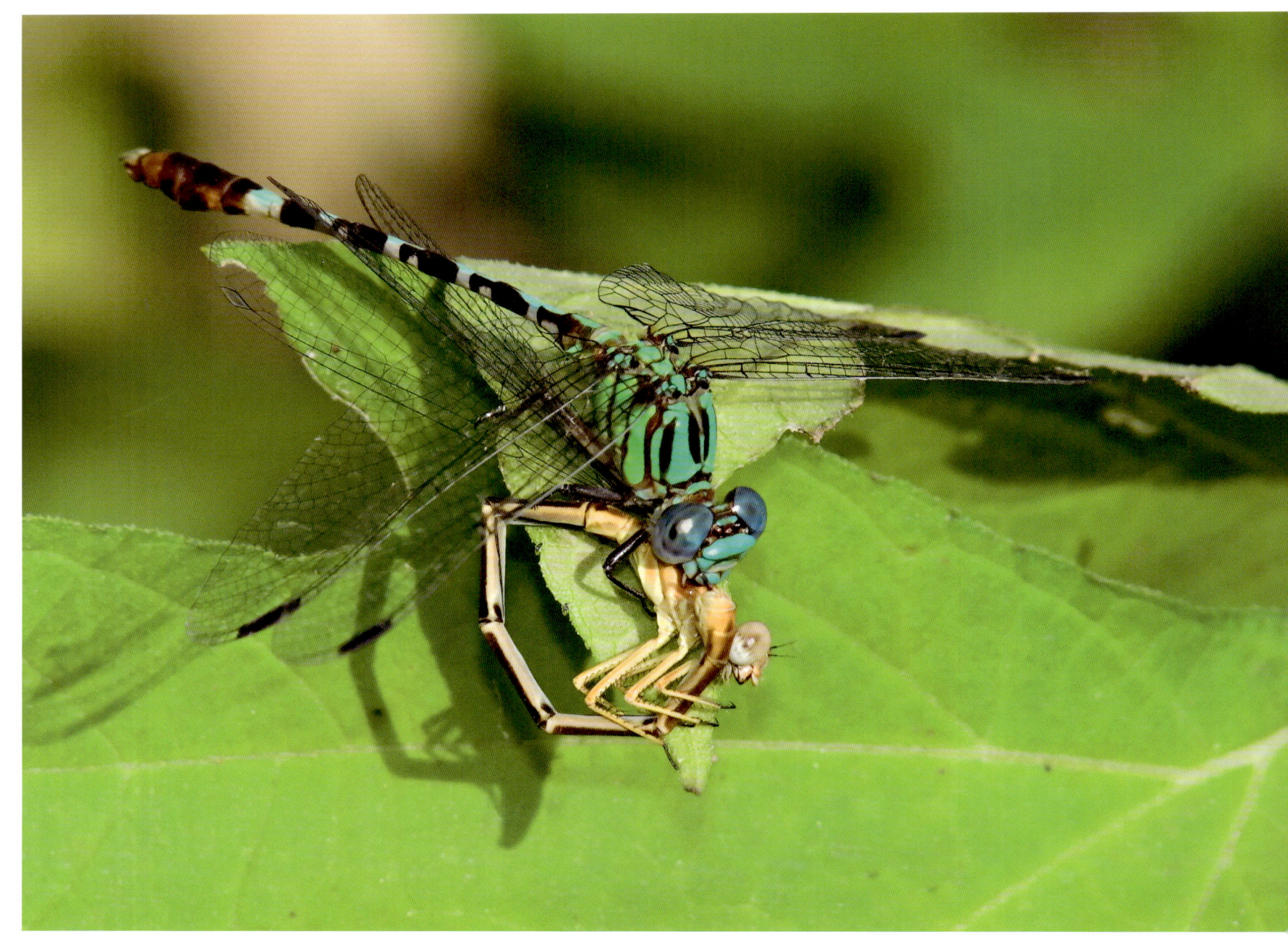

The **Blue-faced Ringtail** *is quite a rare dragonfly. This colorful bug may be found deep into Central America, but within the United States, the species is known from only three Texas counties. I found this male Blue-faced Ringtail eating a Powdered Dancer that it had captured along the banks of the Guadalupe River in Gonzales County.*

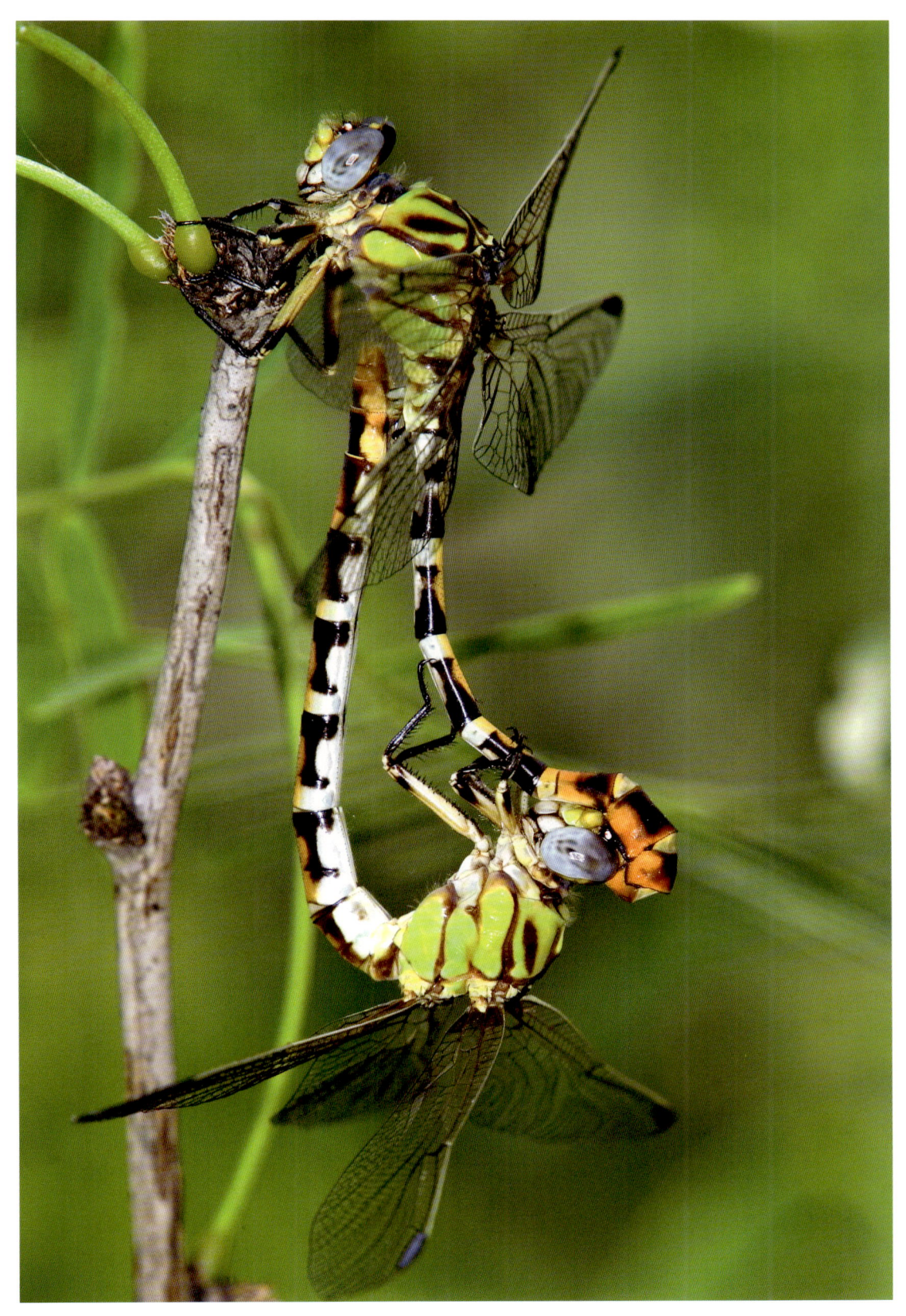

The **Eastern Ringtail** *is a fairly common dragonfly across much of Texas. I found this pair "in copula" on a mesquite twig in Austin. The male's abdomen tip has appendages that allow him to grasp the female on the back of the head while the female brings her abdomen tip forward to contact the male genitalia.*

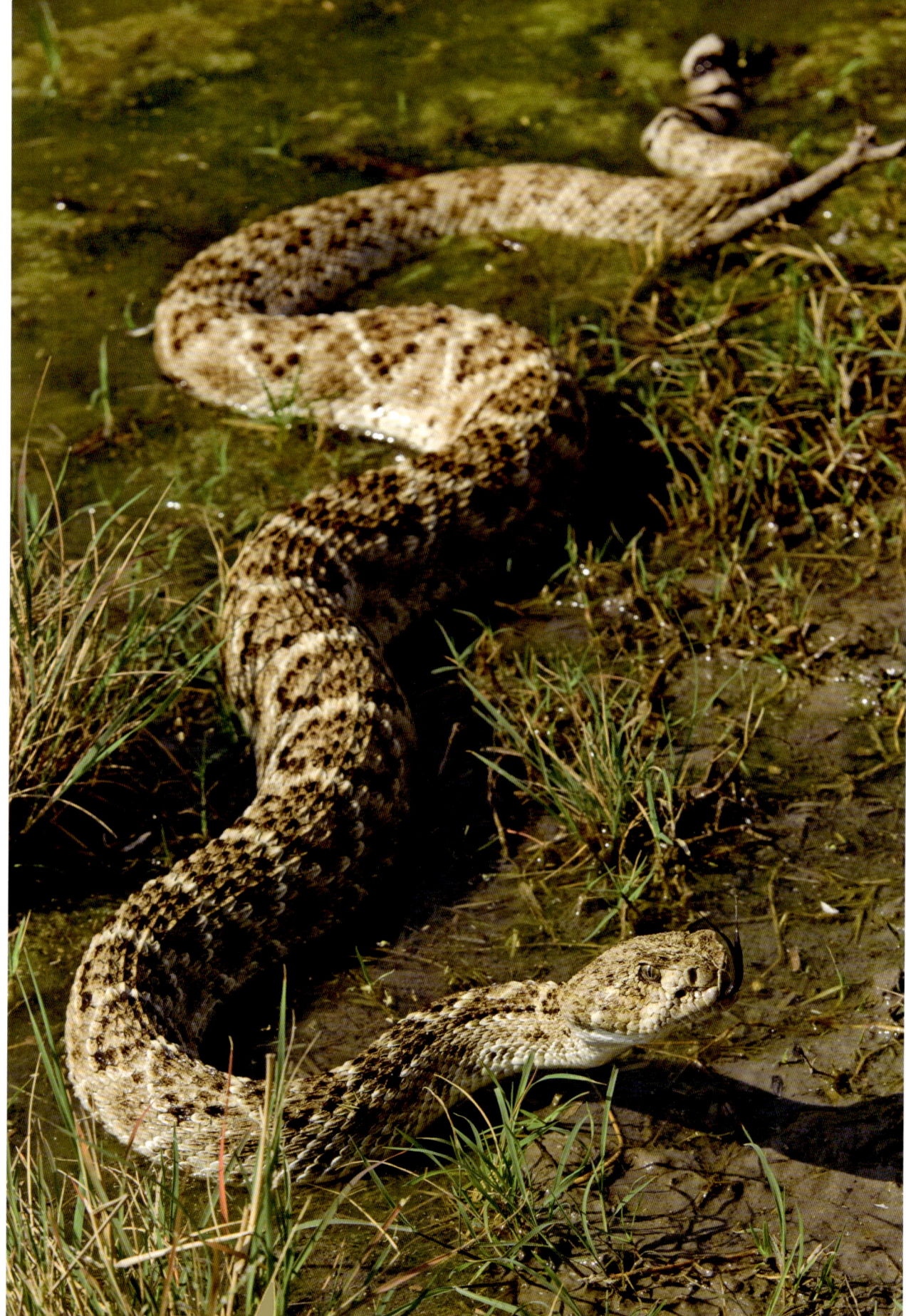

Western Diamond-backed Rattlesnakes *will sometimes visit a water hole to drink. I found this one at the edge of a small pond in Hidalgo County in South Texas. It was a massive brute, well over five feet in length. The snake remained motionless but watched me carefully for several minutes as I took shots of it. After I backed away, the snake slowly disappeared into the thick South Texas brush.*

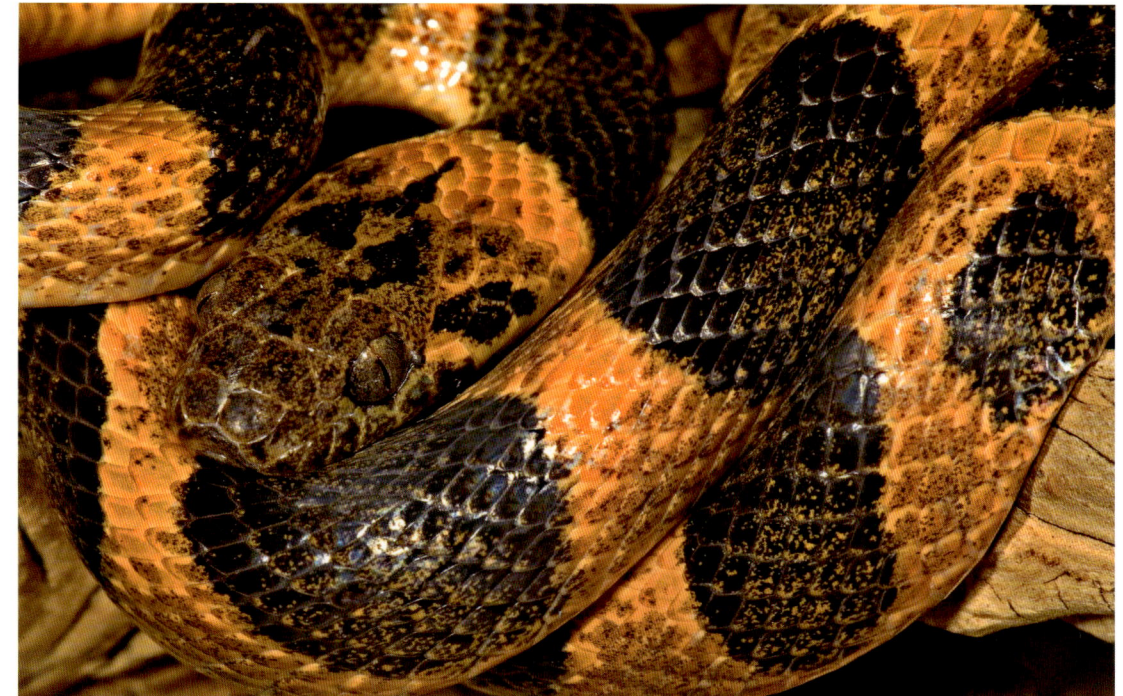

*The **Northern Cat-eyed Snake** is a small, mildly venomous tropical snake that, within the United States, is only found in deep South Texas. It is rare and inconspicuous and usually nocturnal. It is normally an inoffensive snake and simply prefers to be left alone while it hunts for insects or tiny frogs. This one was curled up on a mesquite limb near McCook in Hidalgo County.*

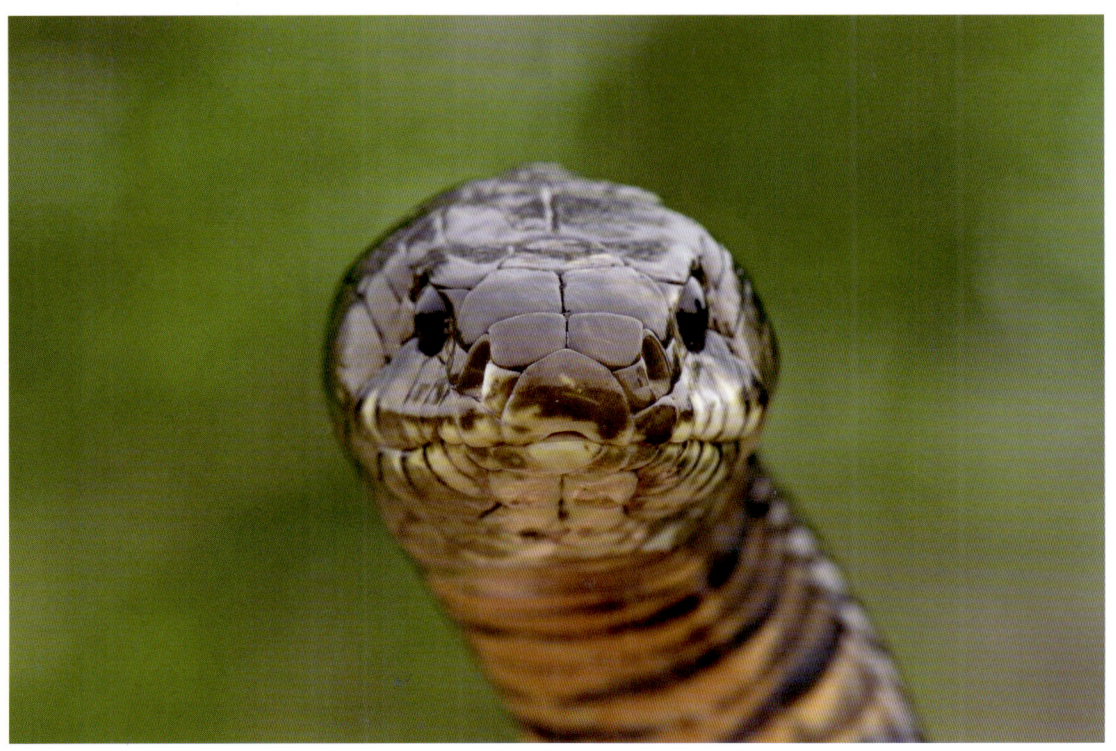

Texas Indigo Snakes
can be huge, but they are not dangerous to people in any way. I have seen this species reach a length of over eight feet, and I promise that is not a "tall Texas tale." The species only occurs in far South Texas, where it sometimes hunts other snakes, including rattlesnakes. It is somehow immune to a rattler's venom. This big fellow peered at me in such a manner that I have always regarded this shot as perhaps the last view that many a rattlesnake ever saw. This shot was taken on a ranch near McCook in Hidalgo County.

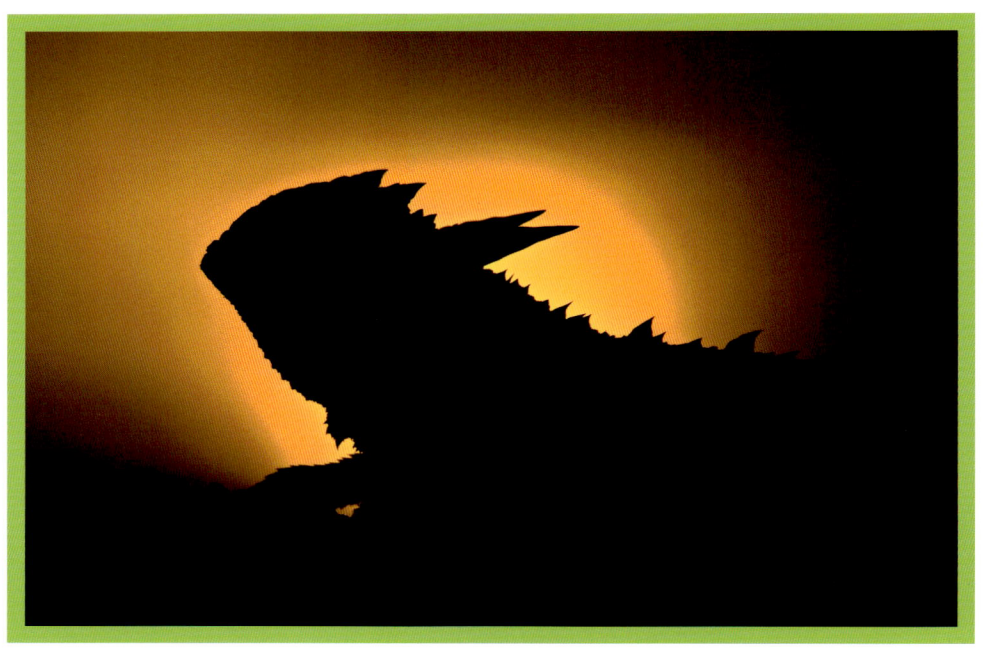

The **Texas Horned Lizard** *was once more common than it is today, but the species may still be found in many areas of the state. The lizard often feeds on our native ants and prefers sandy soils. This Texas Horned Lizard was on the ground near a rocky outcropping at sunset in Hidalgo County, providing a unique silhouette.*

Opposite: While driving along a ranch road in Hidalgo County, I saw something that appeared to be a flying green gemstone pass in front of my windshield. Stopping to investigate, I found this wonderful **Longhorn Beetle** *of the genus* Plinthocelium *perched on a nearby Texas ebony. The green and gold colors of the beetle against the green foliage of the ebony were striking.*

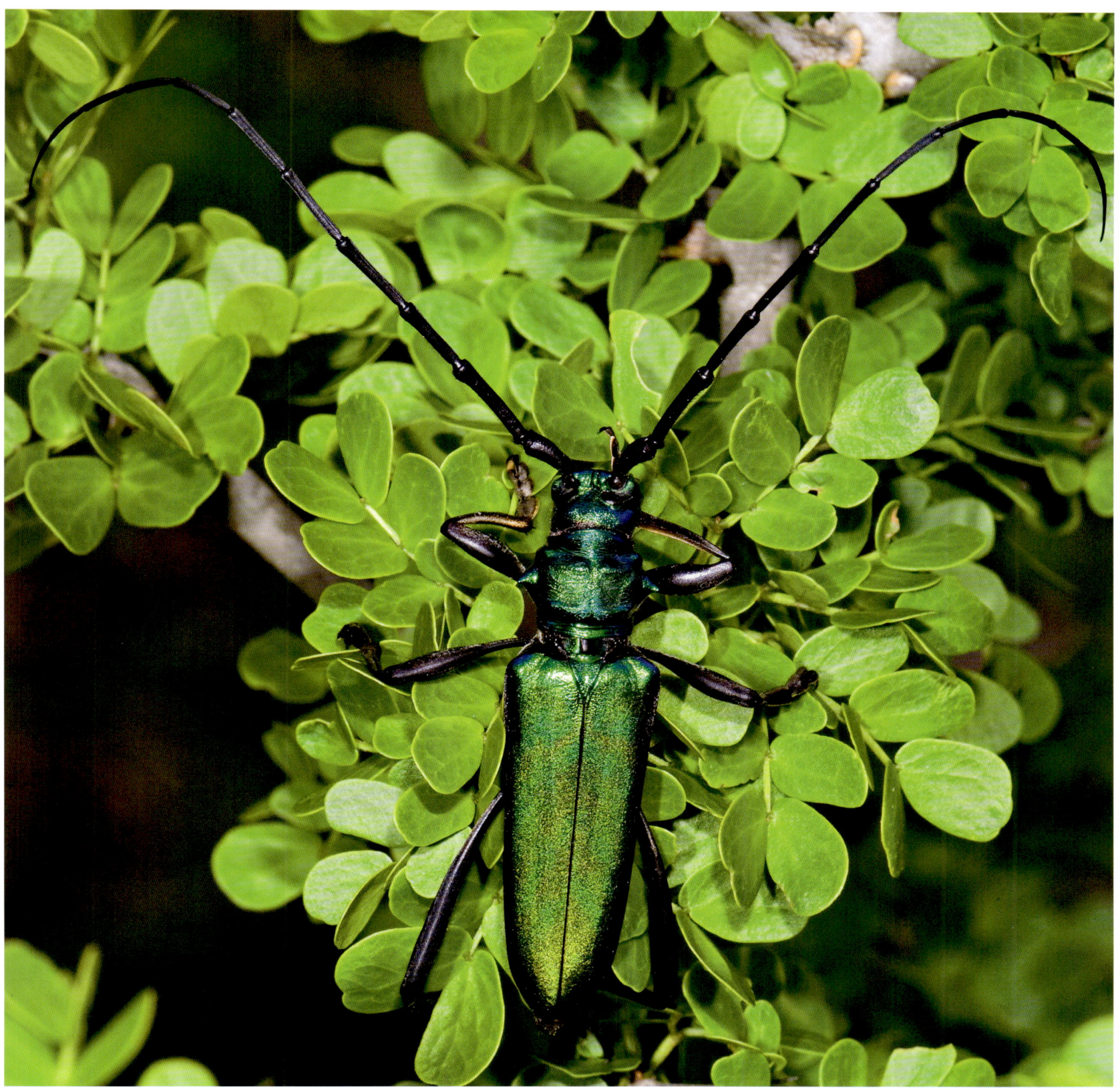

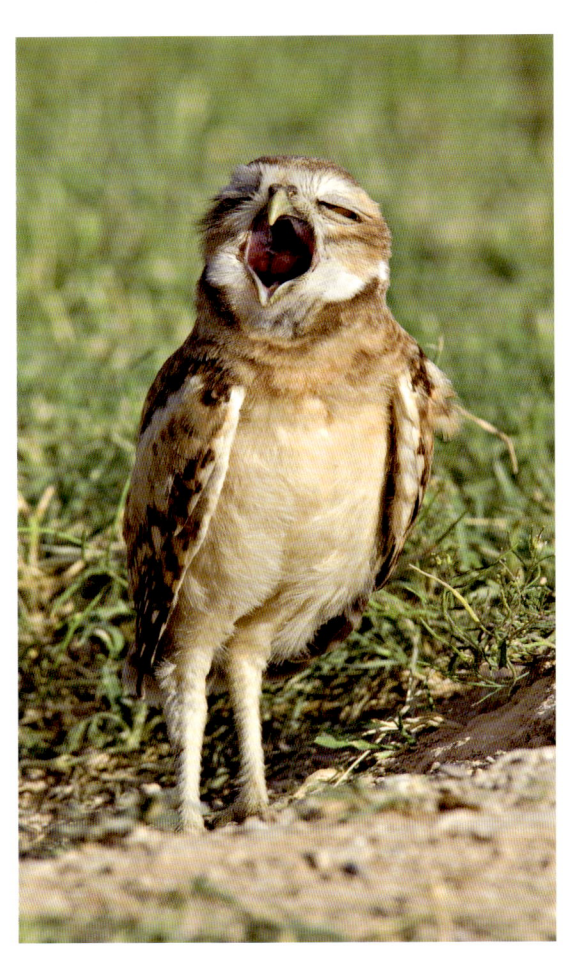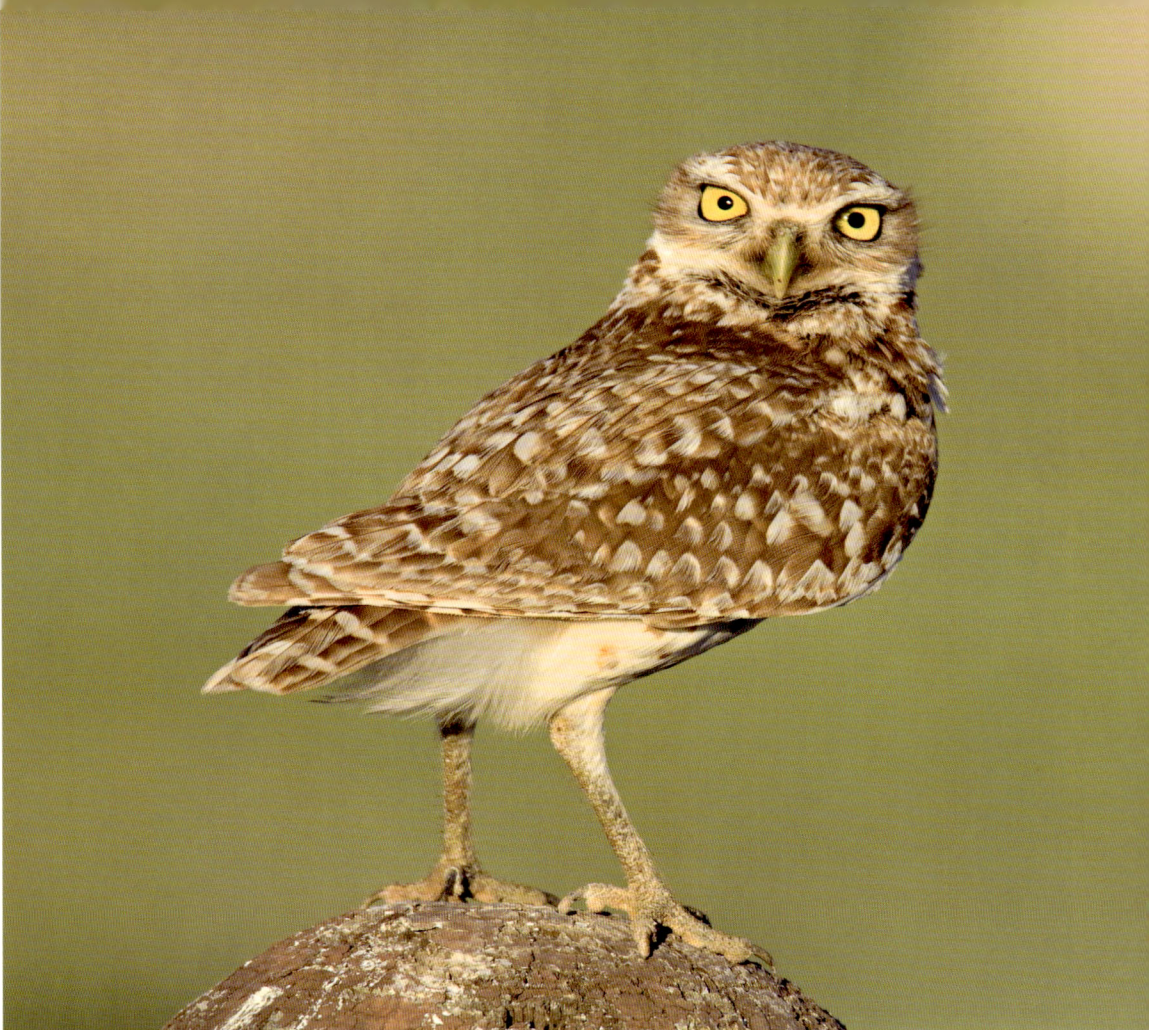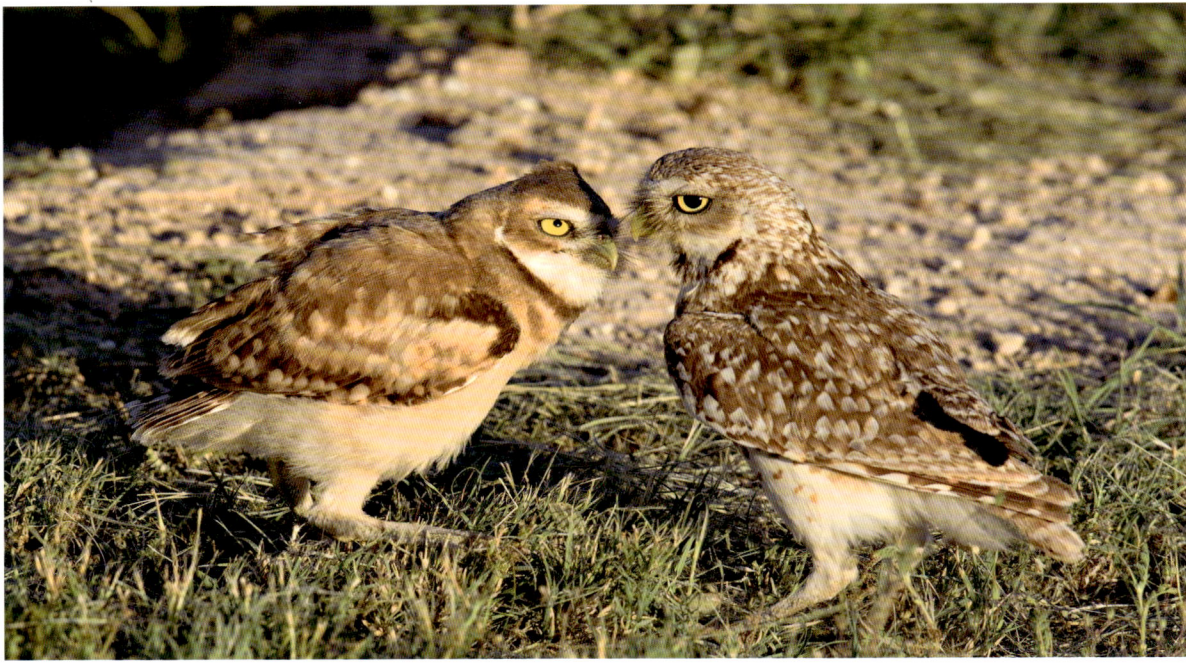

On an early June day, I stopped in Fort Stockton in Pecos County to spend the night. I had visited the area many times and knew of a small population of **Burrowing Owls** *in town. In the late afternoon, when the sun began to get low in the sky, I decided to see if I could find some to photograph. I went to a couple of known burrows and saw adult birds in the vicinity, so I parked my truck in a position to allow me to use a large telephoto lens from a bean bag support on the open driver's window. For about an hour, I took numerous shots of adult Burrowing Owls as they perched on a fence post or stood on the ground near a burrow. Suddenly, some motion out of the corner of my eye drew my attention. A juvenile Burrowing Owl, probably only a few weeks old, had emerged from a nesting burrow and was standing nearby staring at me. I had the impression this young bird was looking at my big white truck and wondering what on earth the thing was. After a while, the young owl seemed to accept my presence and went on about its business. It yawned several times, as if still just waking up from its slumbers. Thrilled as I was with this baby owl to photograph, I then saw two more youngsters peering at me from their burrow. Soon this pair came out into the open. The three young birds stayed close to one another while exploring their new world. At one point, they lined up in a stair-step fashion as they waited for the adult to bring in a meal. The interaction of the adult with the youngsters was rather comical. Sometimes an adult would land on the ground near the young birds and one of the youngsters would tackle the adult in a playful way. At one point, one of the adults perched on a nearby post and looked back at me with an exasperated expression. It is usually fallacy to assign human emotions to an animal, but I could not help but imagine the adult was thinking, "Do you believe these crazy kids?"*

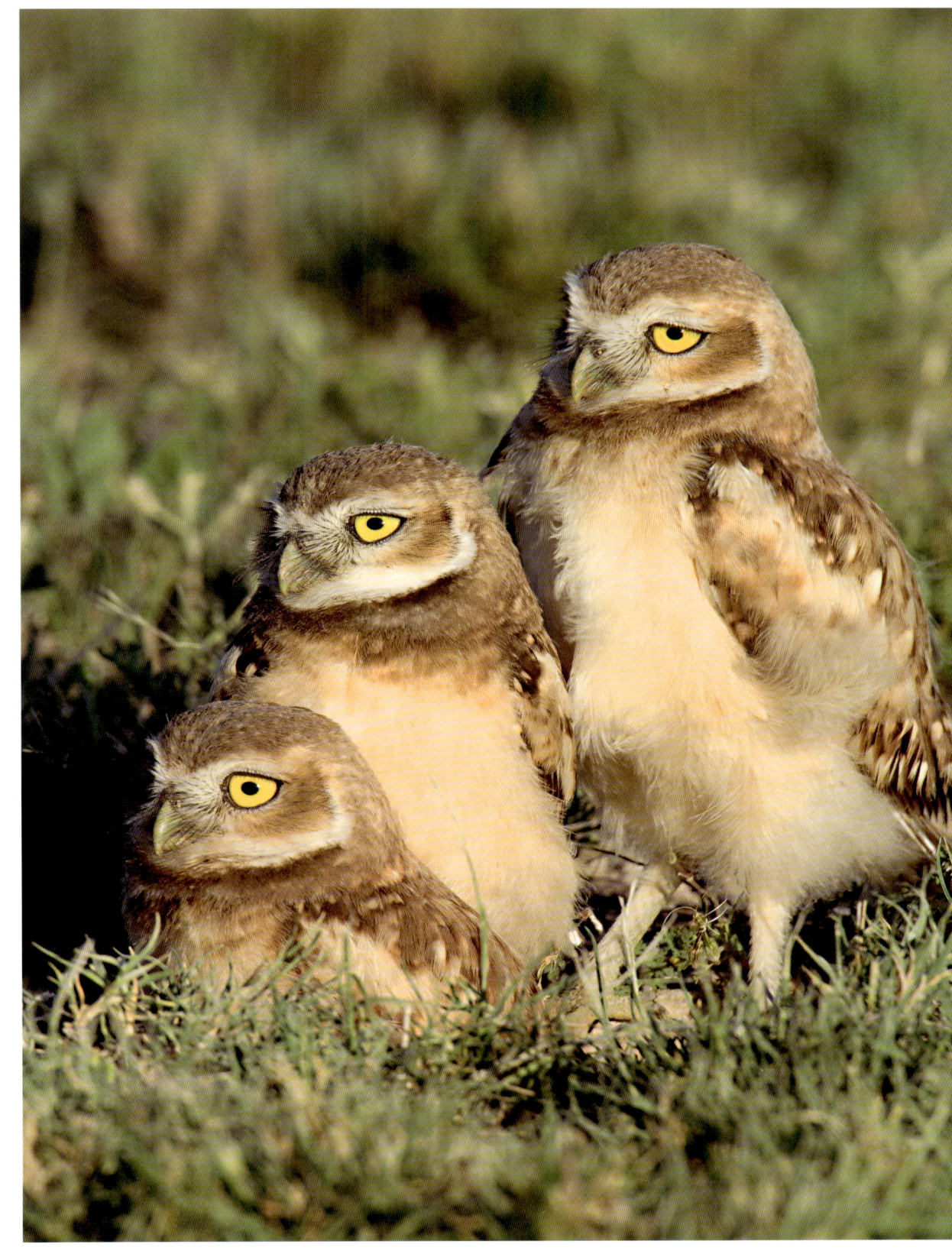

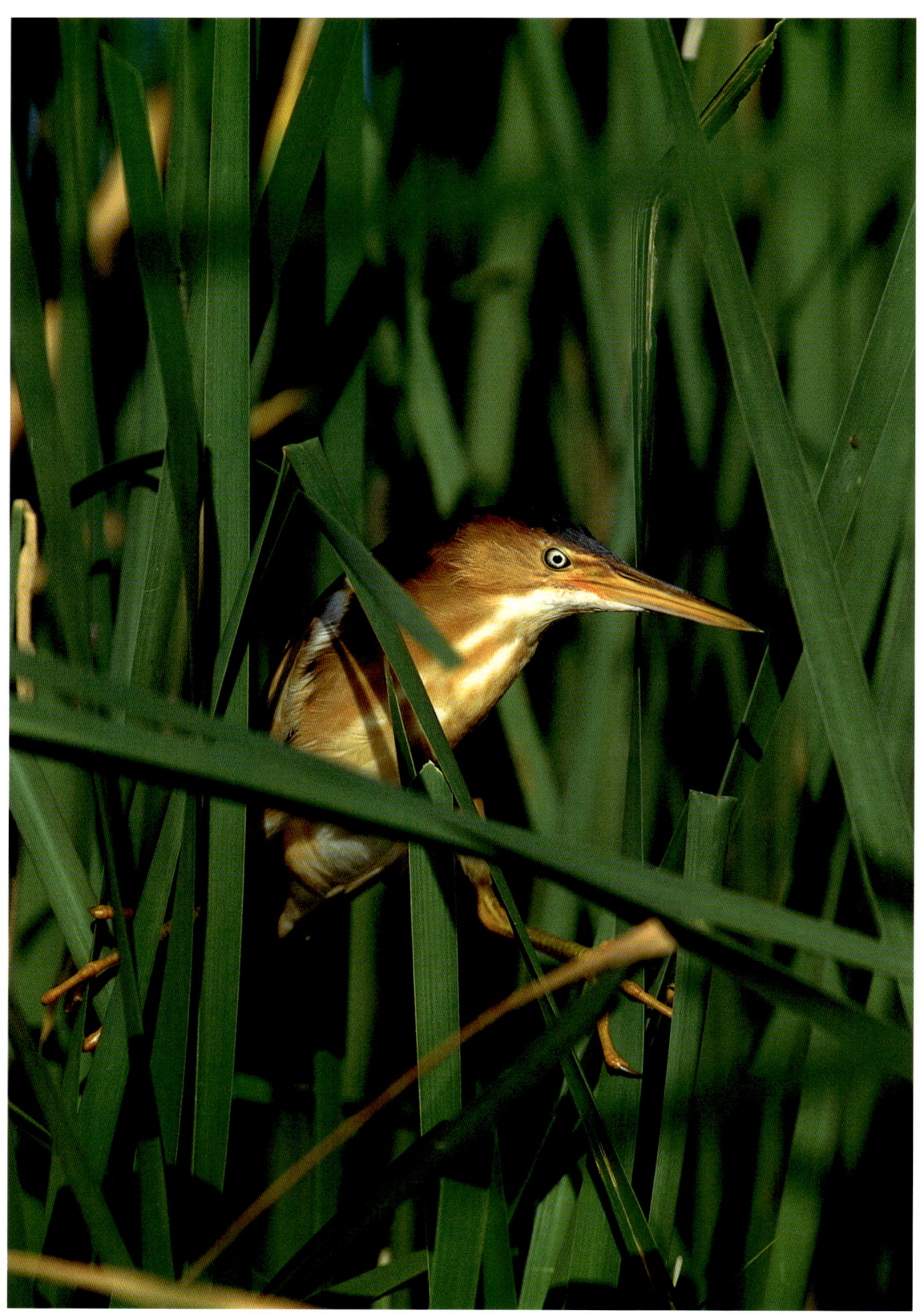

The **Least Bittern** *is a summer resident of marshes and swamps in many areas of South and East Texas. It skillfully moves through marsh vegetation while foraging and may be overlooked if the observer is not paying careful attention. This individual was perched motionless among some cattails on the edge of a pond in Kenedy County as it waited patiently for a tadpole or small frog to come close enough to catch with a lightning-fast jab of its bill.*

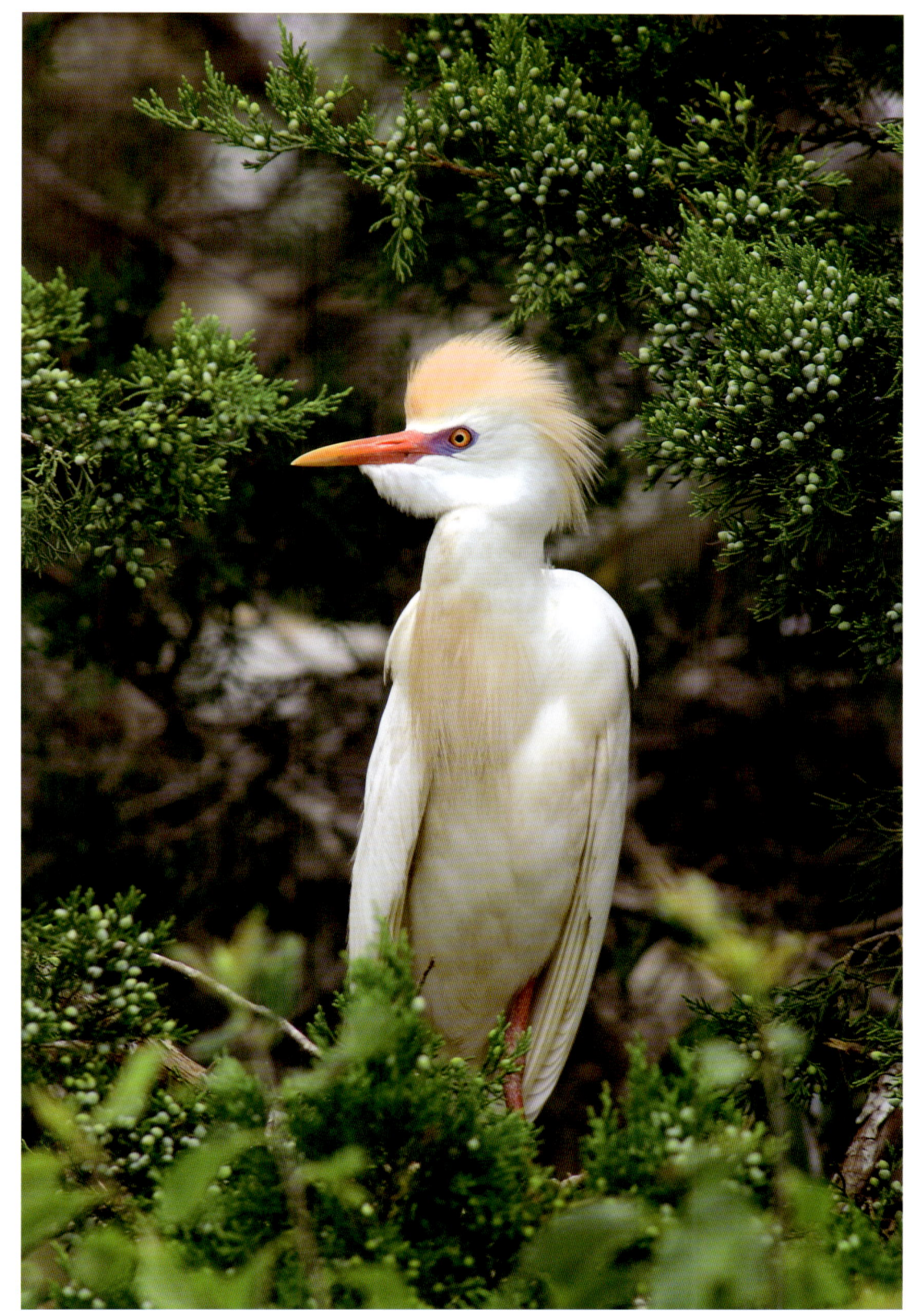

Cattle Egrets *are usually seen in small flocks as they strut through pastures at the feet of grazing cattle or horses to hunt for insects. The species is, however, a colonial nesting bird, and colonies of hundreds or even thousands of individuals may nest in one small area. This breeding plumaged Cattle Egret was near its nest in a grove of juniper trees in Harwood, Gonzales County.*

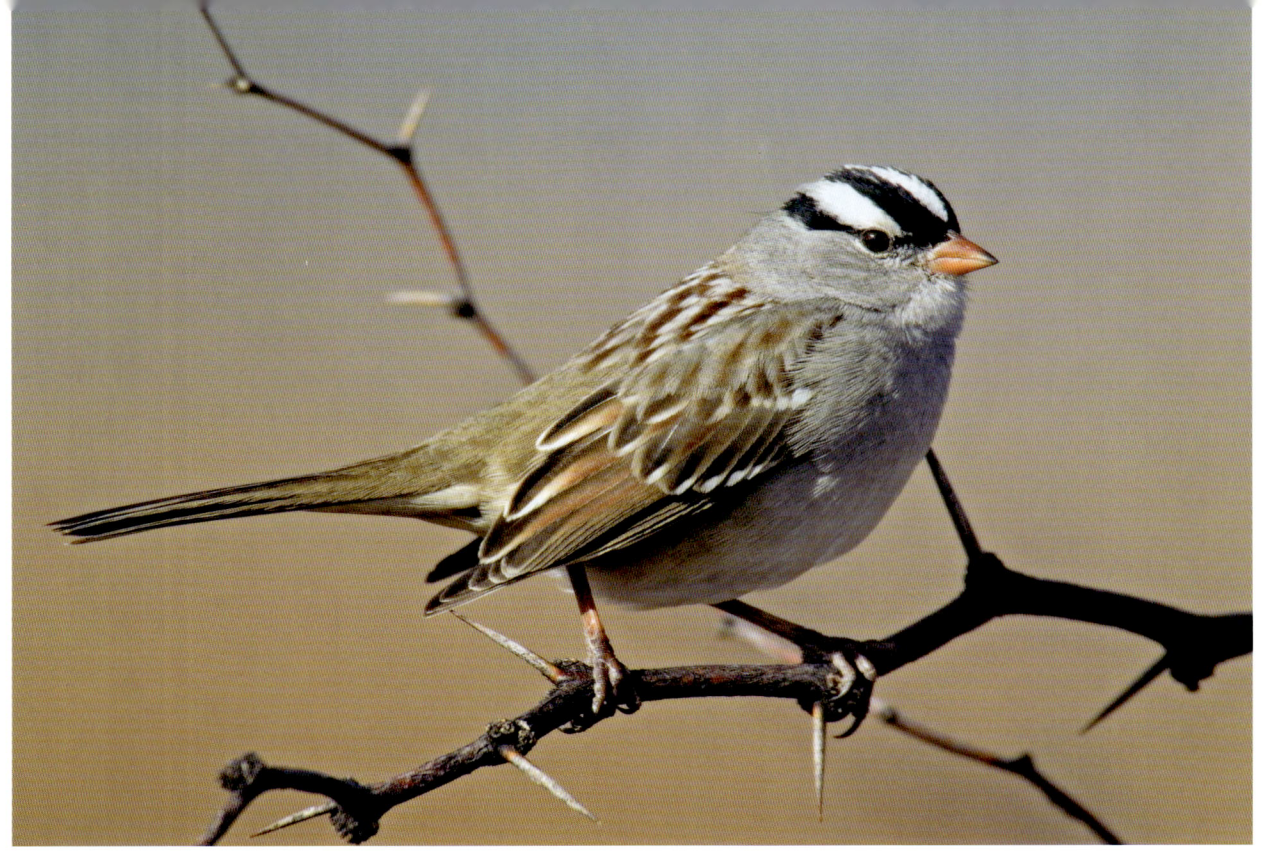

When the first serious cool fronts of fall finally push south into Texas during October, there is a good chance **White-crowned Sparrows** *will arrive at the same time. This bird breeds in the northwestern United States and much of Canada, but it winters in large numbers in Texas. This beautiful adult White-crowned Sparrow was in Caprock Canyons State Park in Briscoe County.*

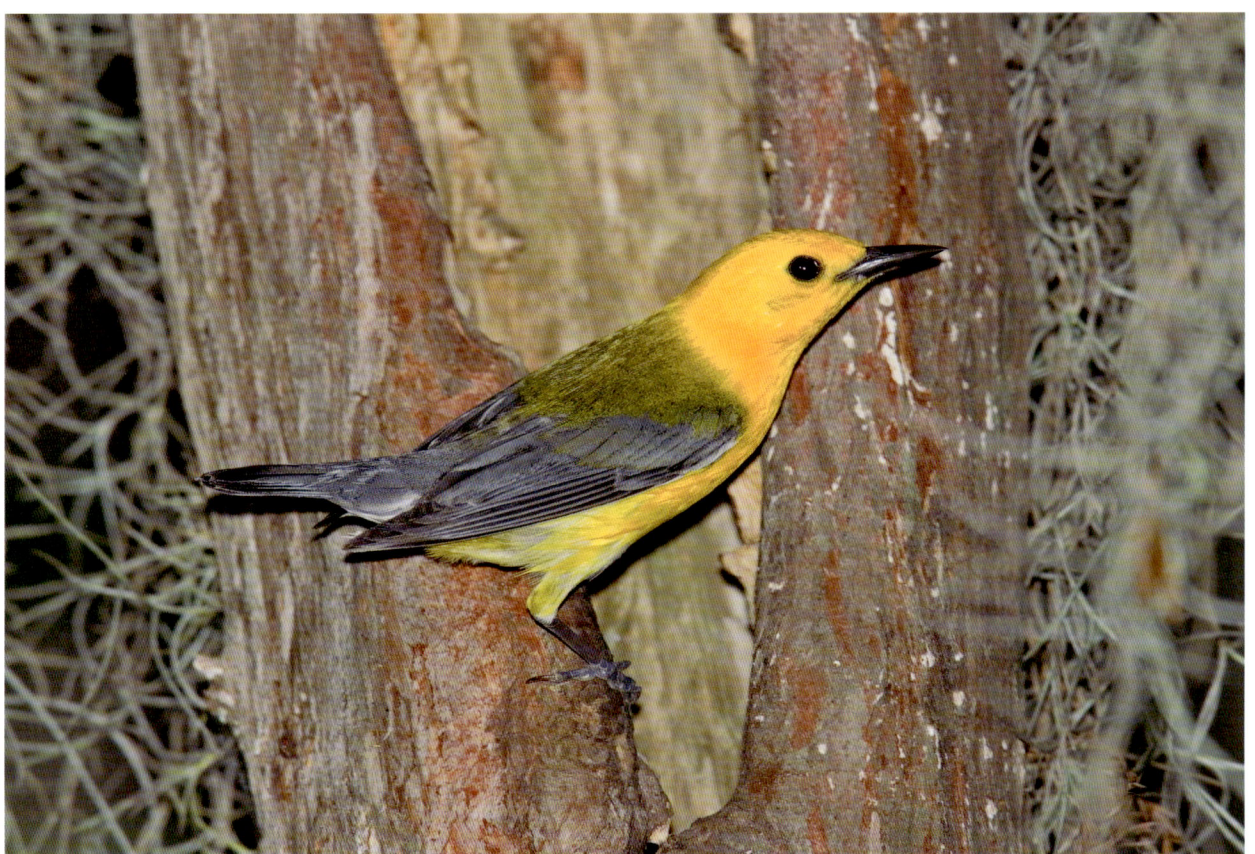

The **Prothonotary Warbler** *nests in wooded swamps across parts of the eastern fourth of Texas. Its loud, ringing song is a familiar sound in these areas. Prothonotary Warblers are a cavity nesting bird, which means they nest in holes in hollow trees, or sometimes in bird houses built by people. Very early in the twentieth century, this bird was sometimes referred to as the "Golden Swamp Bird," and I still love that name. The male shown here was perched at the entrance to a nest cavity in a northeast Texas swamp near Caddo Lake in Harrison County.*

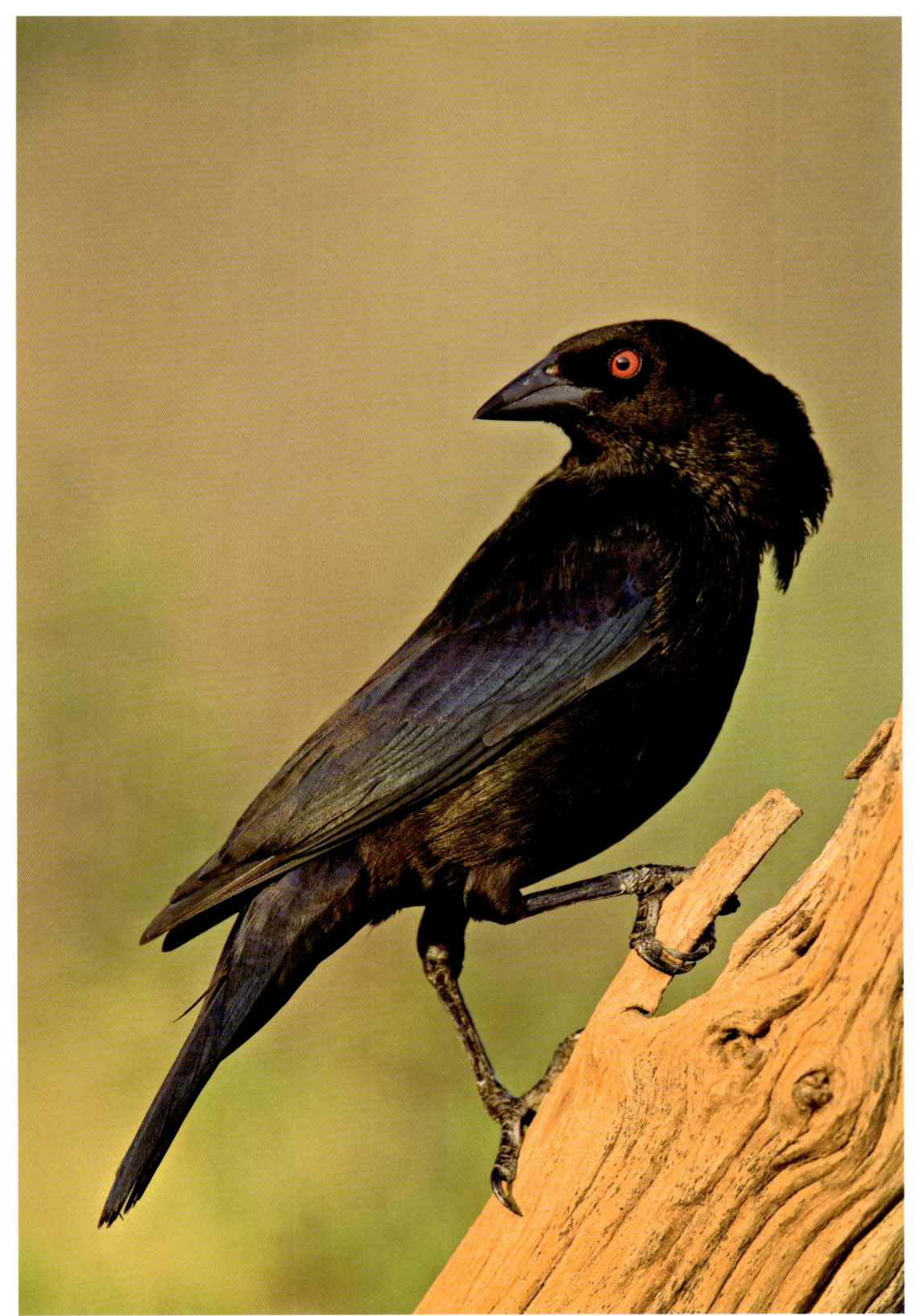

Bronzed Cowbirds,
like their cousin the Brown-headed Cowbird, have a nesting strategy whereby the female lays her eggs in the nest of another species so the host parents raise young cowbirds instead of their own offspring. This has earned both cowbird species quite a bit of bad press because many of the host species are declining, partly a result of cowbird parasitism. Still, when this male Bronzed Cowbird perched on a limb in the late afternoon sun and struck a pose that showed off its bronze and black plumage and striking red eye, I could not resist getting some shots. This one was taken near Edinburg in Hidalgo County.

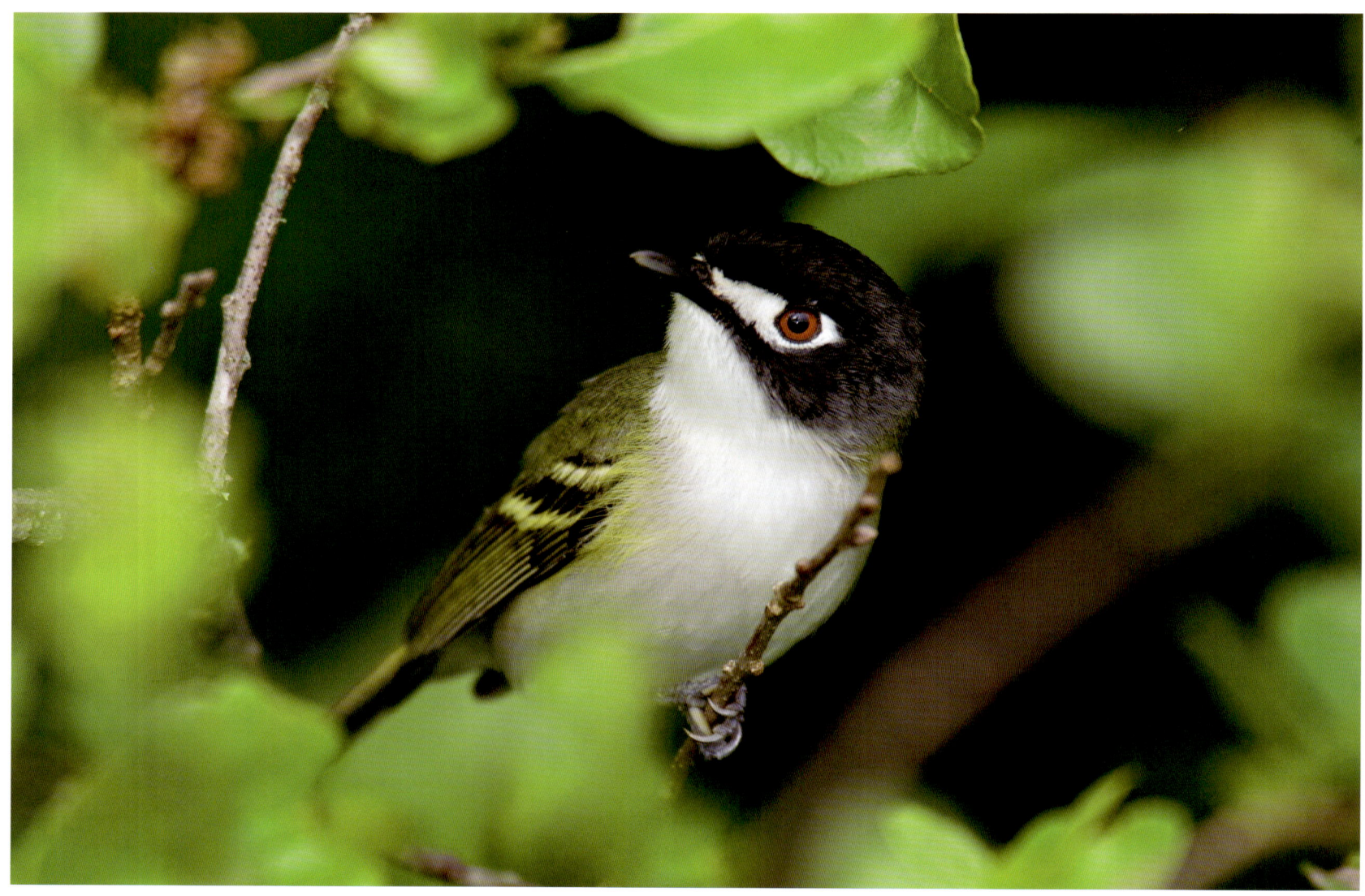

The **Black-capped Vireo** is an endangered species that nests along parts of the Edwards Plateau in Texas. Its breeding range extends into a few areas of Oklahoma, but the majority of the U.S. population nests in Texas. Many bird-watchers in other states travel to Texas hoping to see this species. It is a lively little bird that is usually far easier to hear than to see. This male peered briefly at me from a thicket at a tract of Balcones Canyonlands National Wildlife Refuge in Williamson County.

Opposite: The tiny **Ferruginous Pygmy-Owl** is a tropical species found throughout much of Mexico and Central America. Its range barely enters the United States in far South Texas, and it is much sought after by bird-watchers. This one glared down at me from a tree on a private ranch in Kenedy County.

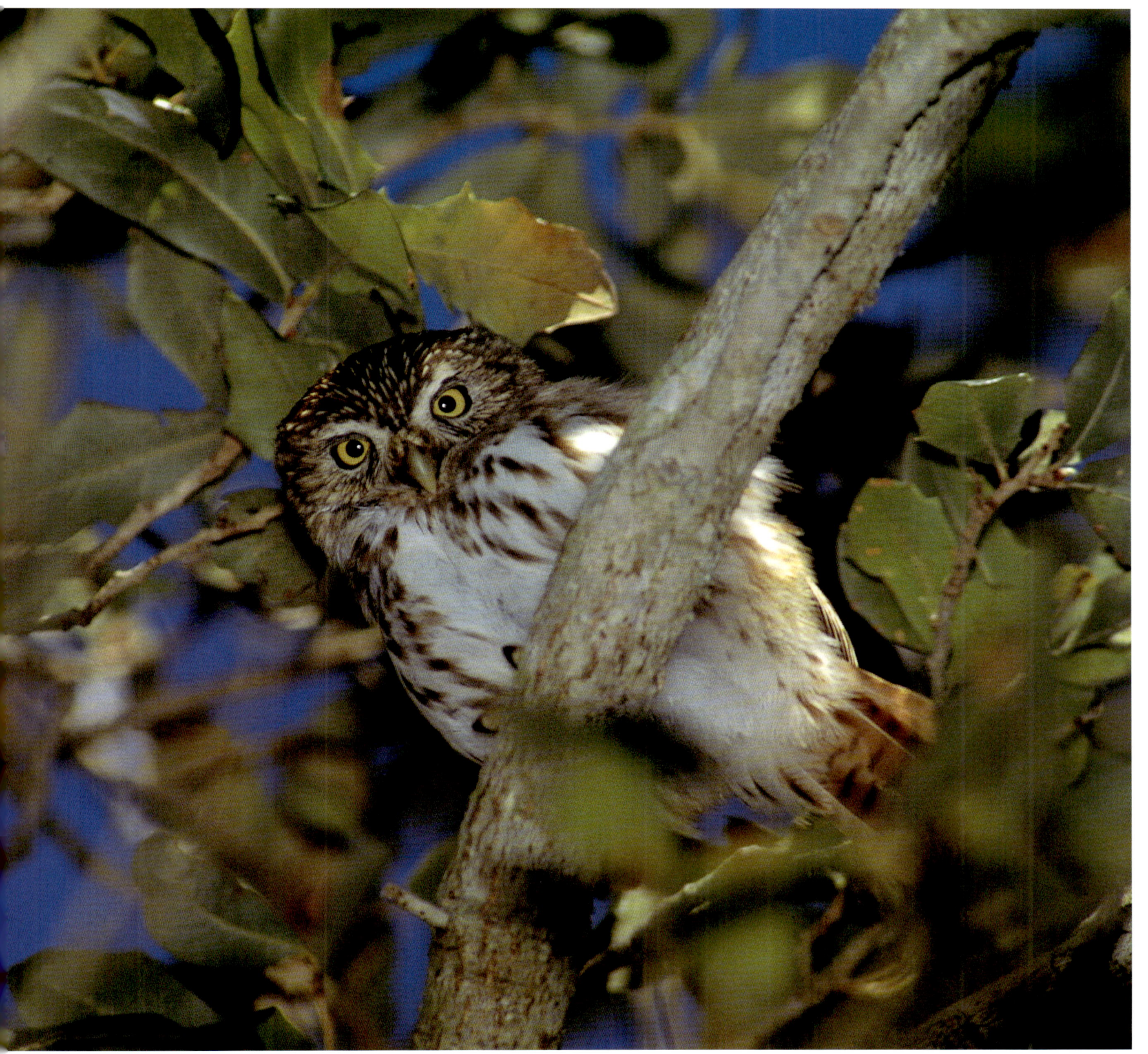

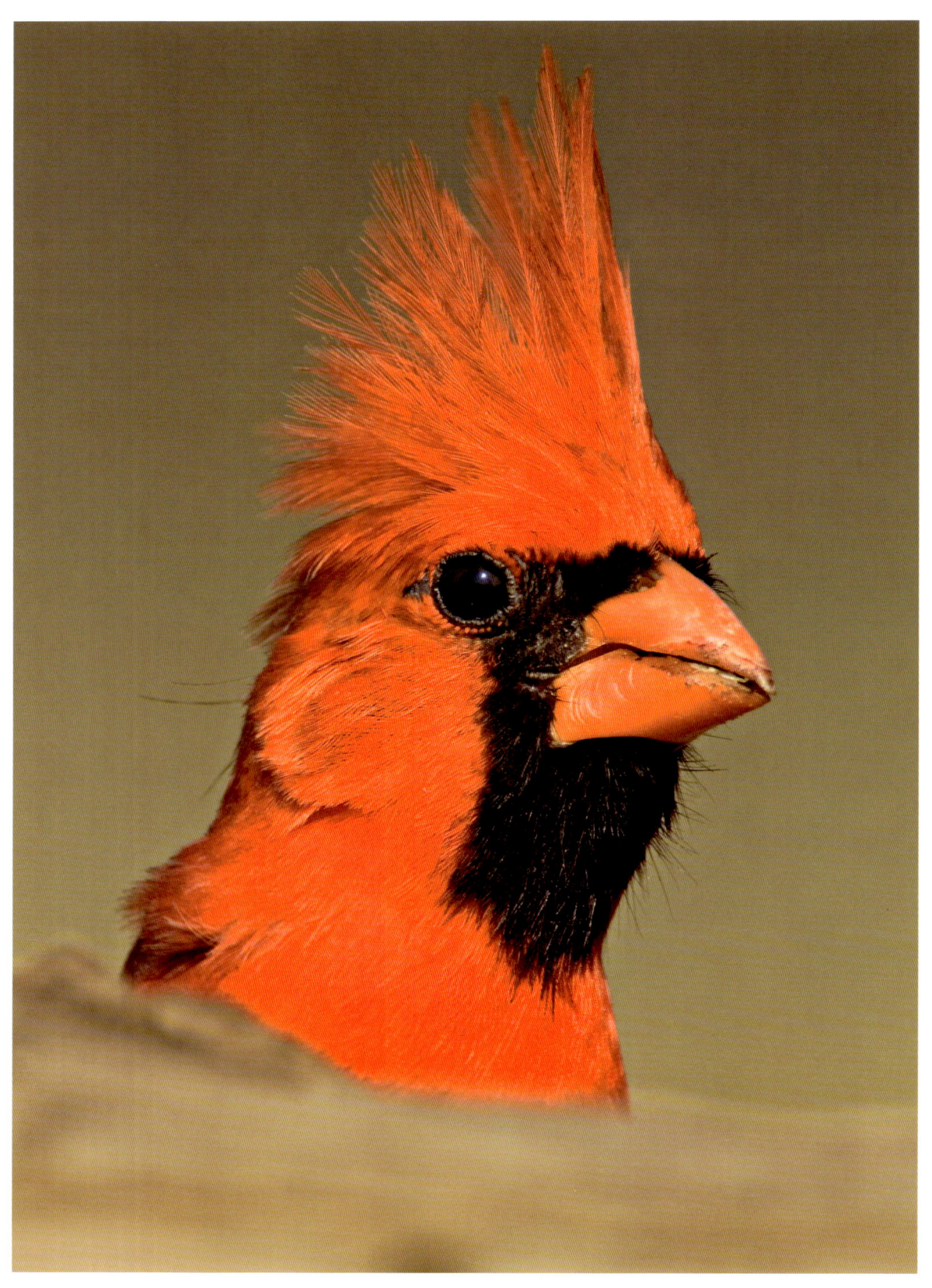

The **Northern Cardinal** *is one of the most familiar backyard birds in the United States. This flashy creature rules over many a bird feeder and has captivated many beginning bird-watchers. I have always liked this shot, which is a real close-up of the face and massive seed-cracking bill of a male Northern Cardinal as he peered over a log to look at me while I was in a blind with a telephoto lens. This photo was taken in South Texas in Hidalgo County.*

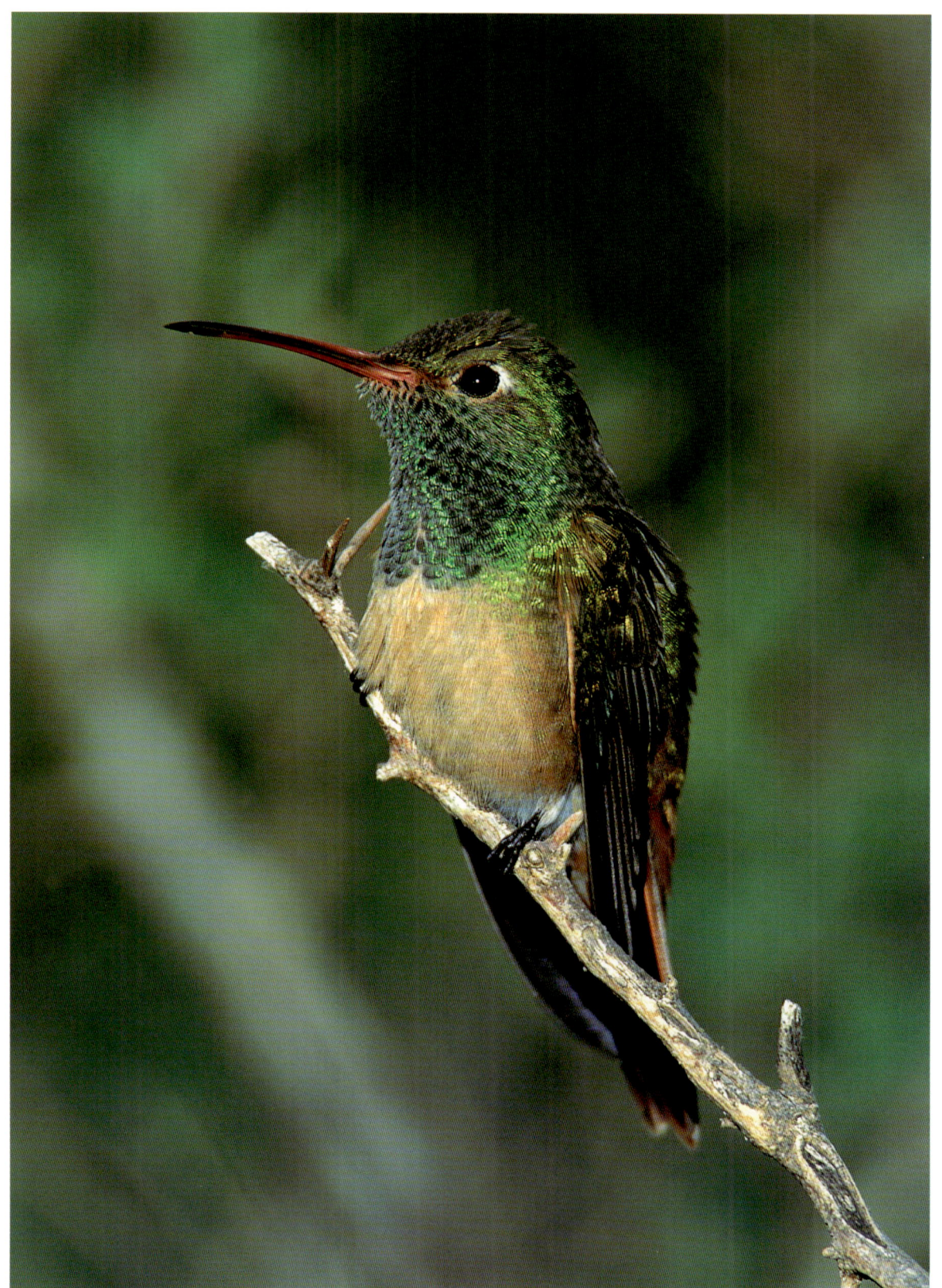

Buff-bellied Hummingbirds *occur across much of Mexico, but within the United States the species normally occurs only in South Texas. Buff-bellieds are a little larger than the Ruby-throated or Black-chinned Hummingbirds, which are more widespread in Texas. It is an attractive bird with a red bill, an iridescent green throat, and a buffy colored belly. The shot here shows a Buff-bellied Hummingbird as it perched near a feeder in Kenedy County.*

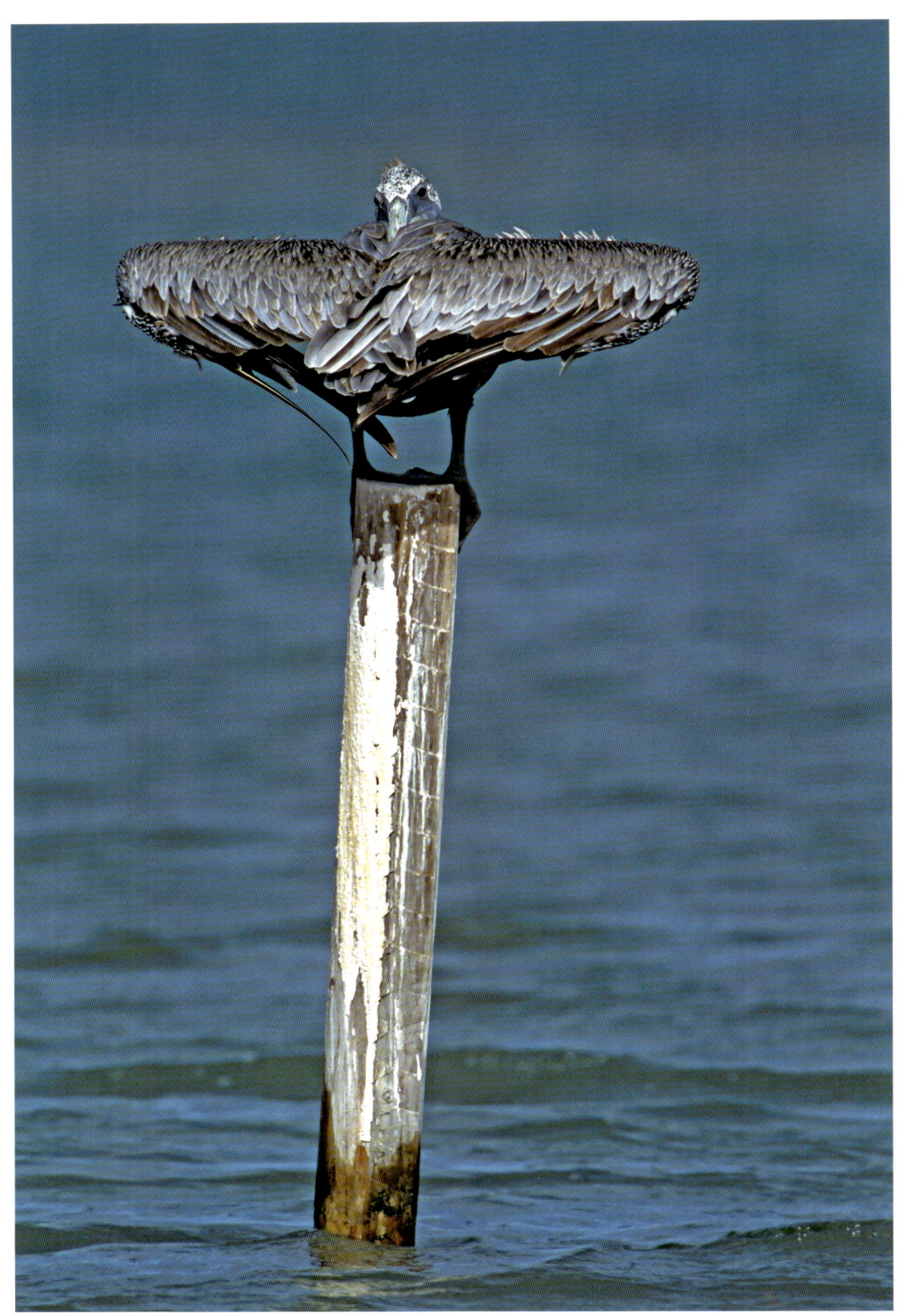

Until the mid-1980s, **Brown Pelicans** were rare along the Texas Coast. Thankfully, the species is now quite common. I was driving along a shoreline at Aransas Pass on a very windy September day when I saw this Brown Pelican perched on a piling with its wings held out as aerodynamically as possible. The bird had its head and bill tucked under its back feathers while its feet tightly gripped the piling. The feathers of the shoulders were vibrating in the wind as the bird stubbornly held its place.

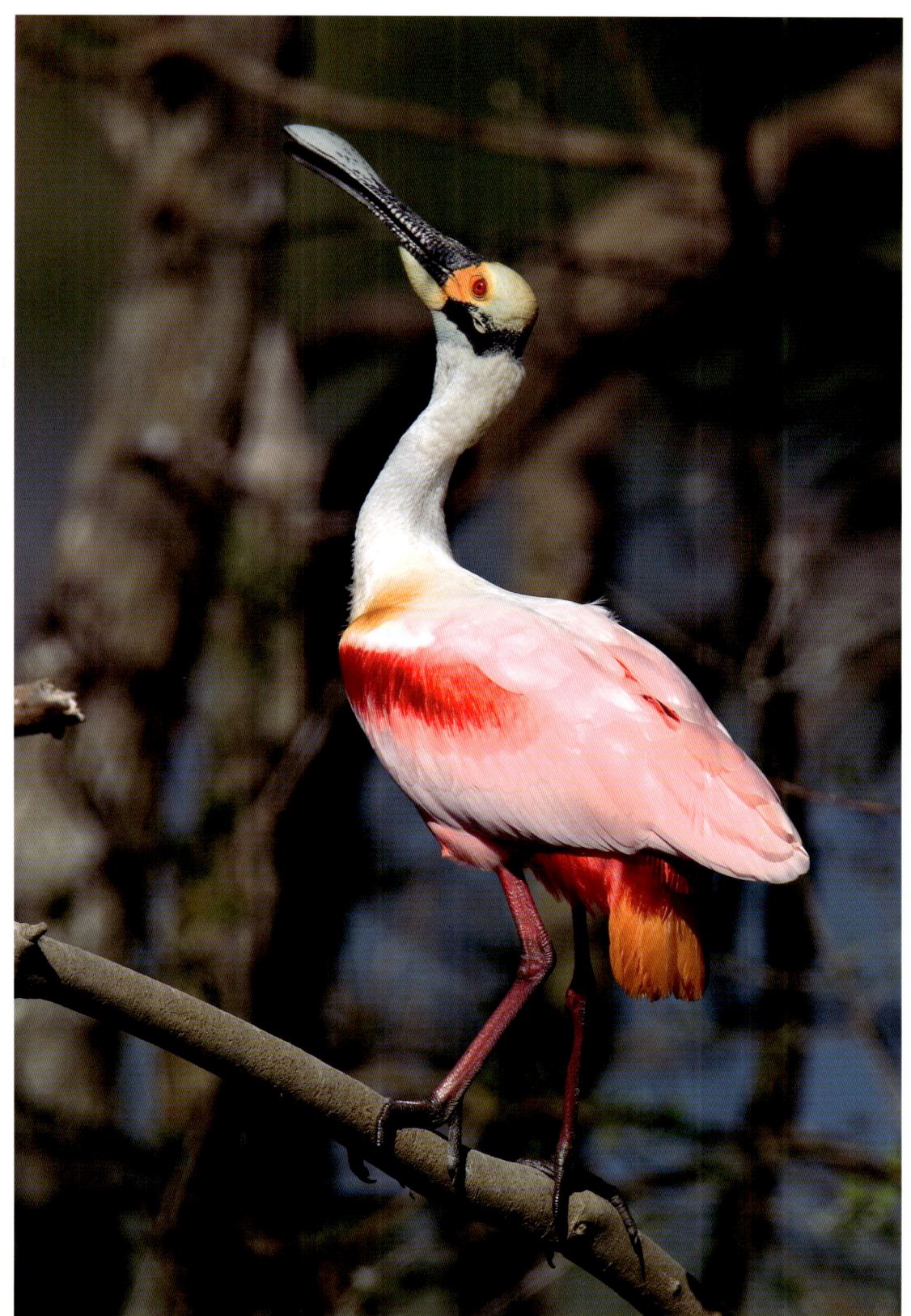

Roseate Spoonbills *can be seen along the Texas coast during most of the year. Spoonbills have amazingly flat, spoon-shaped bills, which they swish back and forth in shallow water while hunting food. Their pink body plumage, accented with red shoulders and rump and popsicle-orange tail, certainly makes them one of our more flashy water birds. This spoonbill was perched at a breeding colony at High Island in Galveston County.*

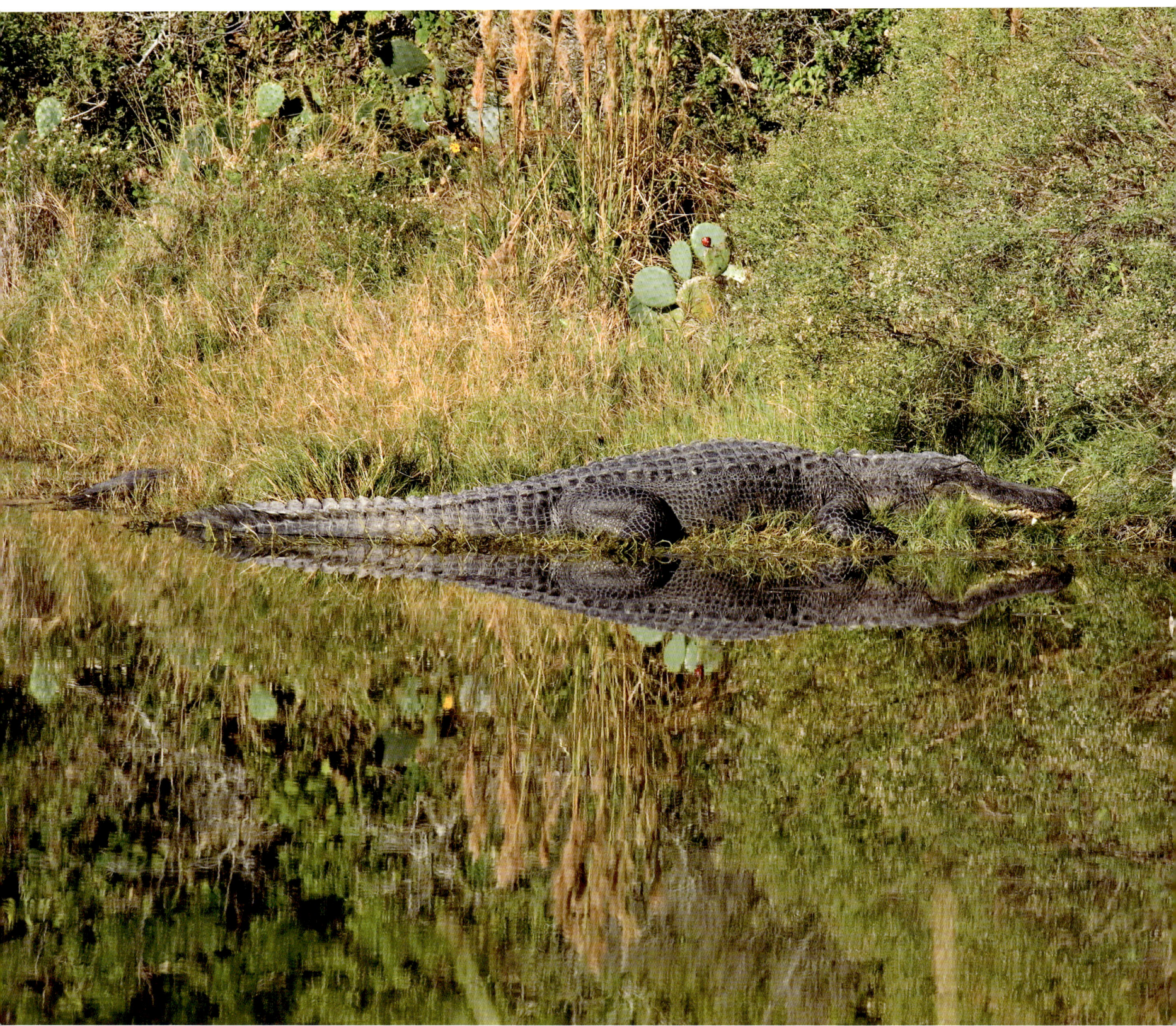

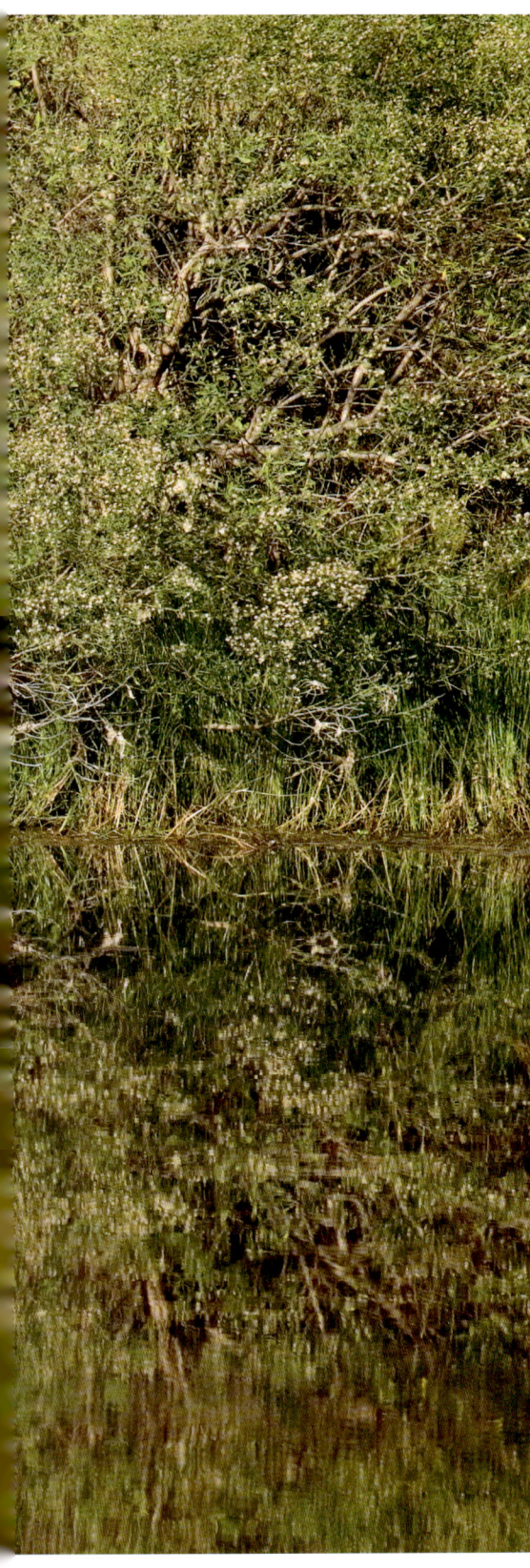

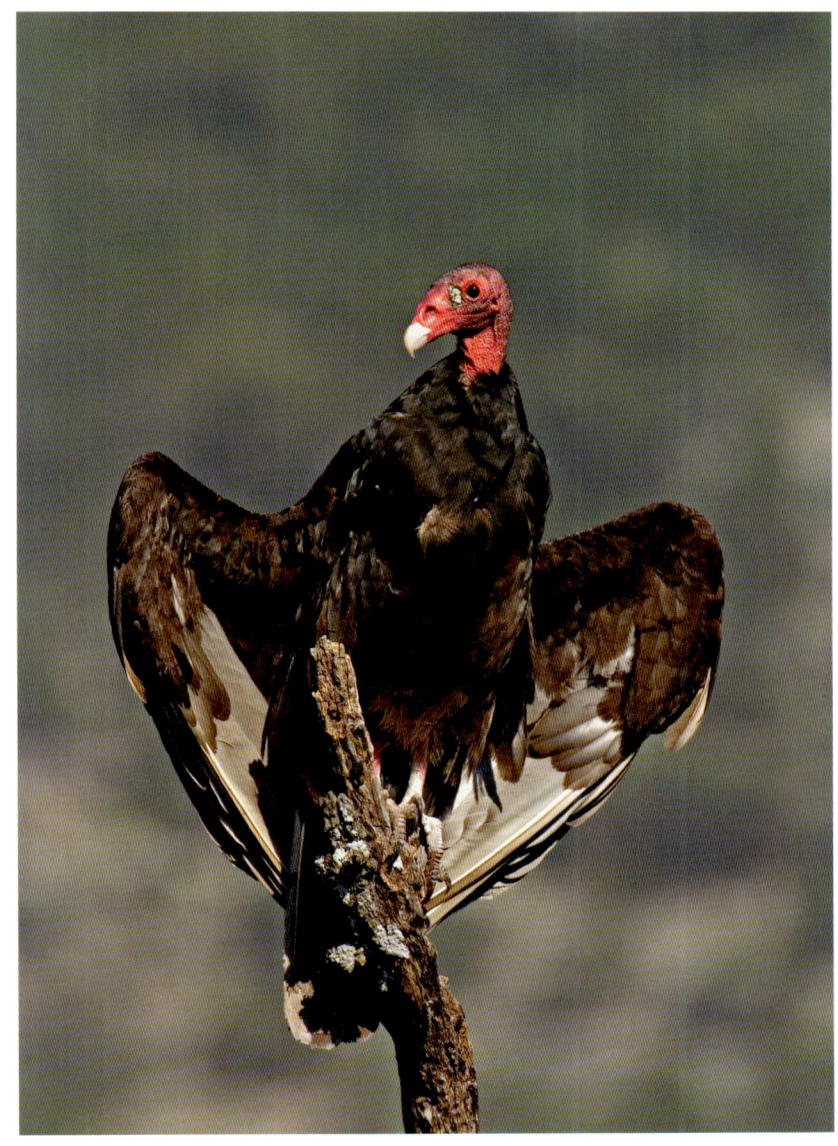

On a cool early morning in November, I came across this large **American Alligator** warming itself in the sun at Aransas National Wildlife Refuge in Aransas County. There was absolutely no wind, and the image of the alligator mirrored itself against the motionless water's surface. The photo seems almost like a pastel and somehow just says "Texas!"

Turkey Vultures are certainly one of the most familiar birds we see as we drive along roads and highways in Texas; their lazy, circling flight may be seen over most of the state. Turkey Vultures feed on carrion, so they perform a very needed service of cleaning up after an animal dies or perhaps is killed along a highway. This Turkey Vulture was warming up on a cool spring morning in Real County in the Texas Hill Country. Many birds will spread their wings to the sun in an effort to take advantage of the sun's rays.

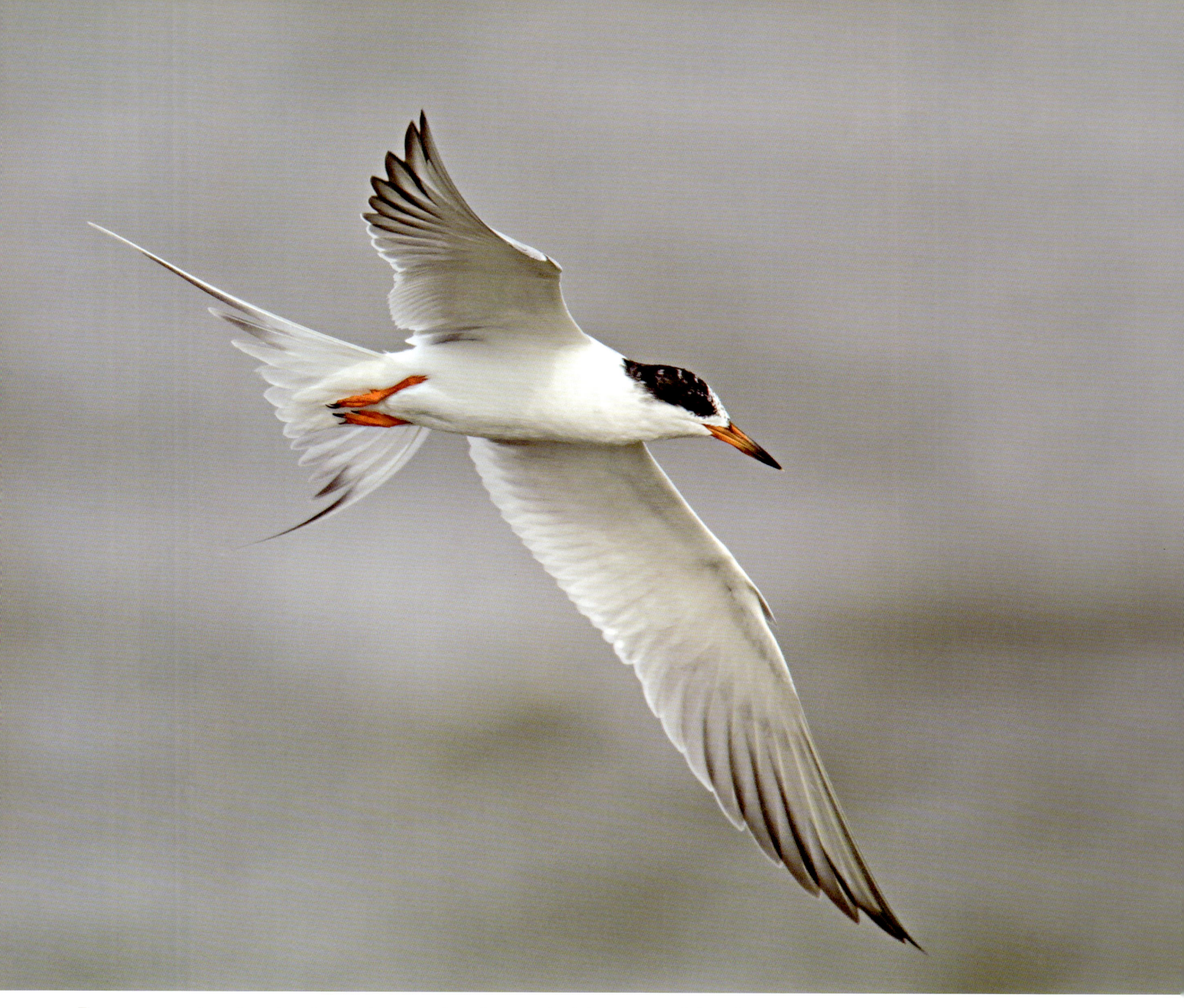

There are a number of species of terns along the Texas coast. One of the most common is the **Forster's Tern,** which may be found throughout much of the year as it fishes along Texas beaches, jetties, and docks. This bird, in winter plumage, was along the Texas City Dike in Galveston County. The bird was patrolling along the water's edge, watching for a tiny fish to try to catch.

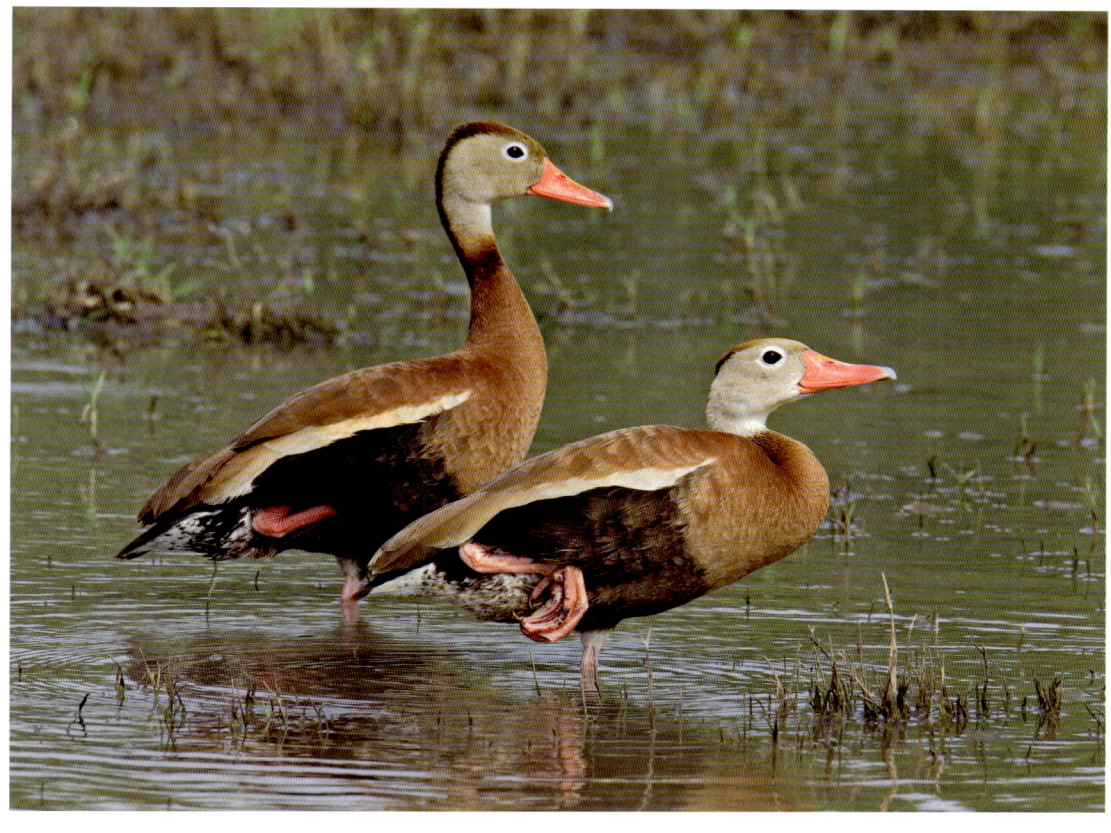

Black-bellied Whistling-Ducks *earn their name from their distinctive whistling voice, as opposed to the "quack" most people would expect from a duck. These long-legged ducks nest in cavities in trees and often use artificial duck boxes for nests as well. They can be common in parts of coastal and South Texas. This pair was resting on the edge of a pond near McCook in Hidalgo County.*

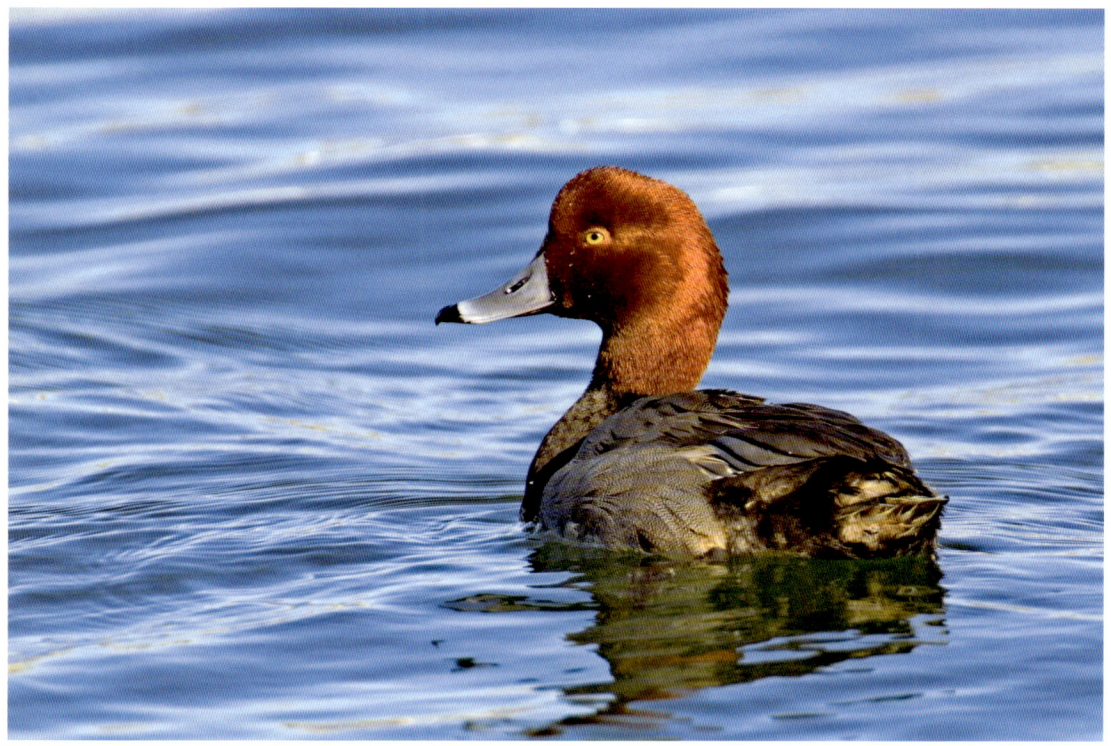

The Gulf Coast of Texas is one of the most important waterfowl wintering areas in the United States. Probably millions of ducks of many species winter in Texas, including the **Redhead.** *Redheads are diving ducks, which prefer deeper water habitats than dabbling ducks such as Mallards or teal. This dapper male Redhead was wintering along the coast at Aransas Pass in Aransas County.*

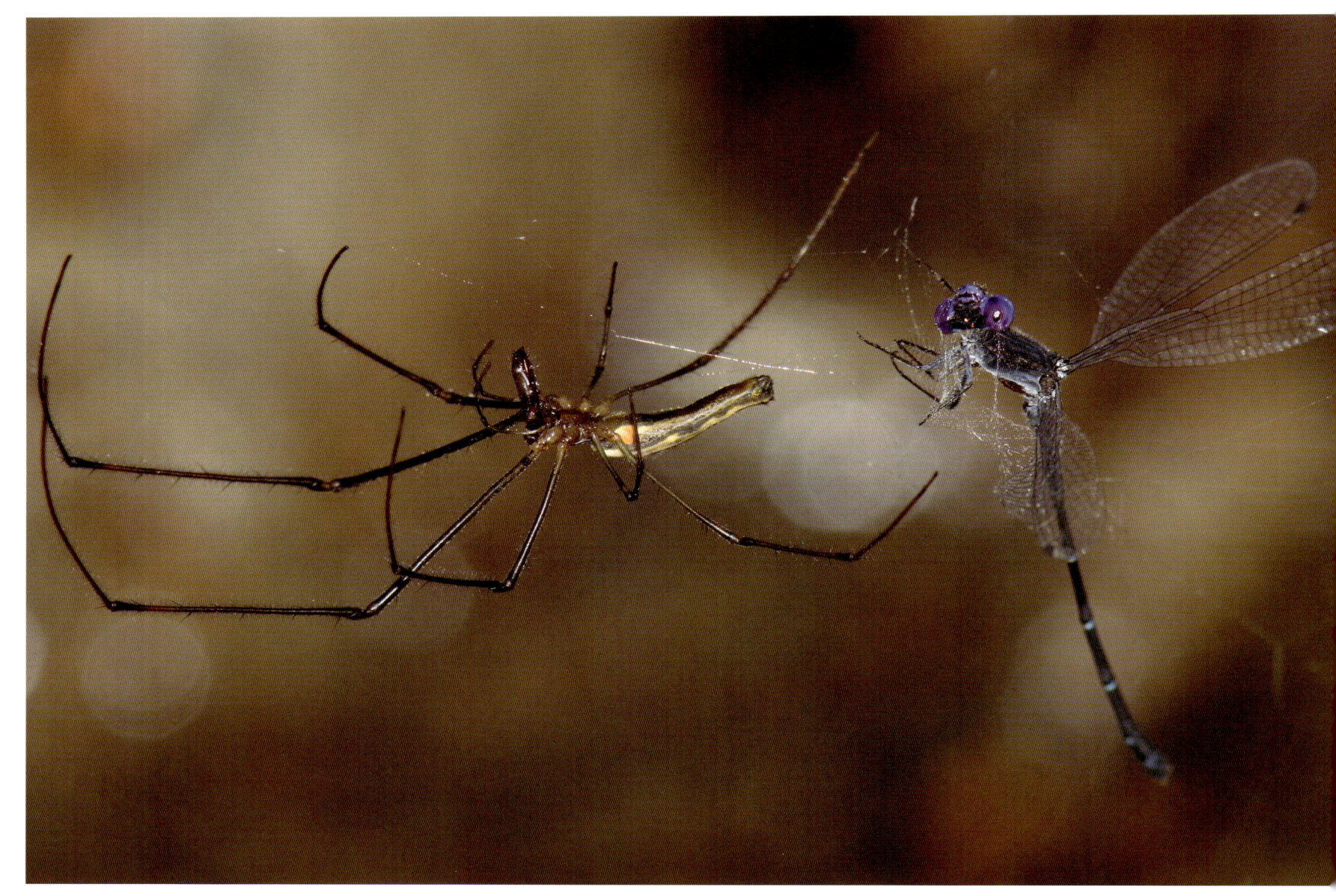

The drama of predator and prey and life and death unfolds thousands of times a day almost anywhere in the natural world. While wading along a portion of Honey Creek in Comal County, I found this **Long-jawed Spider***, which had captured a damselfly called a Dusky Dancer. The spider would soon consume its prey and then get ready for its next capture.*

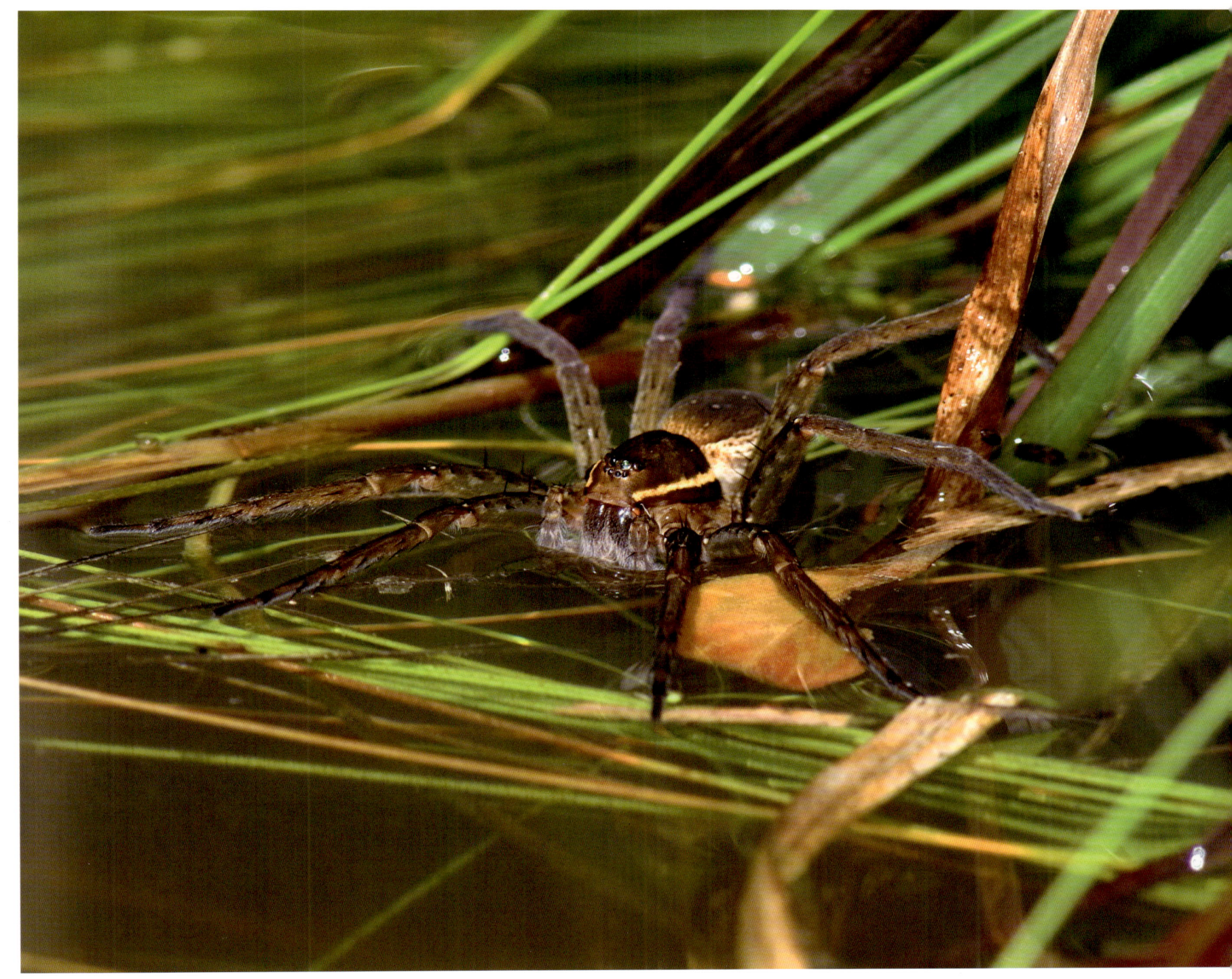

While walking slowly along a creek in western Travis County, my attention was drawn to a sudden movement on the surface of the water near my foot. Looking closer, I spied this **Fishing Spider** *as it lay in wait on the water's surface near the bank. These spiders are able to actually rest on the water's surface to catch minnows or insects that venture too close.*

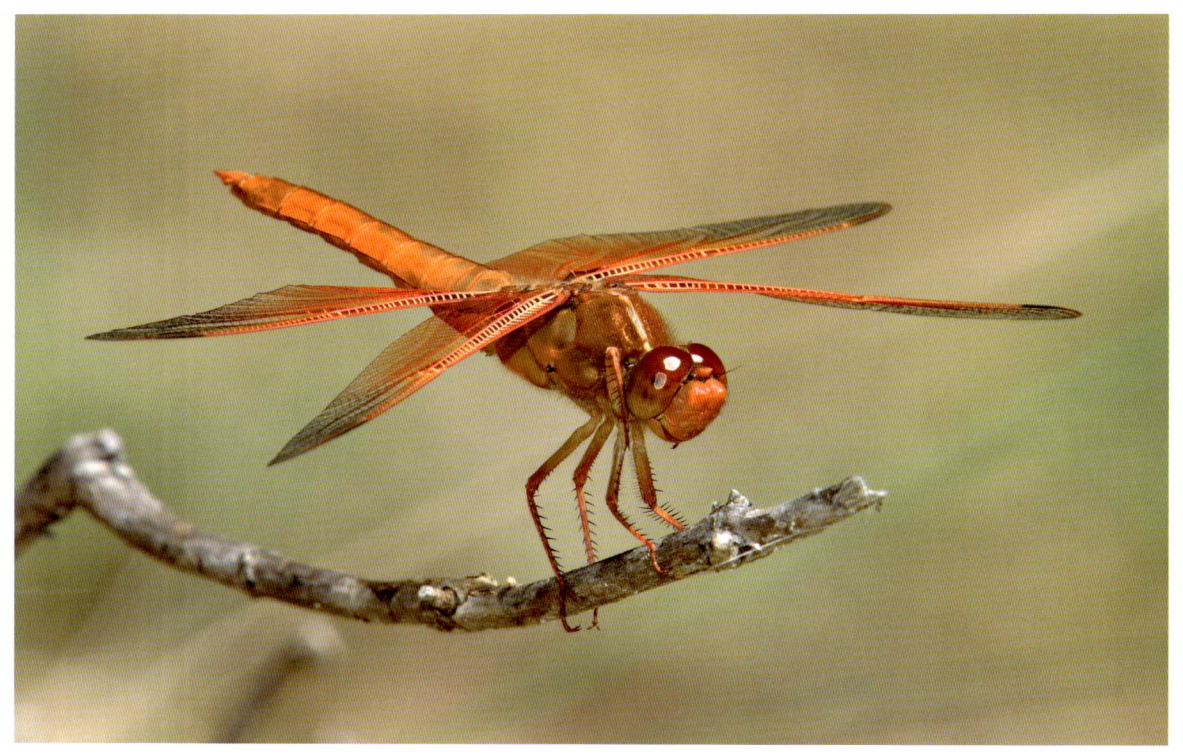

One of the most attractive dragonflies of Texas is the **Flame Skimmer**, which is found in the western half of the state. This bright orange dragonfly can be common along streams or ponds in West Texas and in a few areas of Central Texas. The wing structure of dragonflies is truly an engineering wonder of nature. This individual was in western Travis County, not far from Austin.

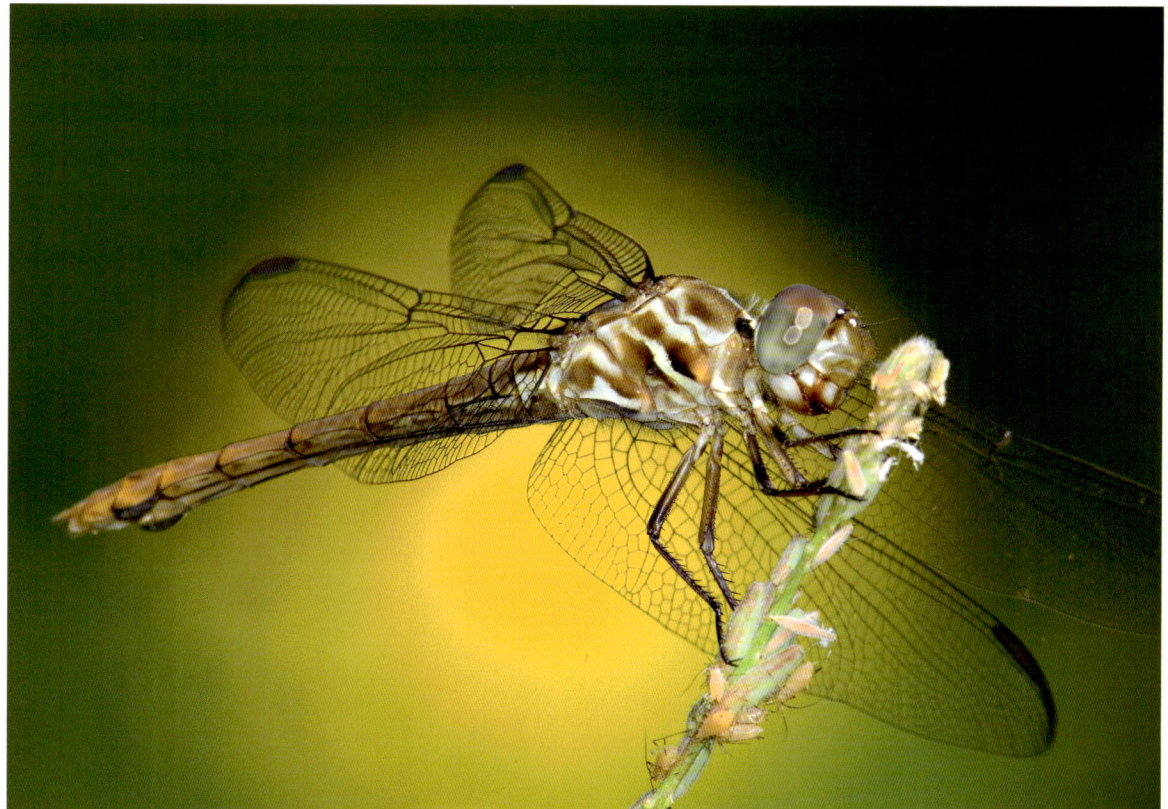

Roseate Skimmers are common dragonflies, widespread across most of the southern half of Texas. The males are a lovely lavender color, but the females are a more mottled brown and white, although still quite interesting. This female Roseate Skimmer was perched on a weed tip in Austin, Travis County. An out-of-focus sunflower in the background adds an interesting splash of yellow to the image.

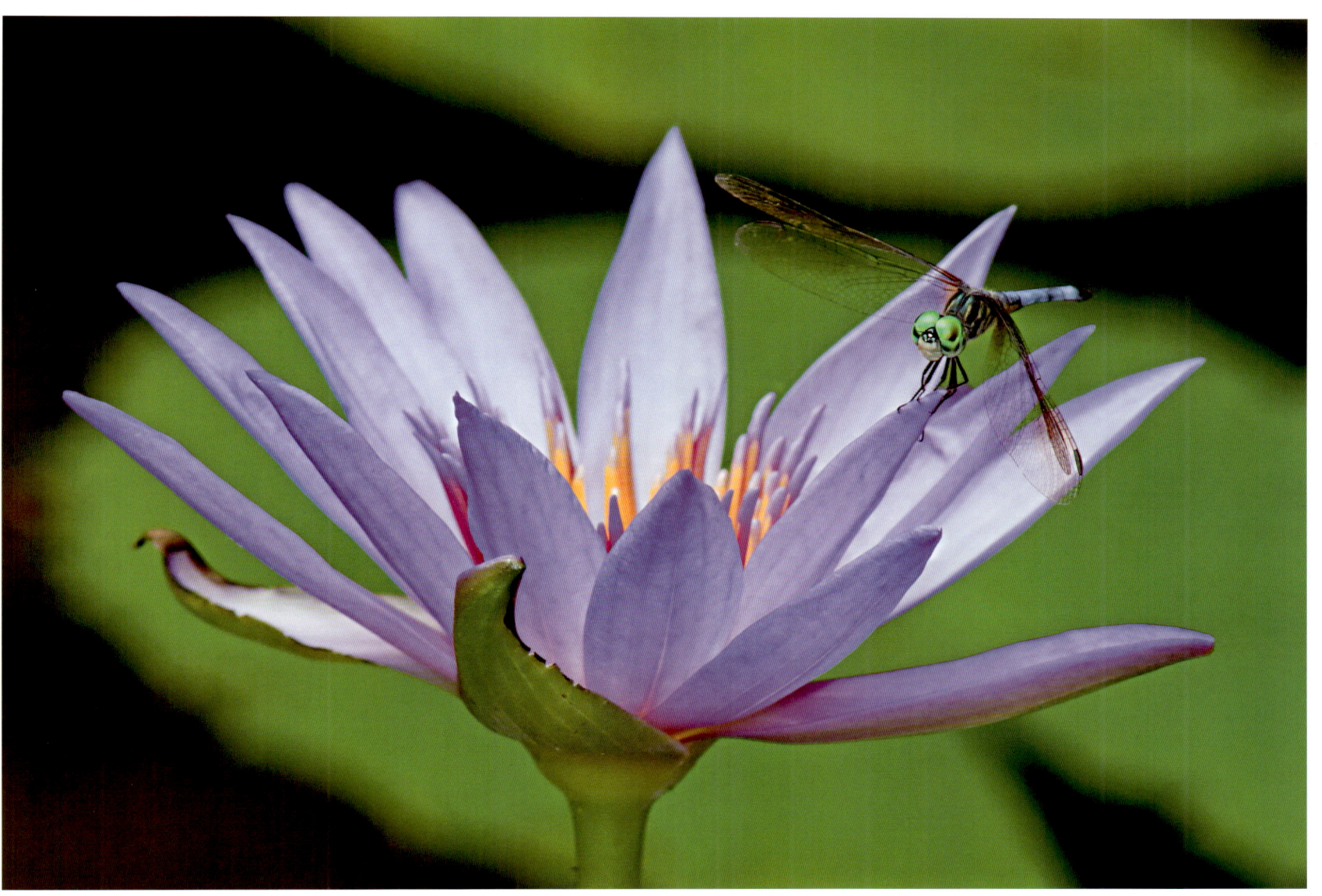

Most of the time when I am photographing dragonflies, I tend to concentrate on the individual dragonfly rather than the overall scene. There are several reasons for this, including the fact that many dragonflies like to perch on sticks or other pieces of vegetation that are not particularly attractive, coupled with the fact that I am often trying to illustrate particular points about the bug's colors or structure. The **Blue Dasher** *is a common dragonfly across much of the United States. On a late summer day, when I was walking through the Oriental Gardens at Zilker Park in Austin, my eye was drawn to a male Blue Dasher perched on a flower of a water lily. Even a very common insect can help create a very beautiful scene—one of the marvelous things about nature that keeps me coming back for more.*

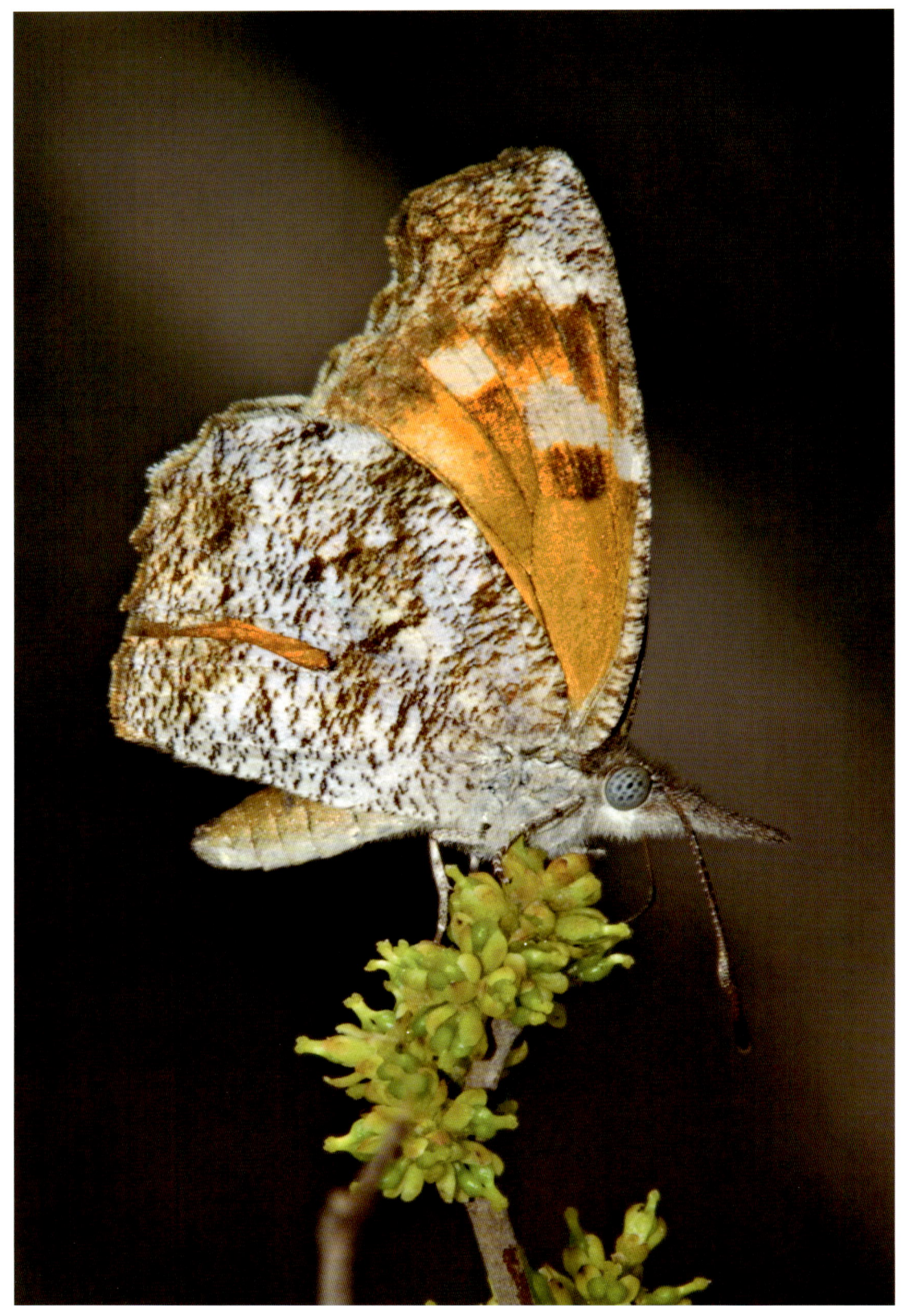

Sometimes, while driving across parts of Texas in the summer or fall, you may encounter swarms of thousands upon thousands of small orangeish butterflies. Chances are good that they are **American Snouts** *on migration. The "snout" on this butterfly can be seen only upon close inspection, but it is a unique characteristic of this species. This image was taken near Edinburg in Hidalgo County.*

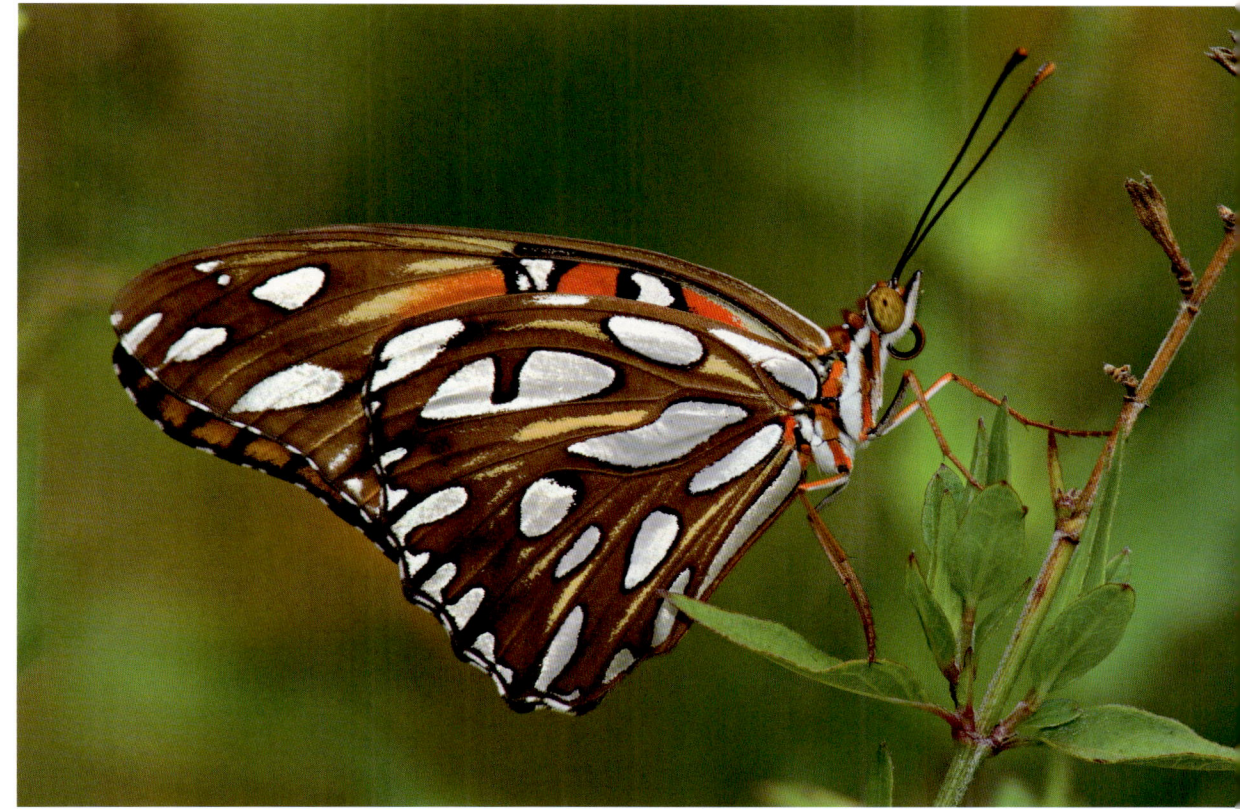

Throughout the spring and summer, butterflies flit around our gardens and yards, but we seldom take the time to admire the exquisite beauty of the patterns, colors, and textures of these winged jewels. This **Gulf Fritillary**, *a species common all over Texas, paused for a few moments in my backyard in Austin.*

While walking through a field of wildflowers near Austin in Travis County on a bright March afternoon, I saw this **White-striped Longtail** *as it worked over a number of the blooms. I had seen the species before in South Texas and along the coast, but I could not recall seeing one in Central Texas. This turned out to be one of the few spring records for the area. The white wing stripe and the long tail of this butterfly are very distinctive.*

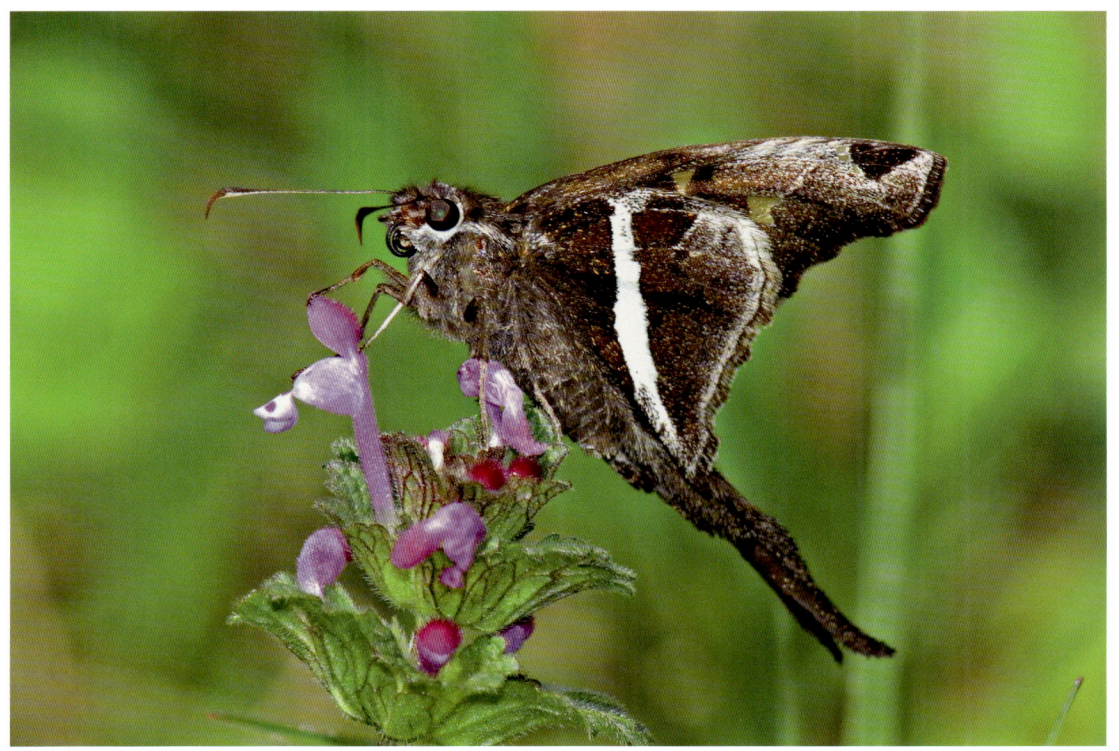

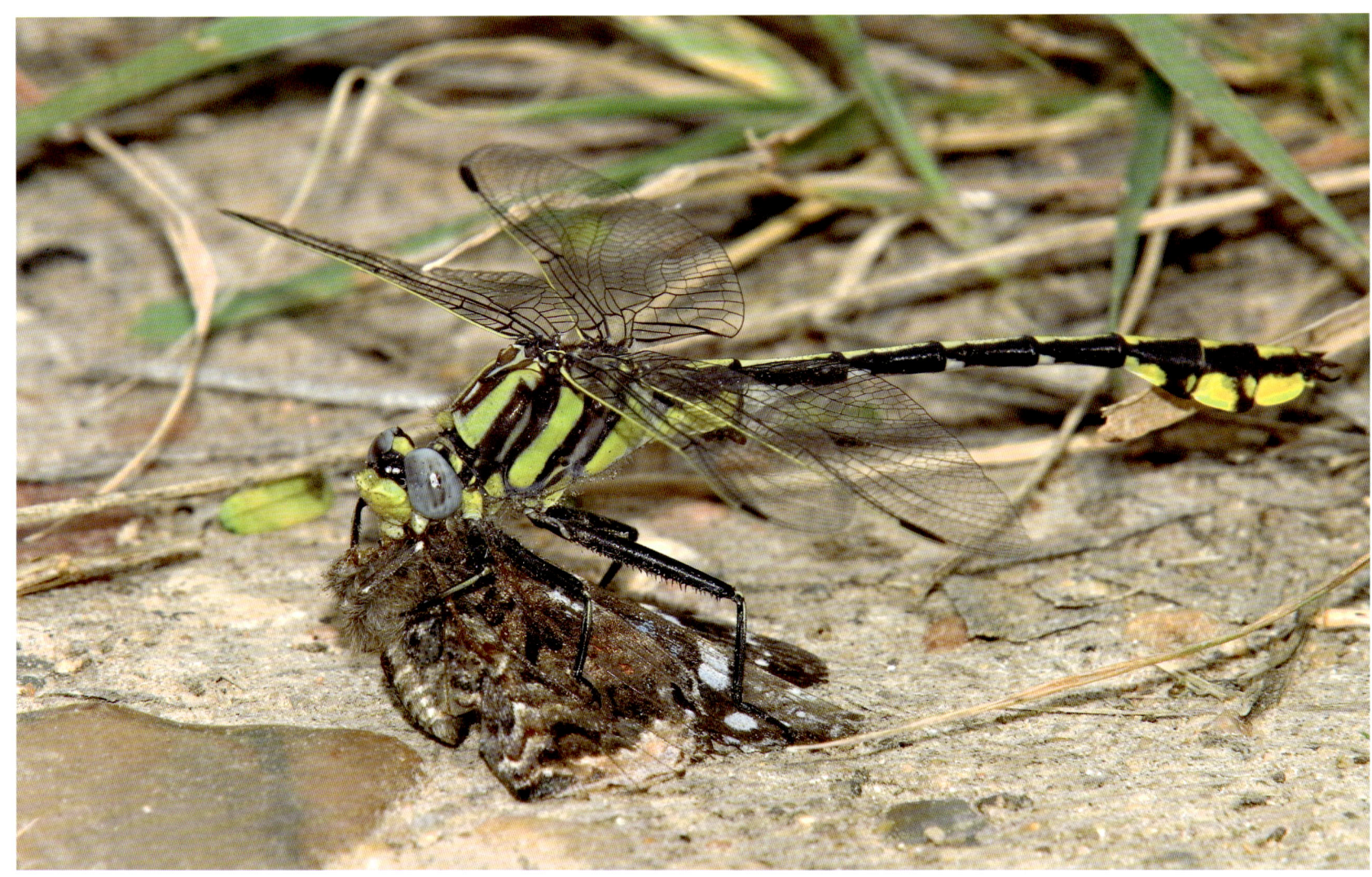

Each spring, as the weather in Central Texas warms up, one of the early emerging dragonflies is the **Plains Clubtail.** *This yellow and black flying predator immediately begins its business of eating and reproducing. This male Plains Clubtail had captured a Red Admiral butterfly and brought it to the ground for dinner. This shot was taken just east of Austin in Travis County.*

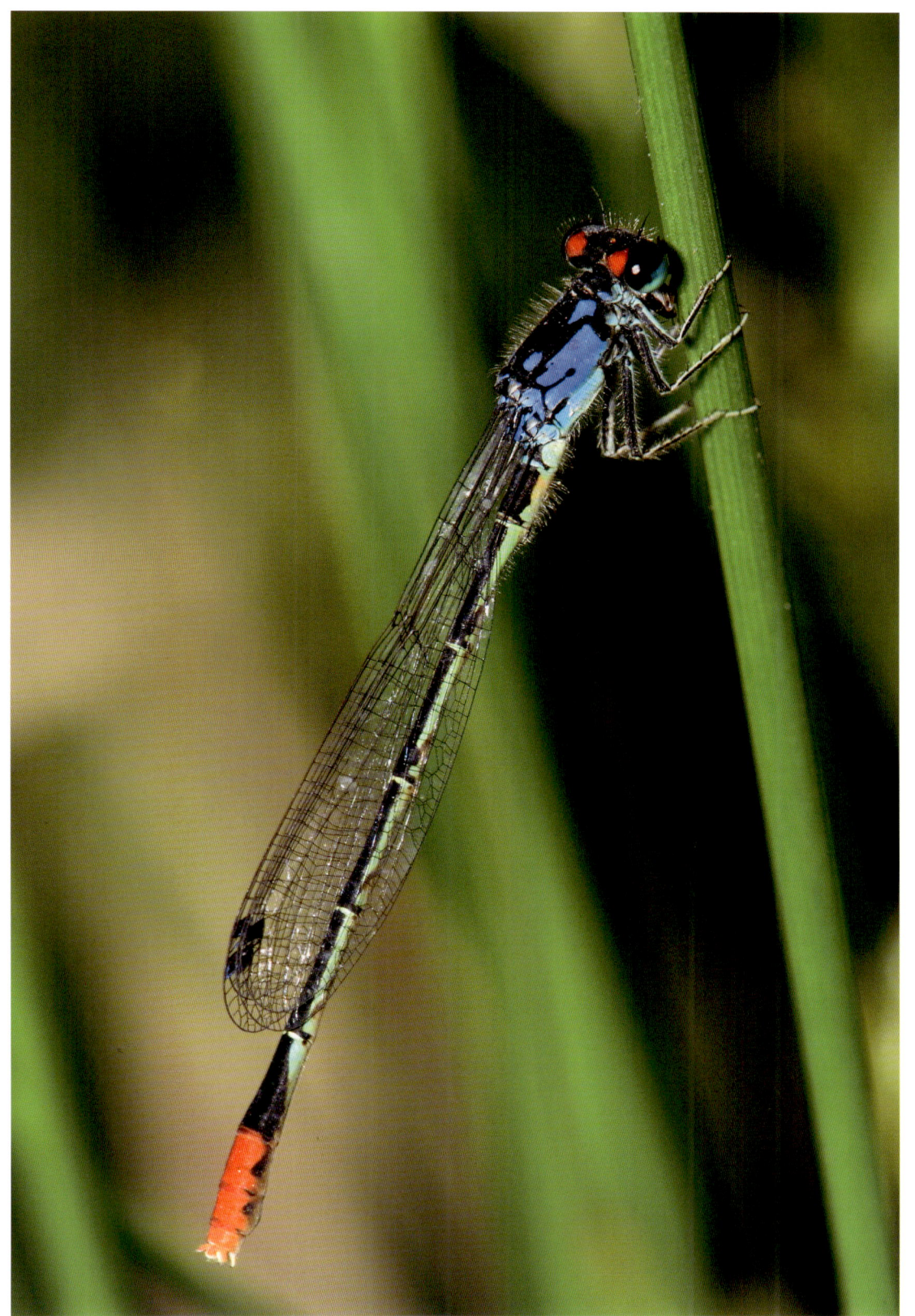

So much wildlife goes unnoticed by the general public because it is small or inconspicuous. For many years, I was focused on birds and failed to see the beauty in our Texas insects. During the past several years, I have tried to be more aware of nature's beauty in whatever form it is presented to us. **Painted Damsels** are only about an inch long, but seen through binoculars or a macro lens, they are incredibly delicate and beautiful with a unique pattern of red, blue, and black. The species inhabits stream sides in some of our western counties and may be seen there often if you look closely enough. This male Painted Damsel was on the Davis Mountains Preserve of the Texas Nature Conservancy, Jeff Davis County.

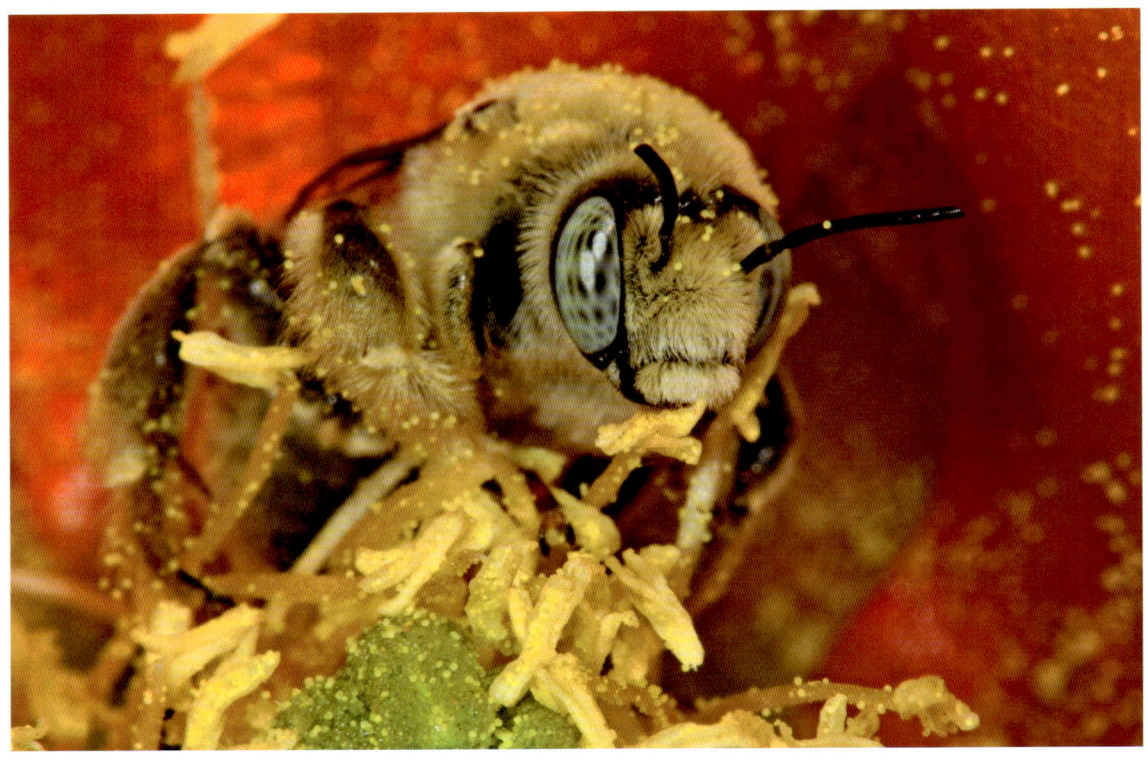

*The **Cactus Bee** is a member of the genus* Diadasia. *There are several similar species, which are all known to gather pollen primarily from prickly pear blooms. Cactus Bees dig burrows into bare ground, and some of their colonies may number in the multiple thousands of individuals. This Cactus Bee was working on the inside of a prickly pear bloom in Hidalgo County and is covered with pollen grains.*

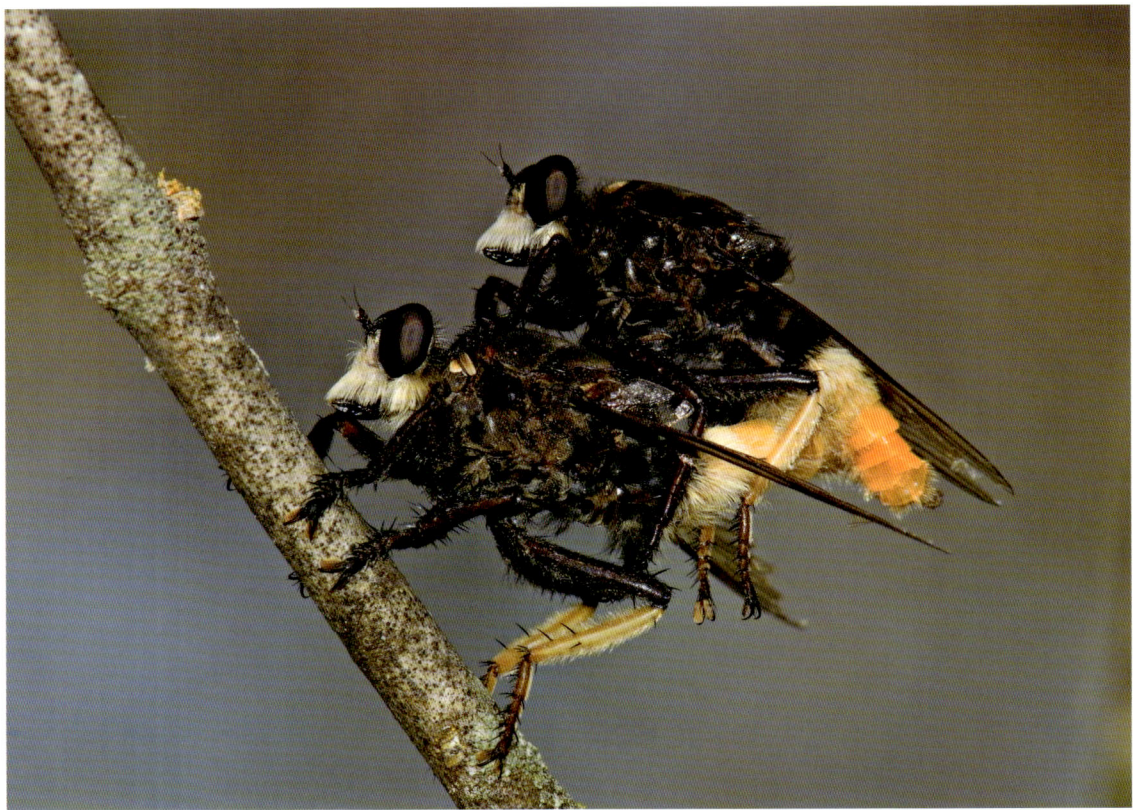

*Opposite: The **Black Saddlebags** is a commonly seen dragonfly across Texas and, for that matter, all of the United States. Even though they may be almost everywhere, it takes a close-up look to appreciate the fine detail of the wing venation and body structure of these fascinating insects. This Black Saddlebags was perched on a weed stalk in Austin and tolerated my camera and me for several minutes.*

*Although **Robber Flies** are certainly not warm and fuzzy or cuddly in any sense of the words, they are quite interesting. All robbers are very efficient predators and are able to capture other insects larger than themselves. This mating pair of robbers, known as* Eccritosia zamon, *was on a twig near Austin, Travis County.*

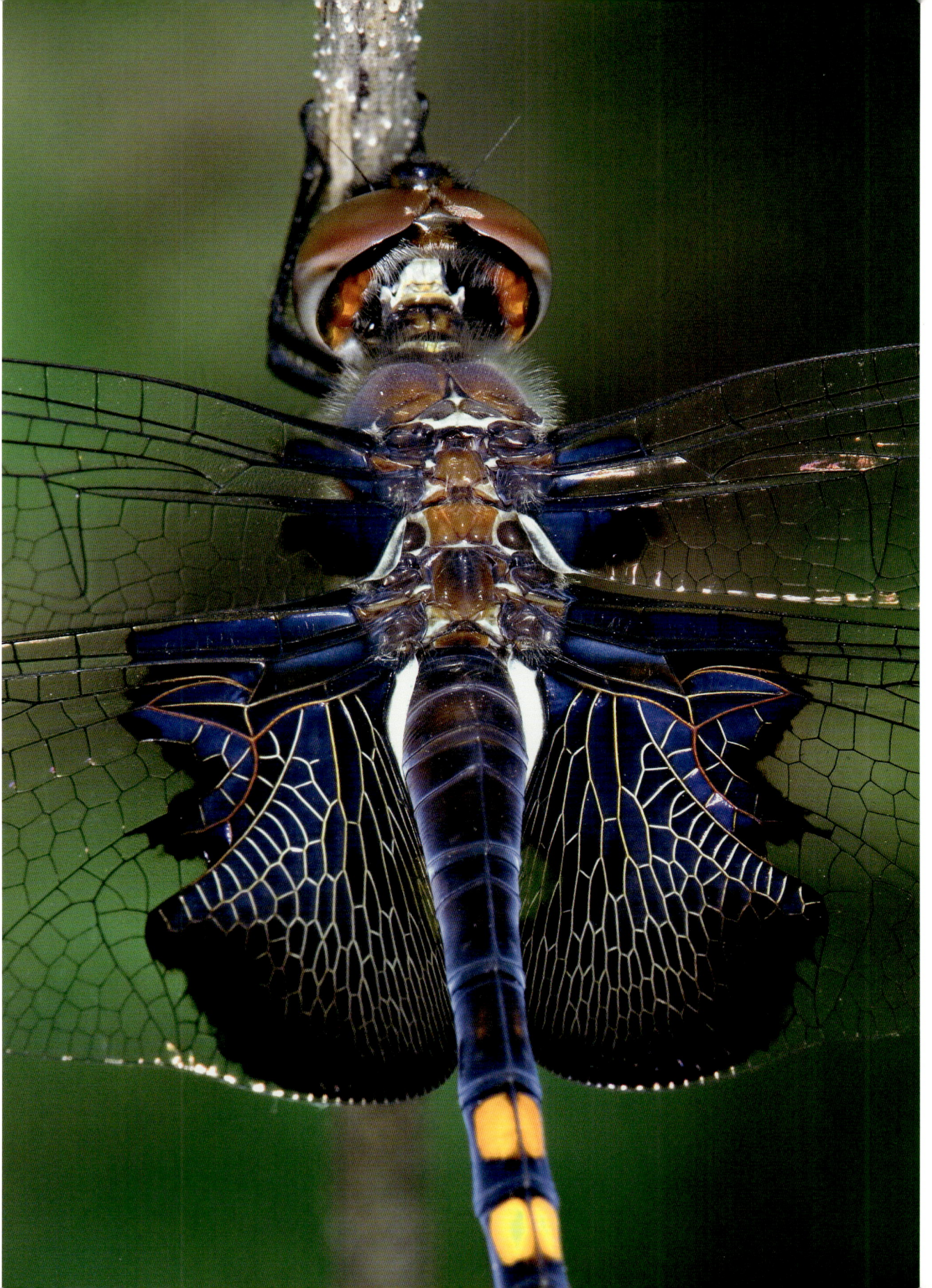

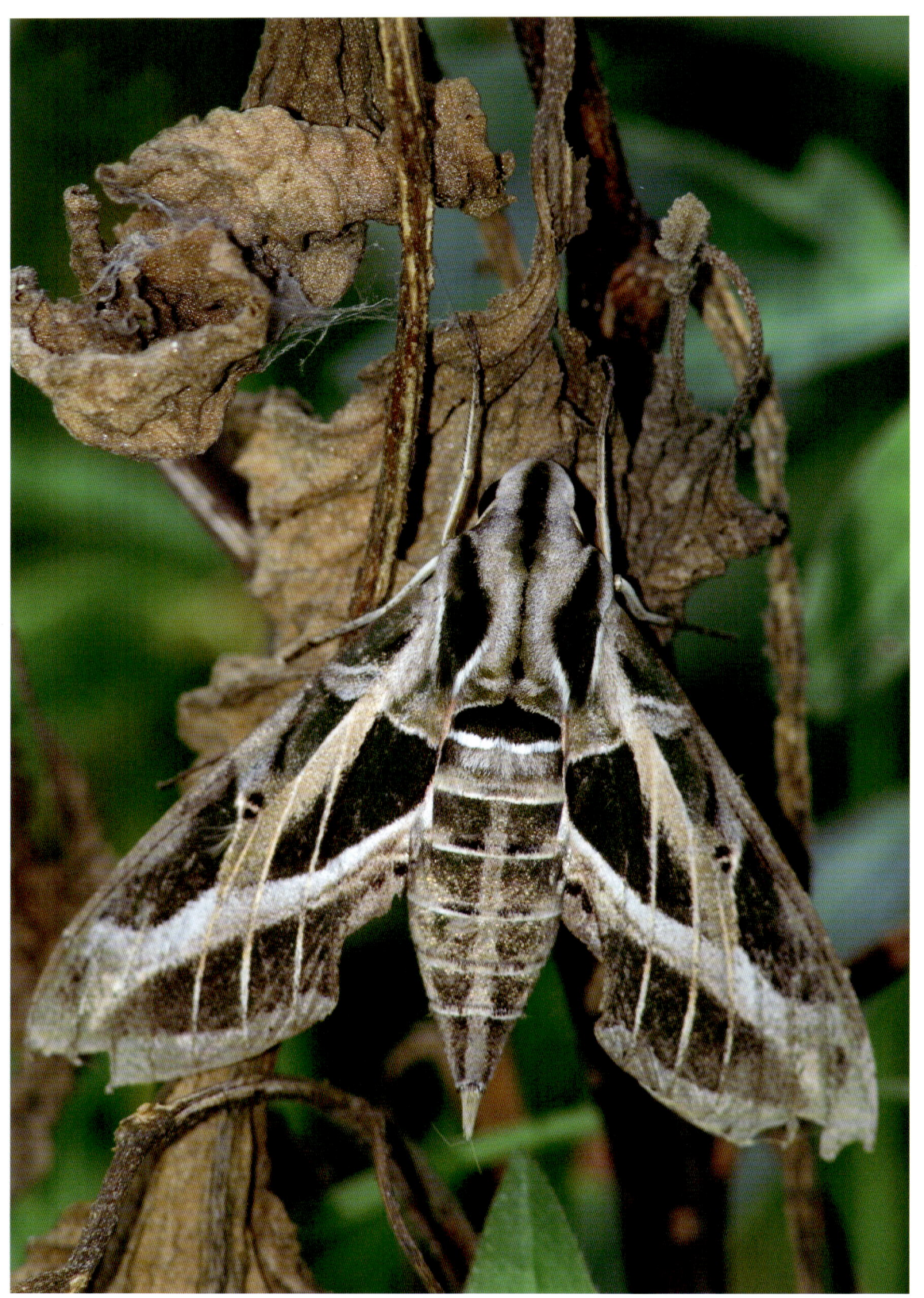

*I was walking along a dirt road near Austin in Travis County looking for dragonflies when I spied this **Vine Sphinx** perched on some dead leaves. These moths may be fairly common, but they can easily be missed since they stay motionless most of the day. By keeping an eye out for small wildlife as well as the larger animals, you will often be rewarded with something special.*

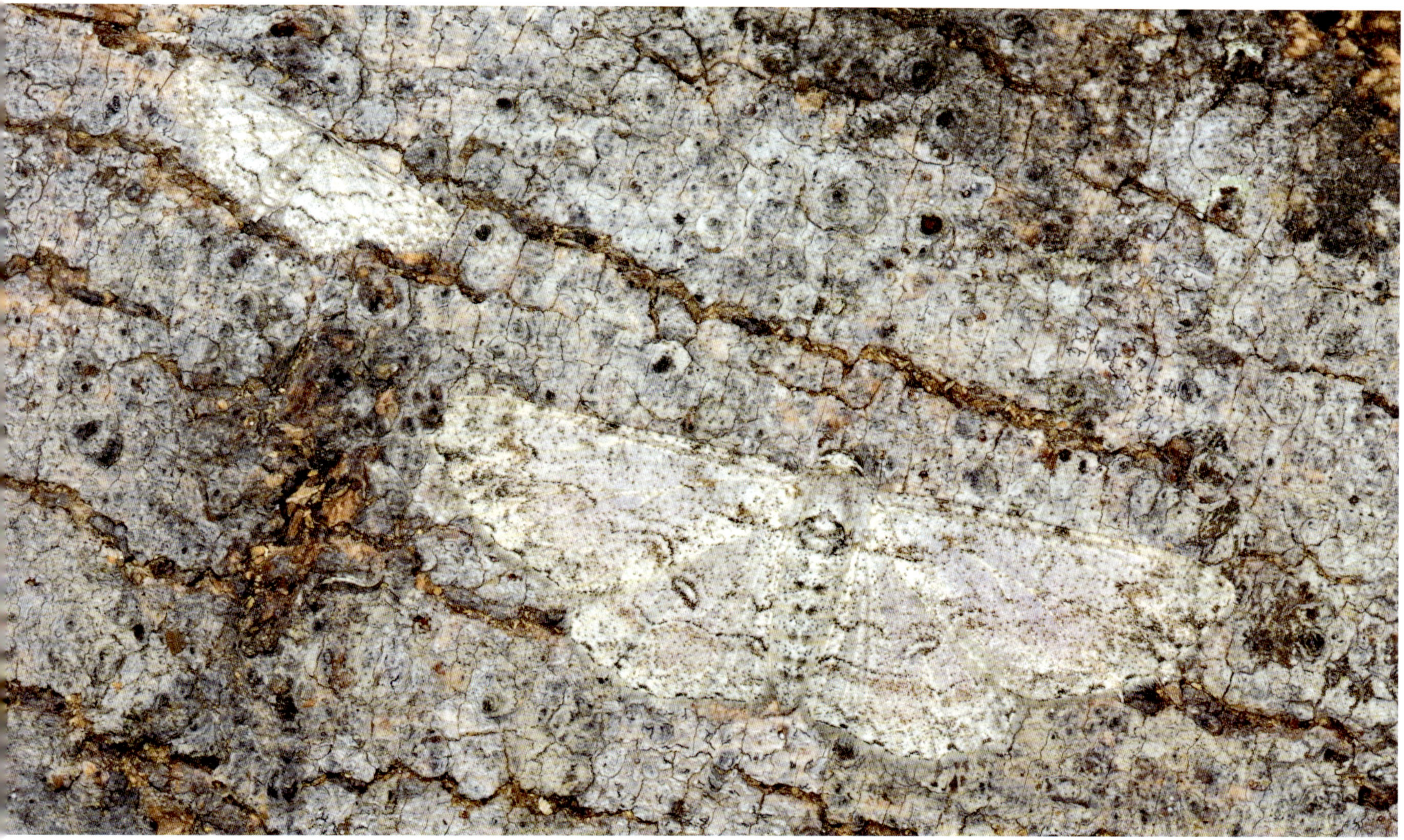

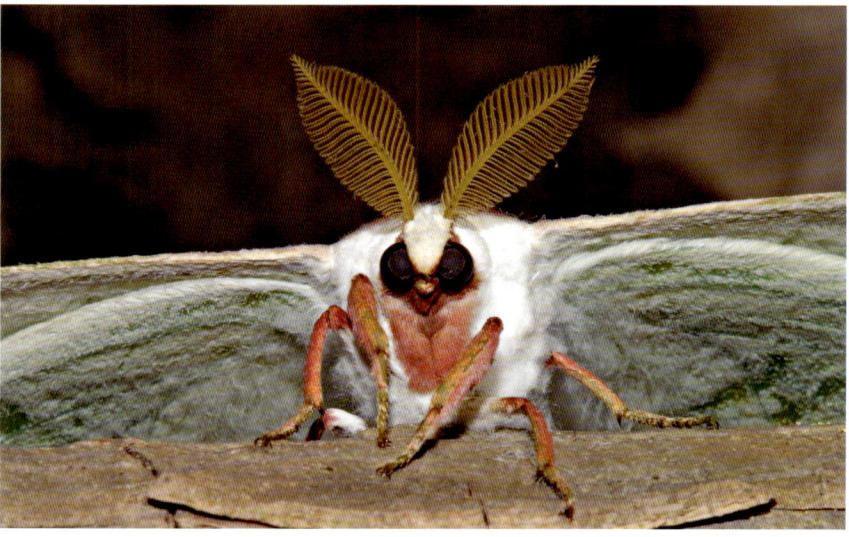

Camouflage is one of nature's ways of helping creatures survive predation. I found these two small **White Moths** on a mesquite limb in Hidalgo County. They blend in against the background so effectively that it is easy to see how a bird or other predator would miss them. These moths apparently have no official common name, but the larger moth is probably of the genus Anacamptodes; the smaller one is of the genus Idaea.

I am always amazed at the size of a **Luna Moth** when I see one. Its six-inch wingspan and large, feathery antennae just captivate me. This one was resting on a log near the San Marcos River in Caldwell County on a warm day in late September.

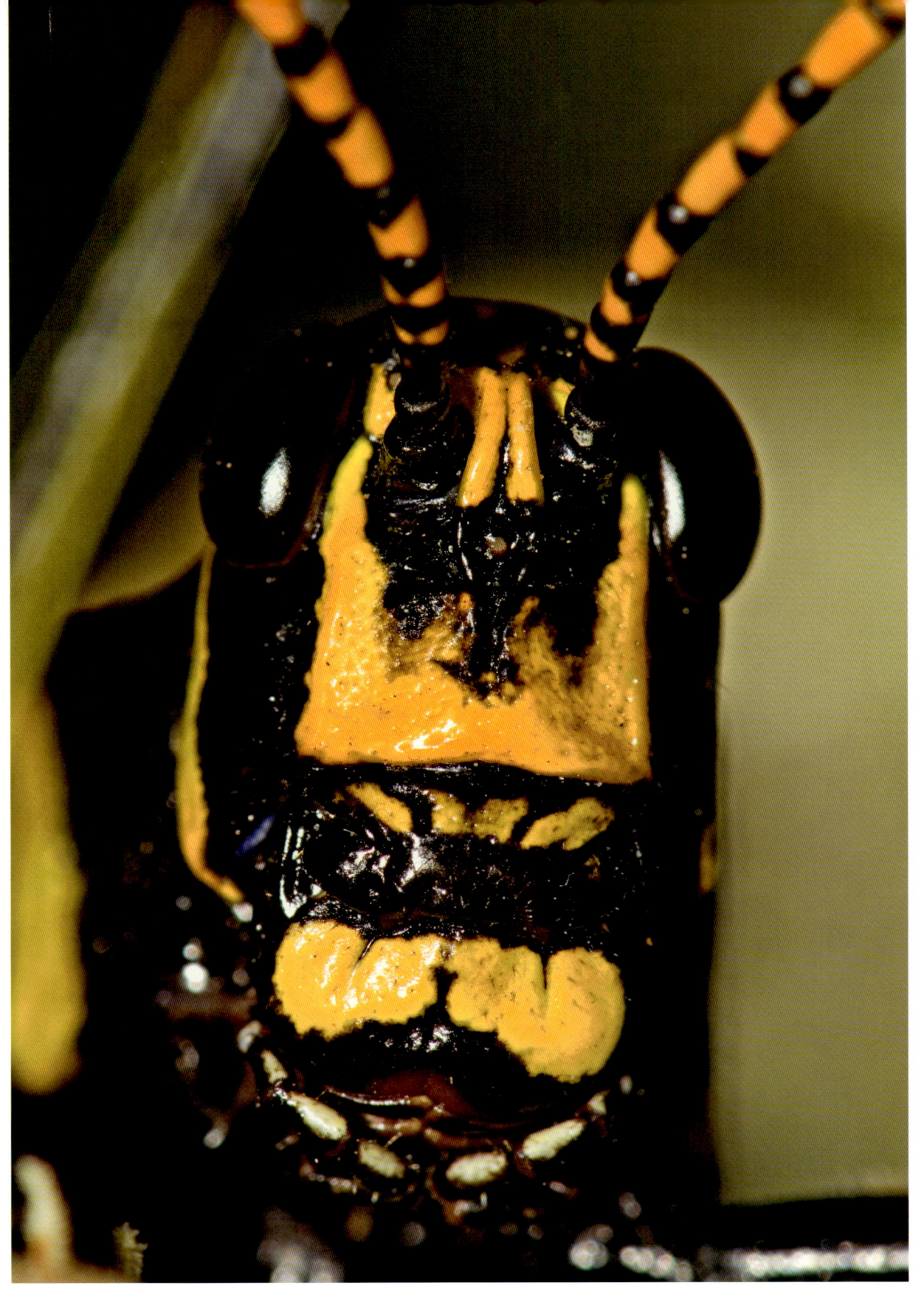

If you visit the Big Bend country of West Texas in the late summer or fall, you may sometimes come across hundreds of huge yellow and black grasshoppers as they move through an area. These large insects, called **Horse Lubbers**, *can be abundant on occasion and many fall victim to passing cars along roadways. This portrait of the face of a big Horse Lubber was taken on Big Bend Ranch State Park in Presidio County.*

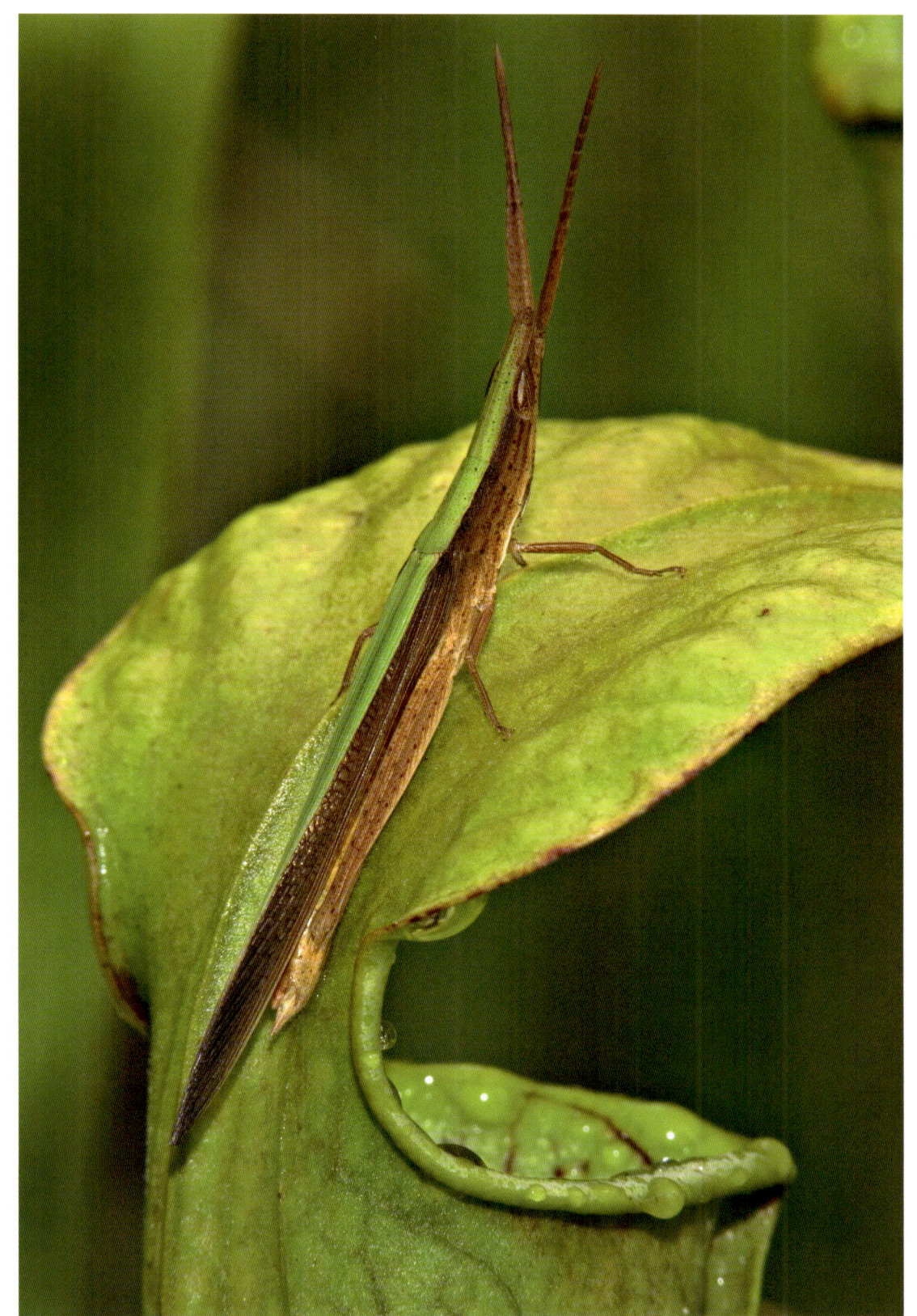

One of the most curious-looking of Texas grasshoppers is called the **Toothpick Grasshopper.** There are a number of different species of these insects, but all have a thin body, which appears quite unlike the grasshoppers we are more familiar with. This one was perched on a pitcher plant in an East Texas bog in the Angelina National Forest in Angelina County.

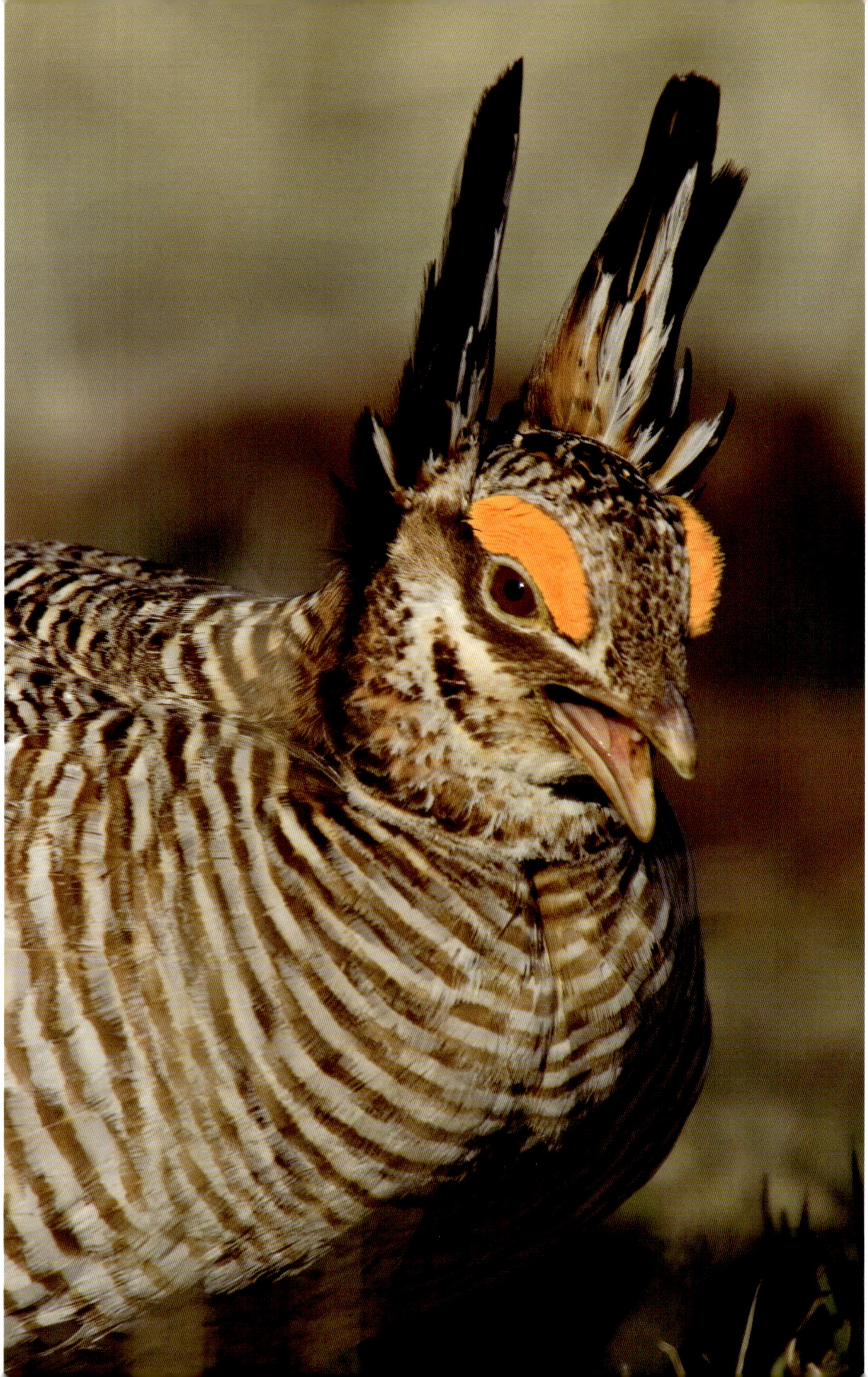

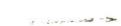

In my mind, **Lesser Prairie-Chickens** are a link to our ancestors. When early explorers first investigated the native grasslands of Central and North Texas, they found these prairie-chickens in abundance across a wide area of our state. Native Americans often imitated the courtship dances of these birds in their own dances. The birds still thrive within our state, but their range is limited to just a few areas in the Panhandle region of Texas. This close-up image of the male shows his bright yellow eyebrows fluffed up during his "booming" courtship dance on his breeding lek at dawn on an early spring morning in the northeast Panhandle near Higgins in Lipscomb County.

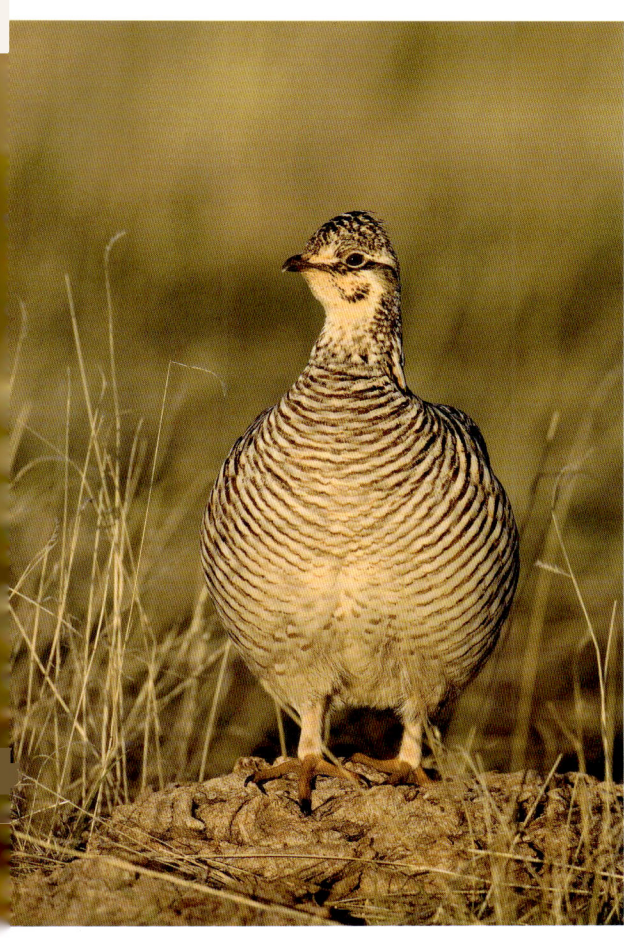

A female Lesser Prairie-Chicken was watching the males perform their courtship dance.

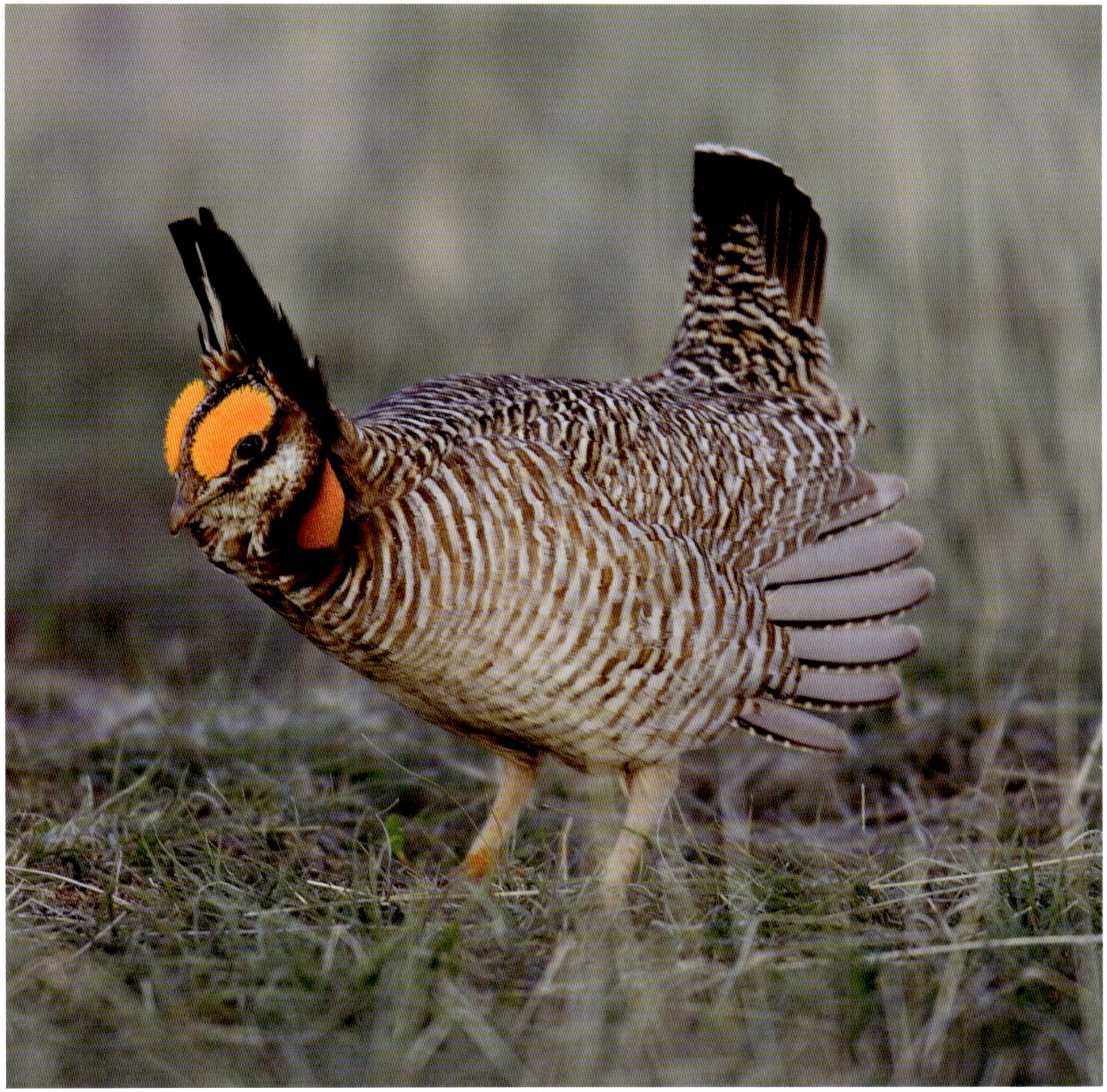

This male had his orange air sacs partially inflated.

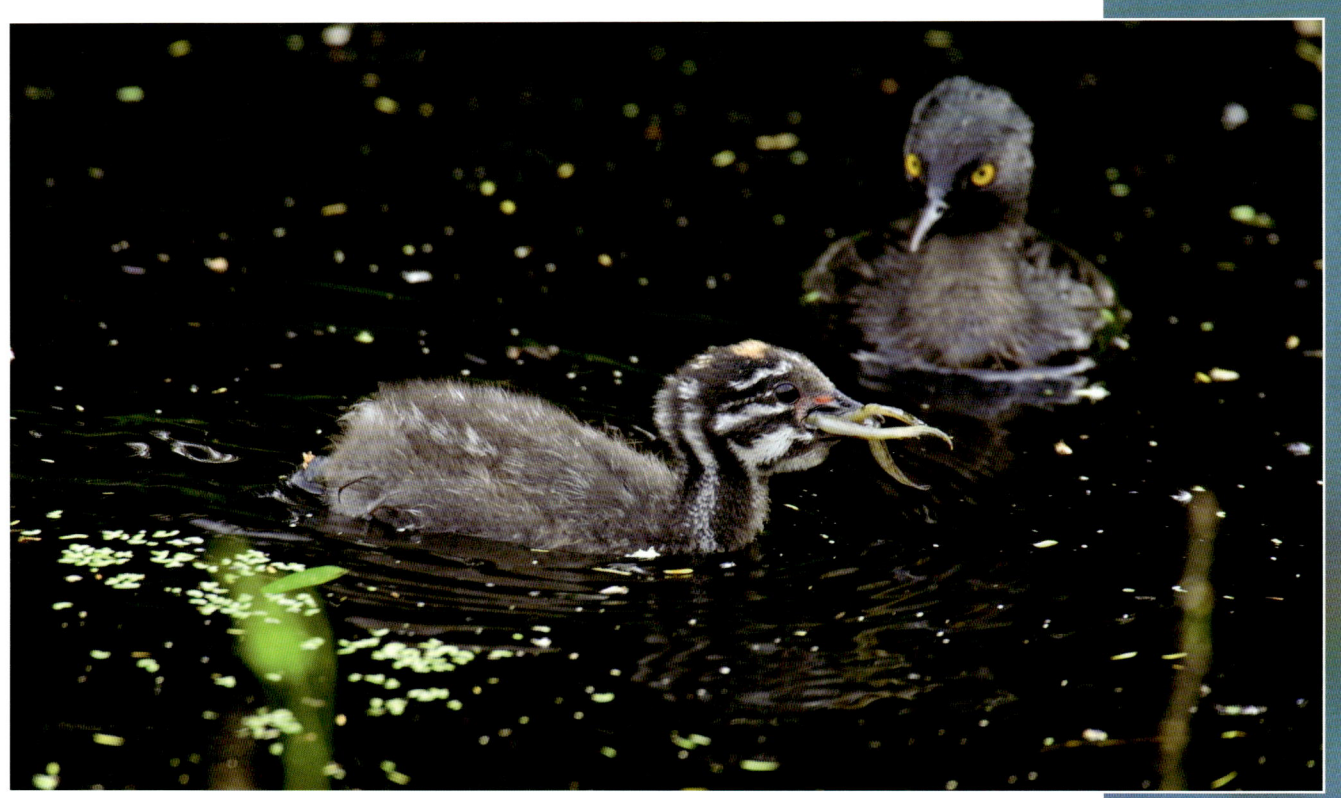

Least Grebe *parents can be extremely busy when trying to take care of hungry youngsters. The adult Least Grebe in the background has just brought a large tadpole to the surface and given it to one of its young. The young bird is in the process of wolfing down its meal. This adult pair had five hungry young birds, so they were kept busy for hours on end trying to take care of growing appetites. I watched the pair of adults catch frogs, tadpoles, small fish, and large insects over an hour or more on a late spring morning at a pond at the National Audubon Society's Sabal Palm Sanctuary near Brownsville in Cameron County.*

The **Least Grebe** *is a very small water bird of South Texas. It dives under the water while searching for food and may be quite difficult to spot among thick vegetation. The bright yellow eye is one of the field marks of this diminutive species. This individual had just popped to the surface of a Kenedy County pond after a dive; the water drops were still rolling off its neck and back, and the pond's surface still showed the disturbance.*

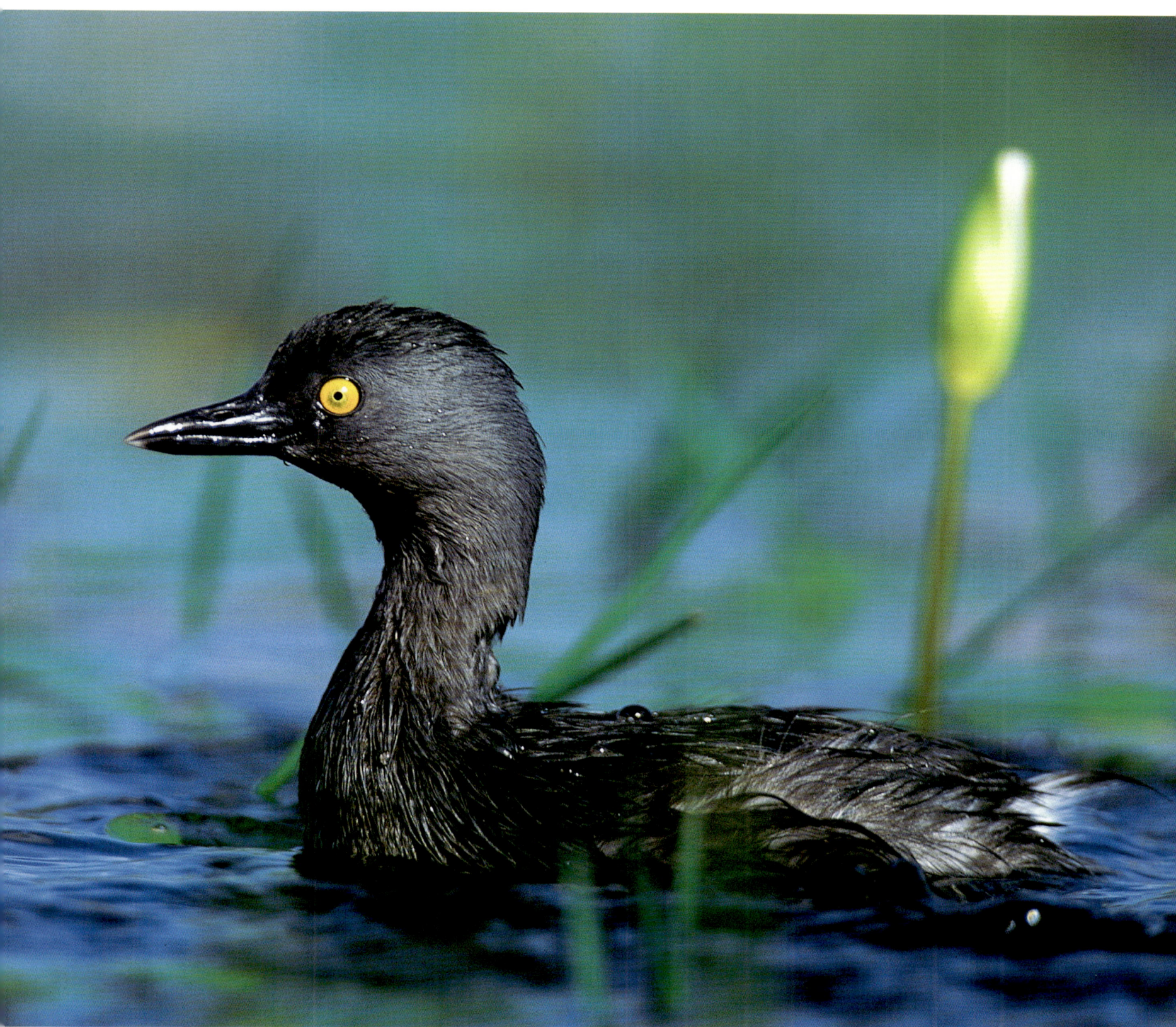

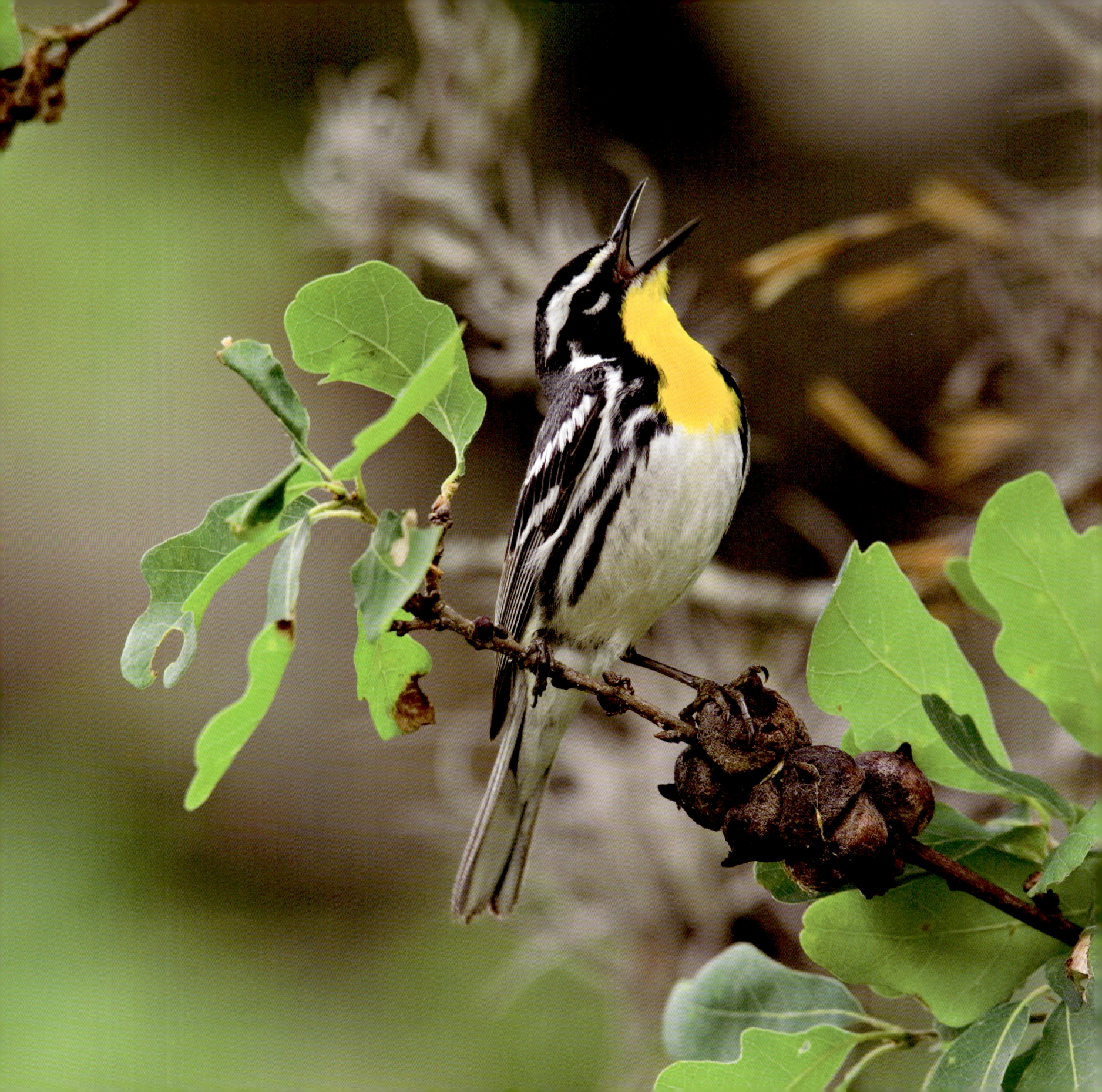

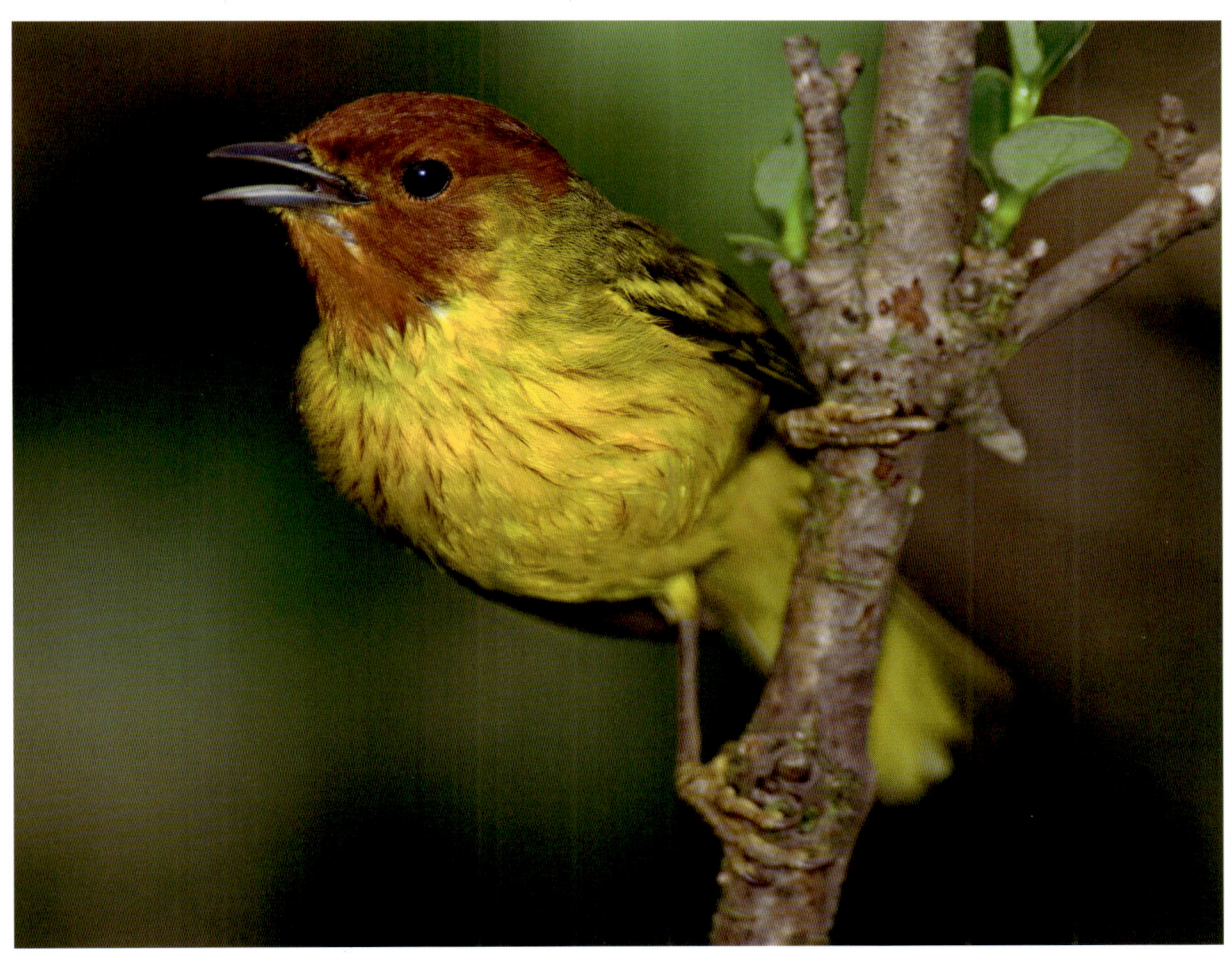

Opposite: **Yellow-throated Warblers** nest in swamps and forests across parts of the eastern fourth of Texas. Their breeding range also extends westward into the Texas Hill Country along the cypress-lined rivers and streams that wind their way through the Edwards Plateau. The bird is boldly patterned with black, white, and yellow and is among the most beautiful of Texas' breeding warblers. The male Yellow-throated Warbler here was singing from a large oak tree near Vanderpool in Bandera County.

Most **Yellow Warblers** *in Texas are migrants, heading to or coming from their breeding grounds to our north. There is a distinctive subspecies of the Yellow Warbler, however, called "Mangrove Warbler" that breeds along the coast of Mexico. It looks like a typical Yellow Warbler but has a rusty reddish head. In recent years, a small population of Mangrove Warblers has colonized mangrove trees on some small spoil islands along the extreme South Texas coast near Port Isabel and South Padre Island. The singing Mangrove Warbler in this image was on one of these islands near Port Isabel in Cameron County.*

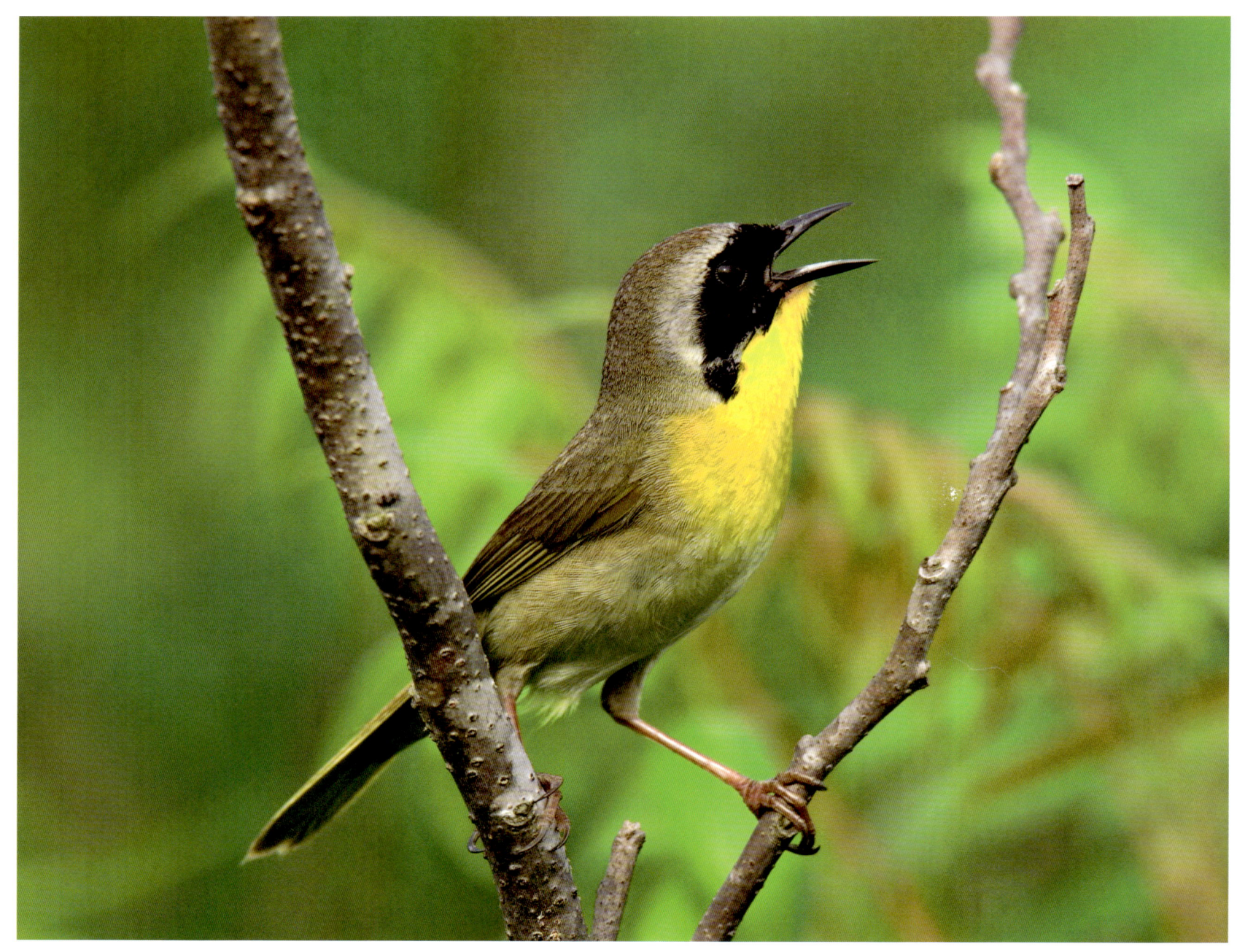

The **Common Yellowthroat** *is a warbler that may be found in marshes or brushy fields in a number of areas of Texas. This male Common Yellowthroat was in full territorial song in a brushy field near Zavalla in Angelina County. Unlike most warblers, Common Yellowthroats spend a great deal of time on or near the ground and can move mouselike through very thick vegetation.*

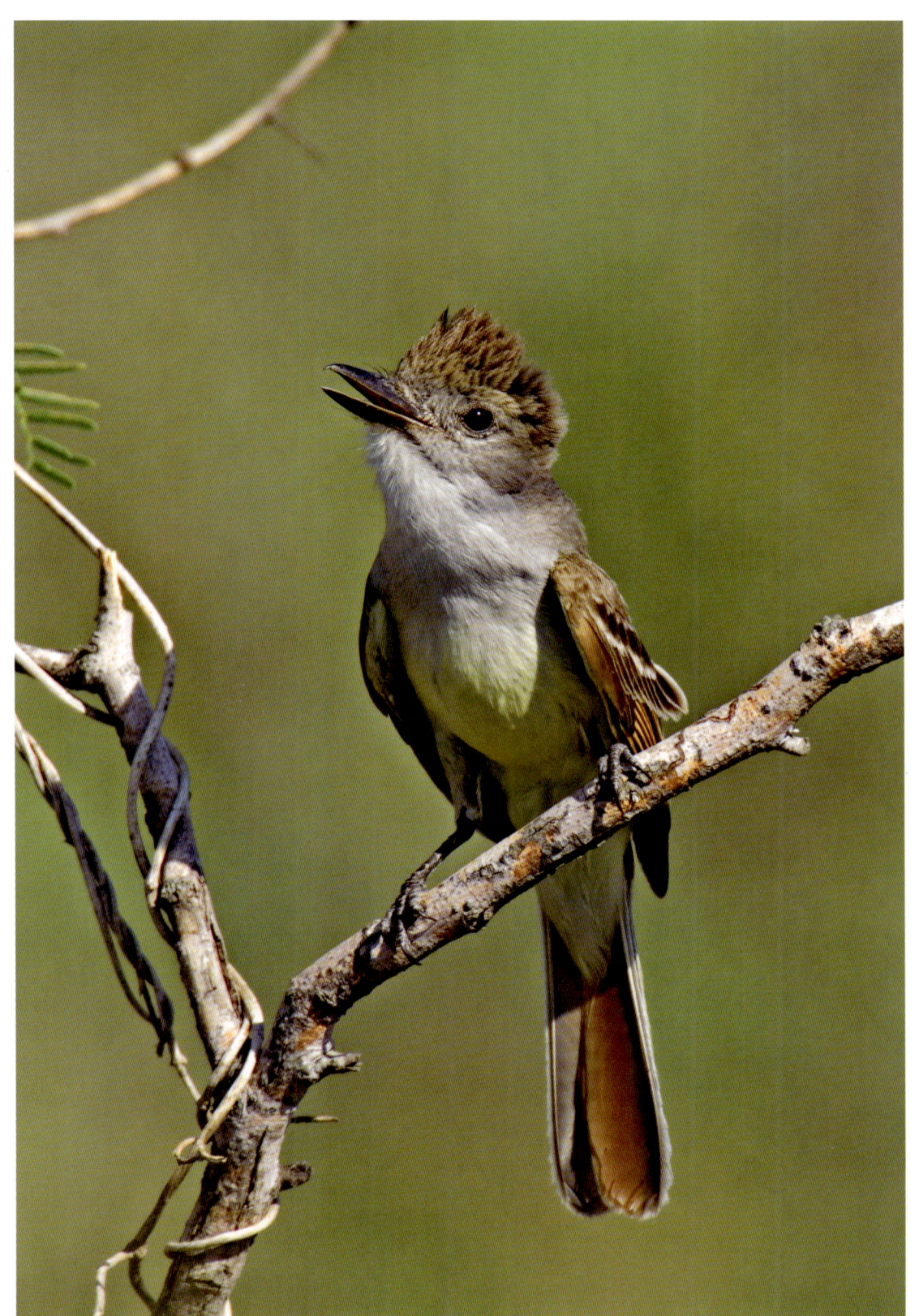

Brown-crested Flycatchers *are summer residents of South Texas, where they nest in cavities in trees such as mesquite or Texas ebony. As the name implies, they feed on flying insects and may often be seen chasing after grasshoppers or other insects. This male was calling from a perch in mesquite woodland in Hidalgo County near McCook.*

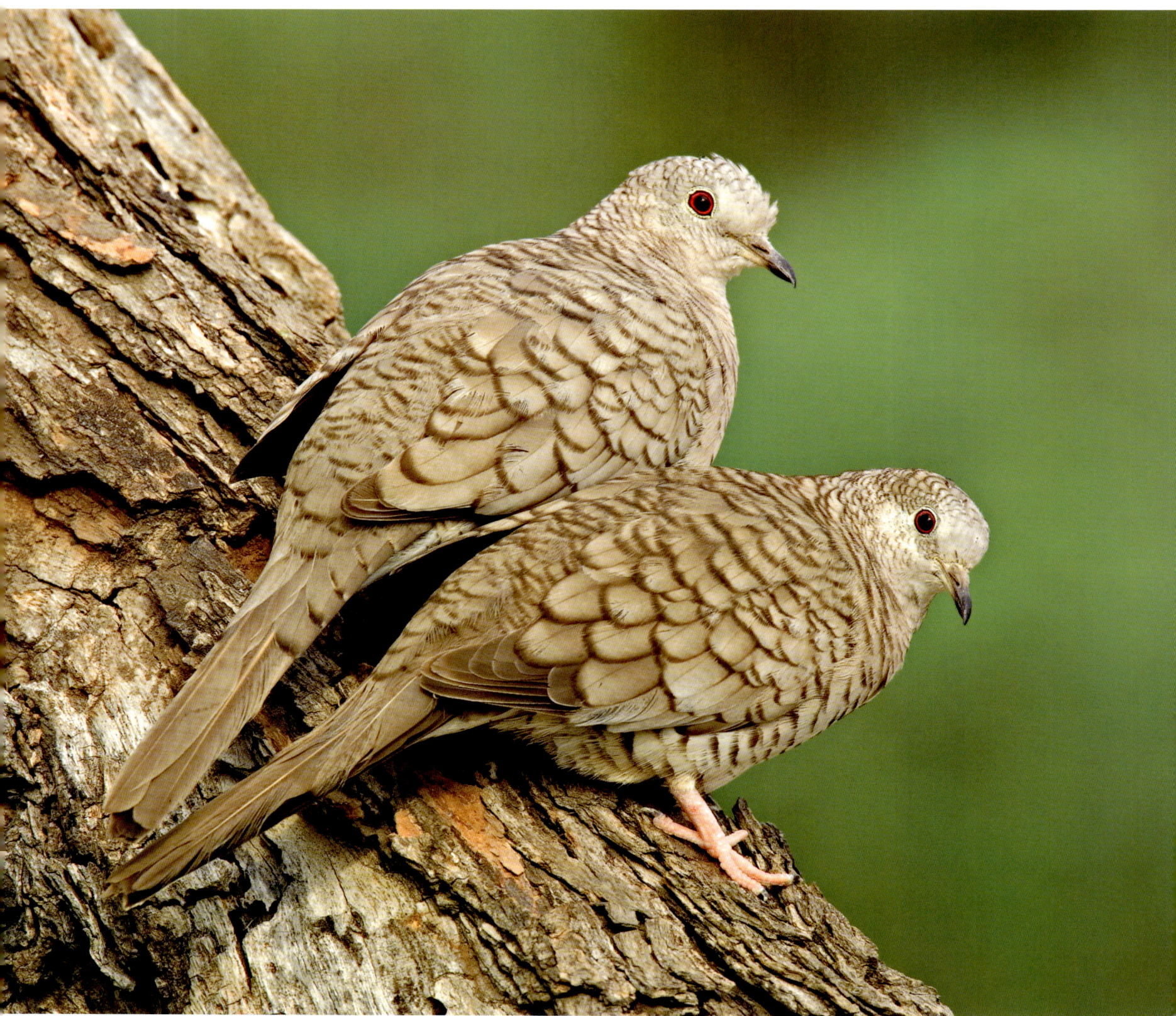

Opposite: **Inca Doves** *are a small cousin of the more familiar Mourning Dove. Incas are mainly found in the southern and western parts of Texas, where they may be quite common in some locations. Incas seem to enjoy sitting together, and a pair of birds on a limb is a fairly typical sight. This pair was resting on a log along a ranch road in Hidalgo County.*

One of the most beautiful signs of early spring in Central Texas is the blooming of the Texas redbud trees. Add a colorful male **House Finch** *and some blue sky and you have a photo to bring back memories of a special day. This House Finch was in a redbud on a section of Balcones Canyonlands National Wildlife Refuge in Travis County.*

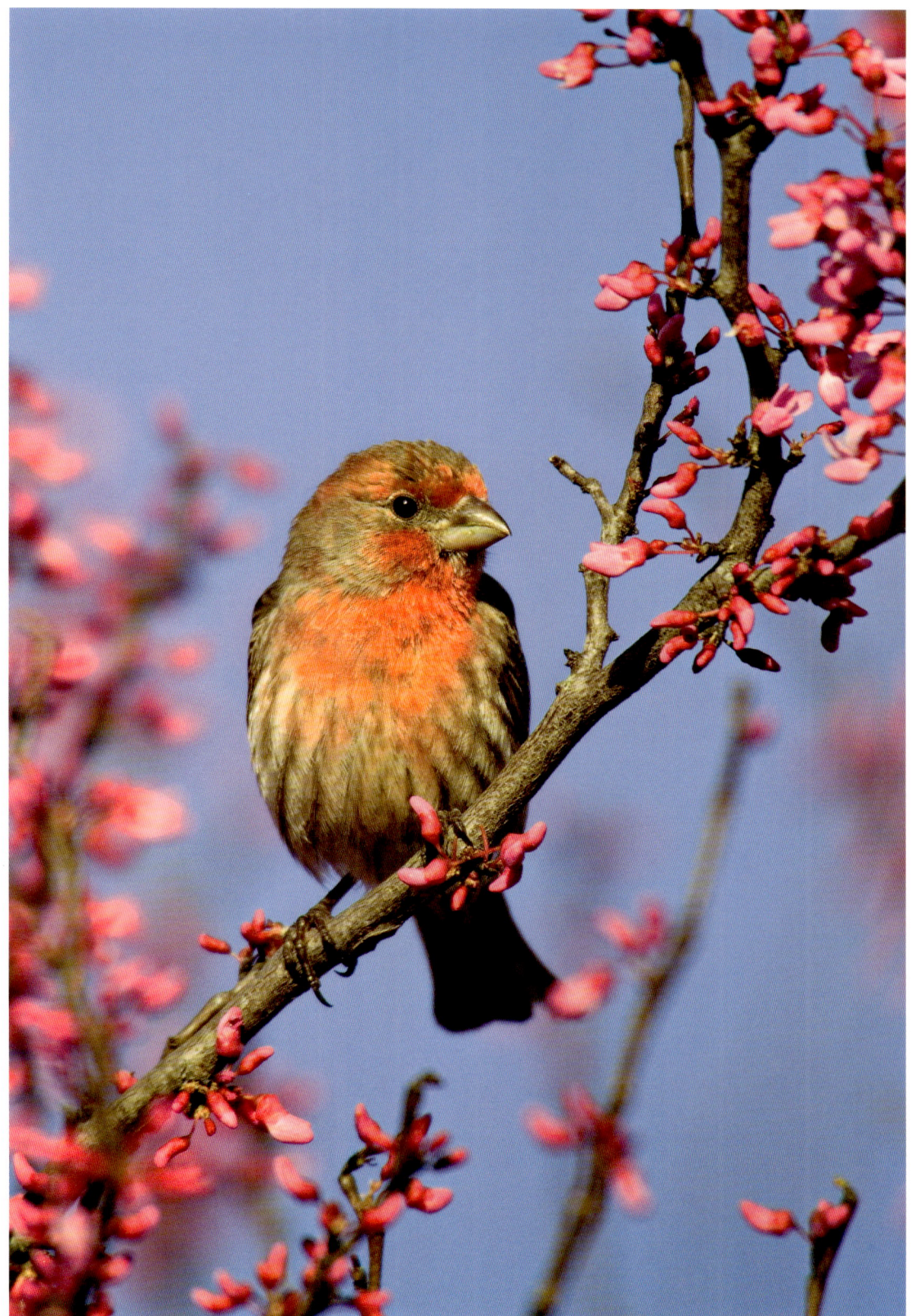

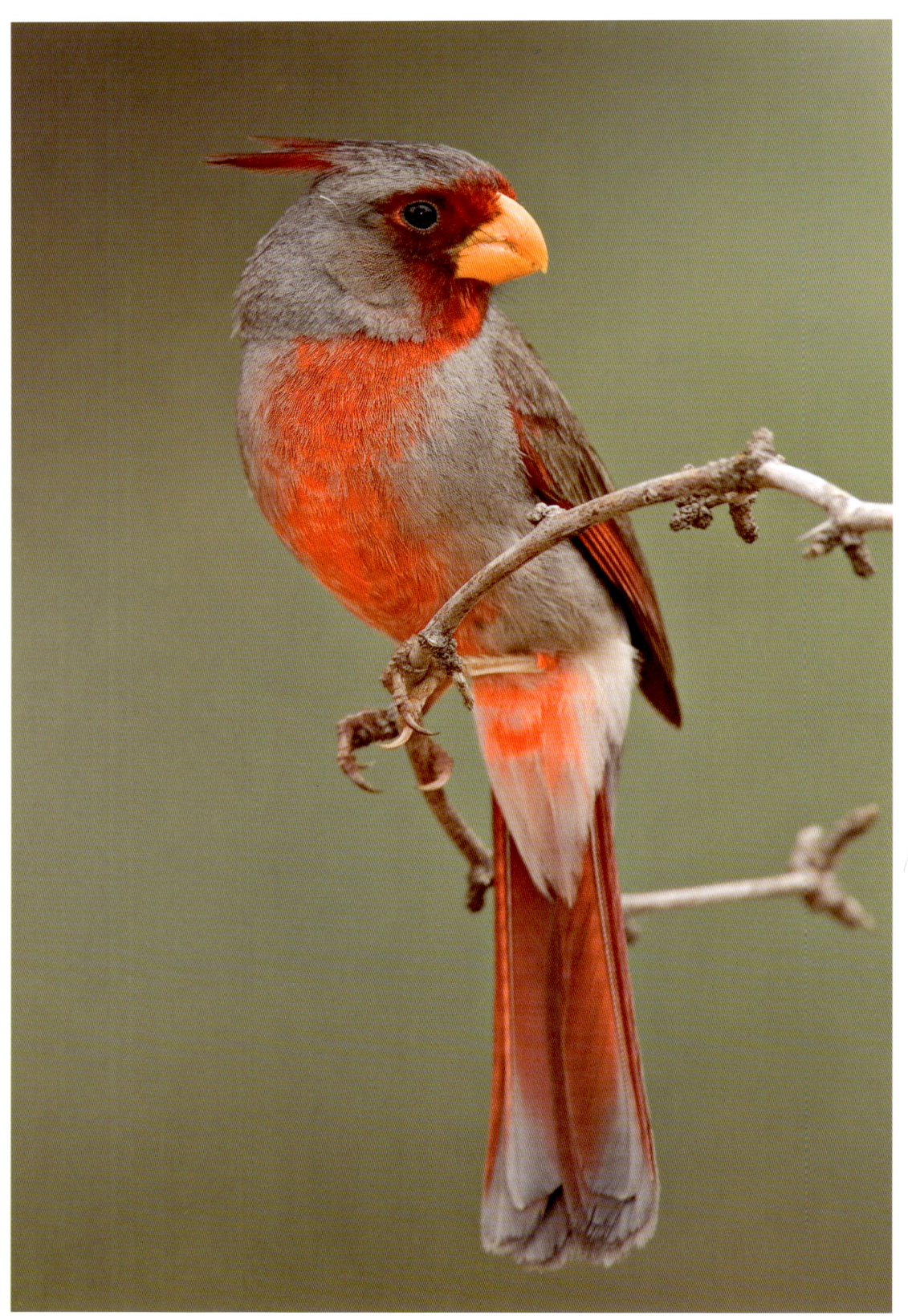

The **Pyrrhuloxia** is a close relative of the more familiar Northern Cardinal, and is, in fact, sometimes called Gray Cardinal. It is typically more western in distribution than Northern Cardinals, and it often occupies more arid habitats. The bird's loud, ringing song may be heard throughout much of the year in parts of South and West Texas. This male Pyrrhuloxia perched on a twig in Hidalgo County to survey his surroundings.

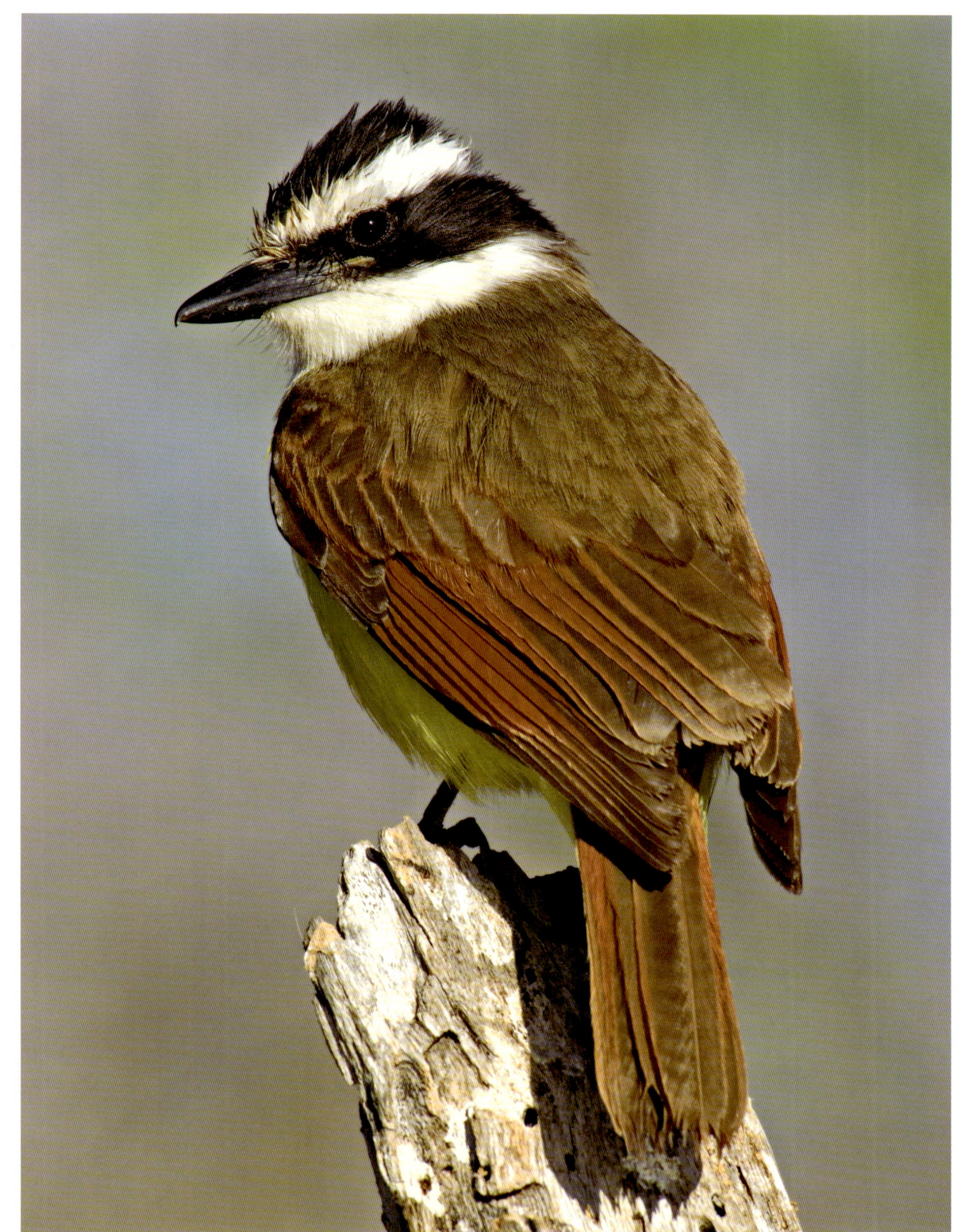

The **Great Kiskadee** is a tropical flycatcher widespread in Central and South America but, within the United States, found only in deep South Texas. The species may often be found near water, and it is known to forage on frogs, lizards, fish, and other prey items in addition to large insects. This Great Kiskadee watched me over its shoulder as it perched near a pond in Hidalgo County near Edinburg.

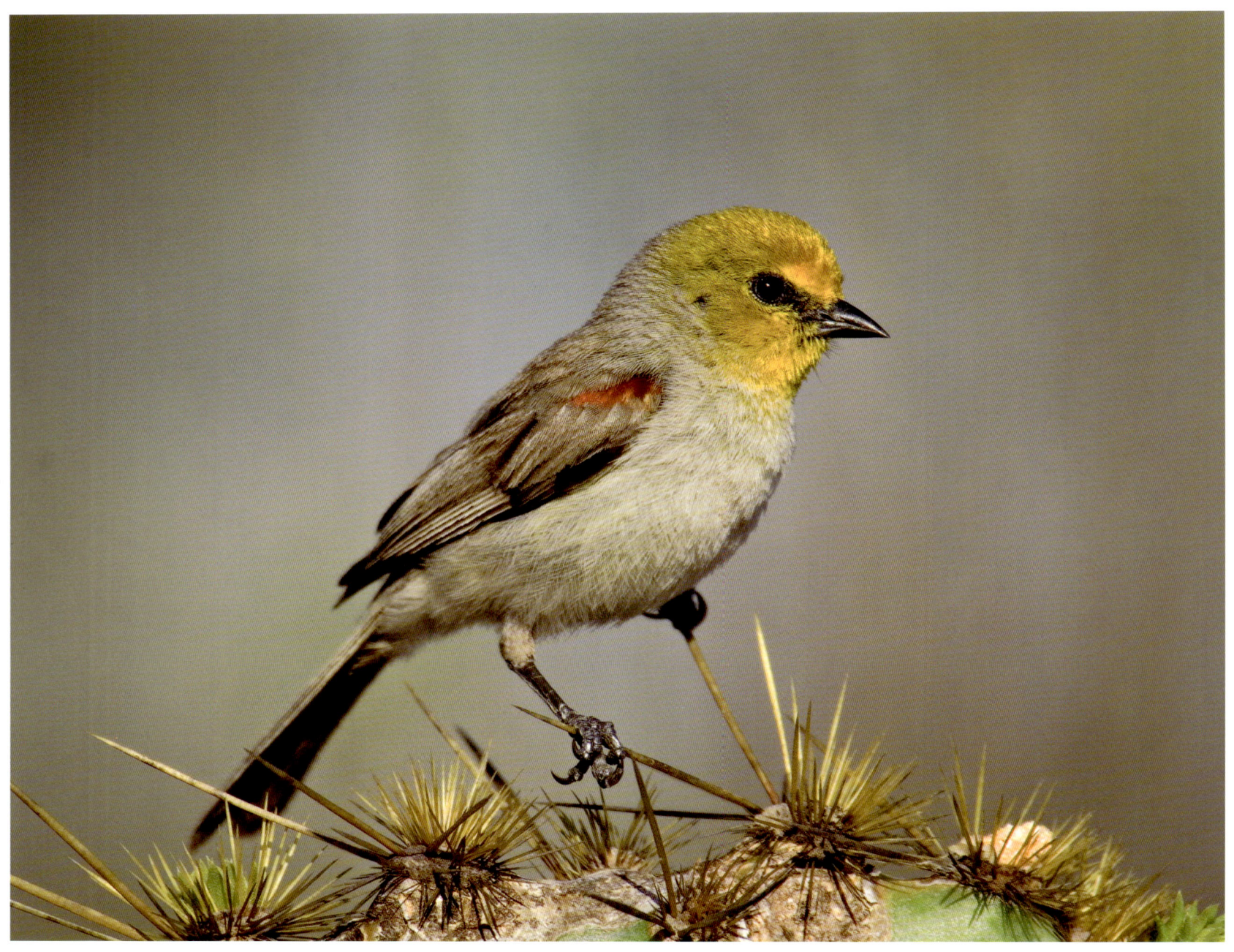

The desert and semiarid portions of South and West Texas host a number of birds and mammals that are only found in those types of habitats. The **Verdin** is a fairly common little desert bird, and its "tink, tink" call notes are heard often. Seldom do most people ever get a good look at this bird, however. Its tiny size and quick movements cause most of us to see only a tiny gray flash as the bird moves through the mesquite and cactus habitats where it lives. It is, however, a stunning little bird with a bright yellow head and a rusty colored shoulder patch, if you can ever get a close look at it.

This Verdin was in some mesquite brushland in Hidalgo County in South Texas. You can get an idea of its diminutive size when you see the bird's feet clutching the spines of a prickly pear cactus for a perch.

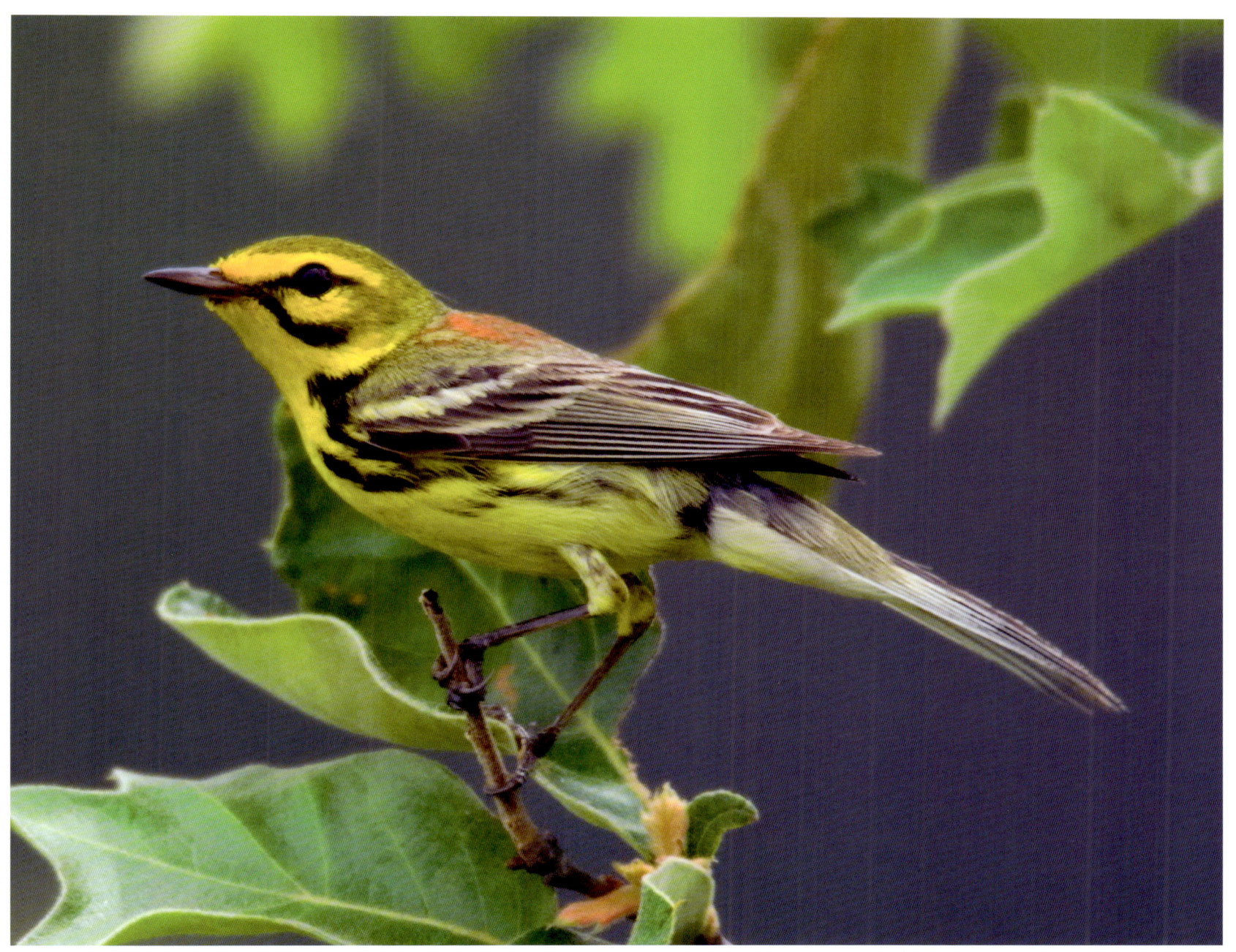

In far East Texas, there is a beautiful warbler that nests in small clumps of trees in scrubby habitats. The **Prairie Warbler** *is widespread across much of the eastern United States, but within Texas it is usually only found on the eastern edge of the state. This male Prairie Warbler was in a small oak tree near Zavalla, Angelina County.*

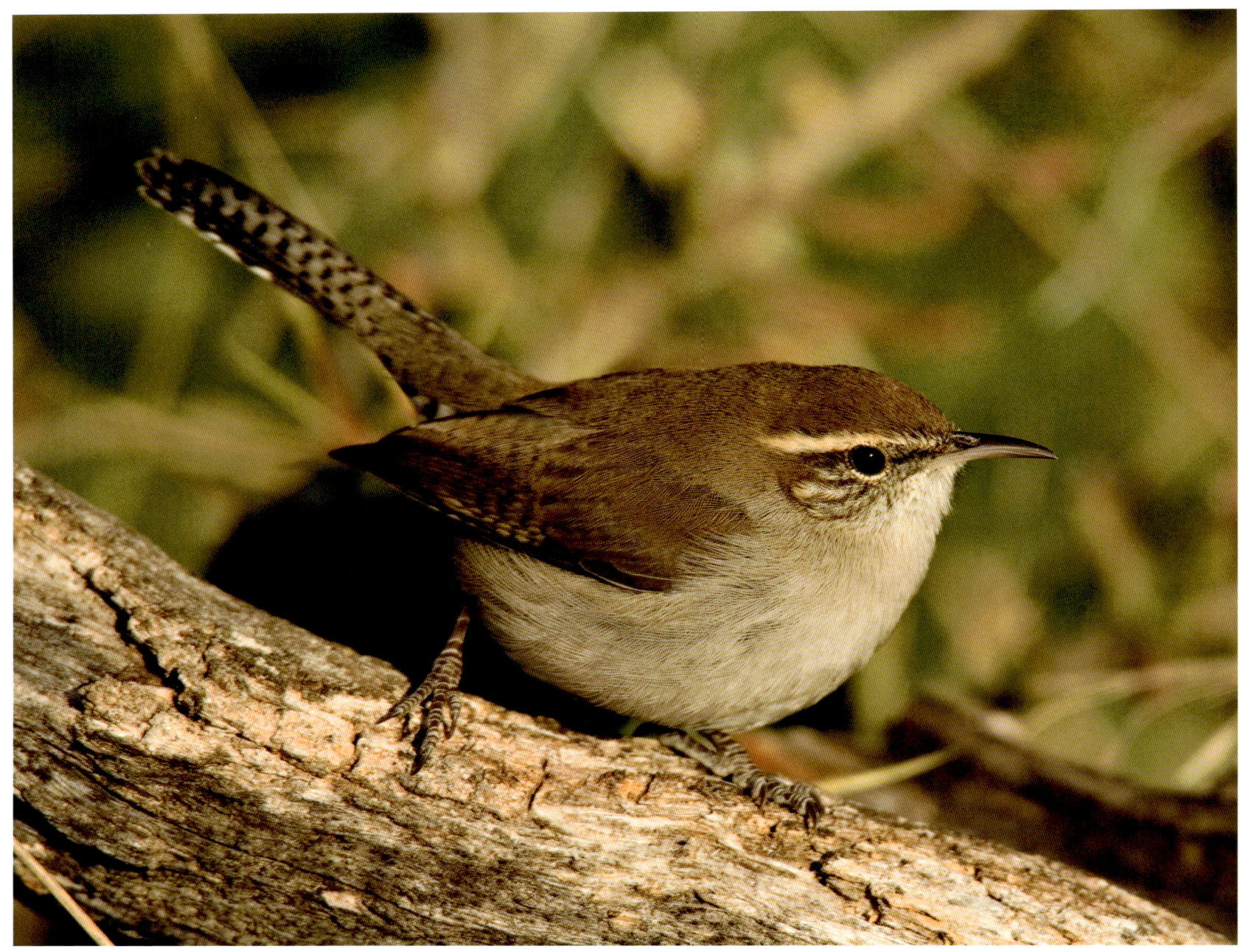

Bewick's Wrens *are common across most of Texas, and their loud song is a familiar sound in many backyards as well as in more rural areas. The species sometimes is known to nest in curious places such as a flower pot, an old boot, or perhaps a hanging basket. Bewick's Wrens seem to have a lively personality, and many people enjoy having them in their suburban yards. This one was investigating a woodpile at Buffalo Gap in Taylor County.*

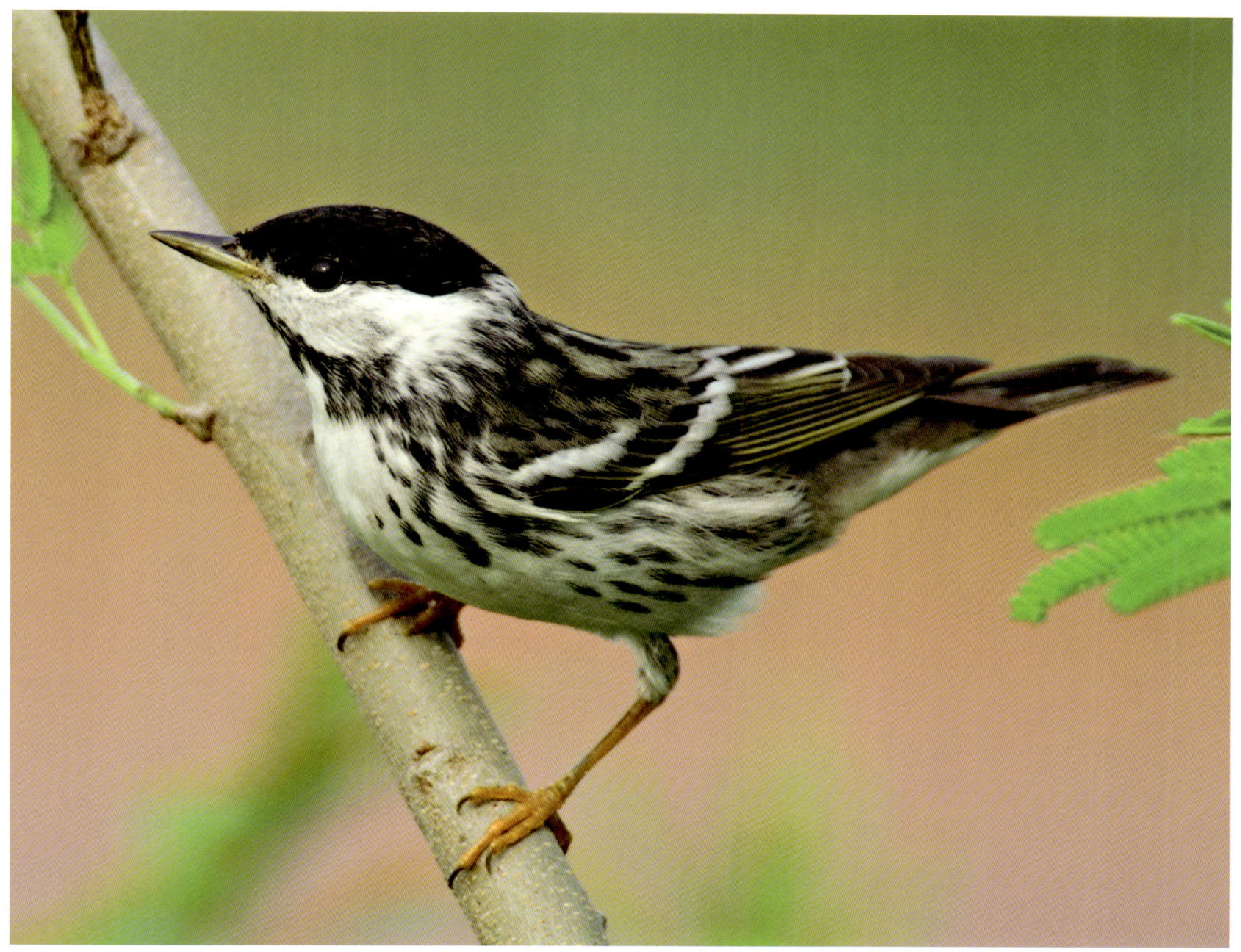

The Texas Gulf Coast is well known as a resting and feeding area for migrant birds. During the spring, hundreds of thousands of migrants may stop along our coast as they head northward to their breeding ranges. Coastal woodlots from Beaumont to South Padre Island are critical to migrant birds. The **Blackpoll Warbler** is one of the many species that pass through Texas in migration. This bird winters in South America and goes north in the spring to its nesting grounds in the tundra and taiga areas of northern Canada and Alaska. This perky male Blackpoll Warbler was on South Padre Island in Cameron County, where it spent a day in early May before continuing its journey north.

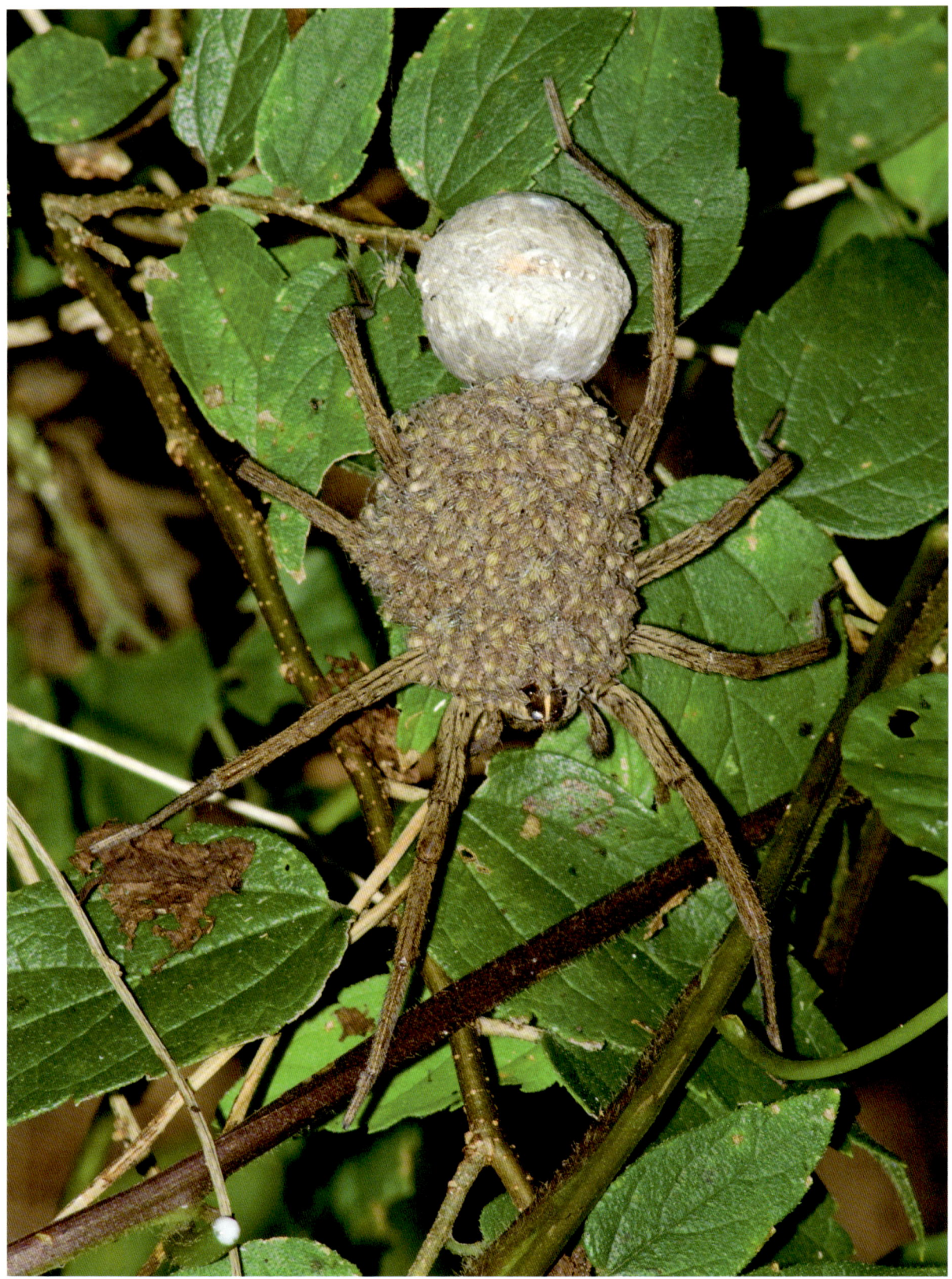

There are many kinds of **Wolf Spiders** in Texas, and the genus and species of a particular one often cannot be determined from photographs. Females carry an egg sack behind them, and when the babies hatch they crawl onto the mother's back. She will carry them in this way for several weeks. Such parental care is not common in spiders. This female with an egg sack was found near the Colorado River in Austin. Many hundreds of tiny spider babies made the adult spider look almost fur-covered.

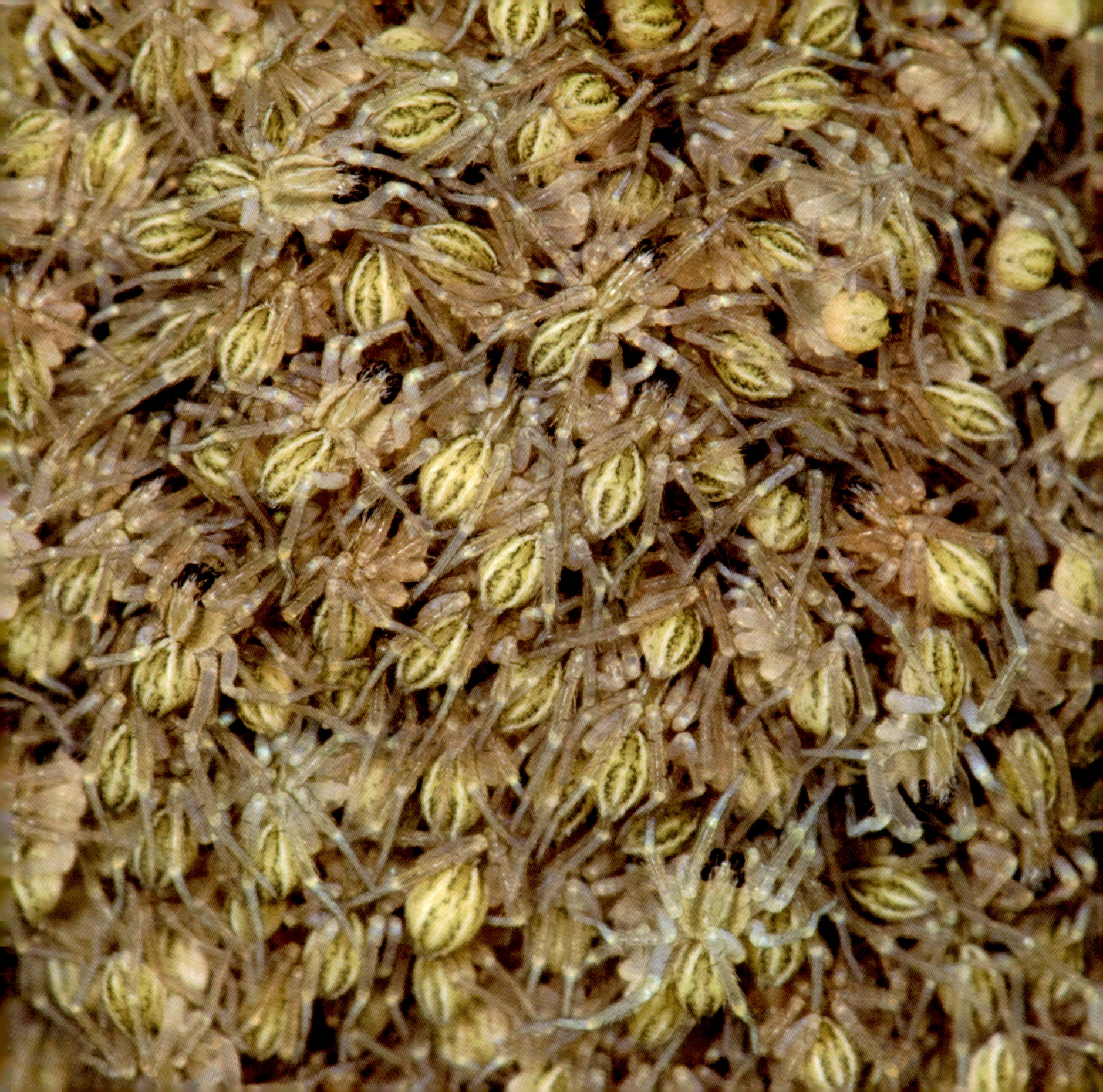

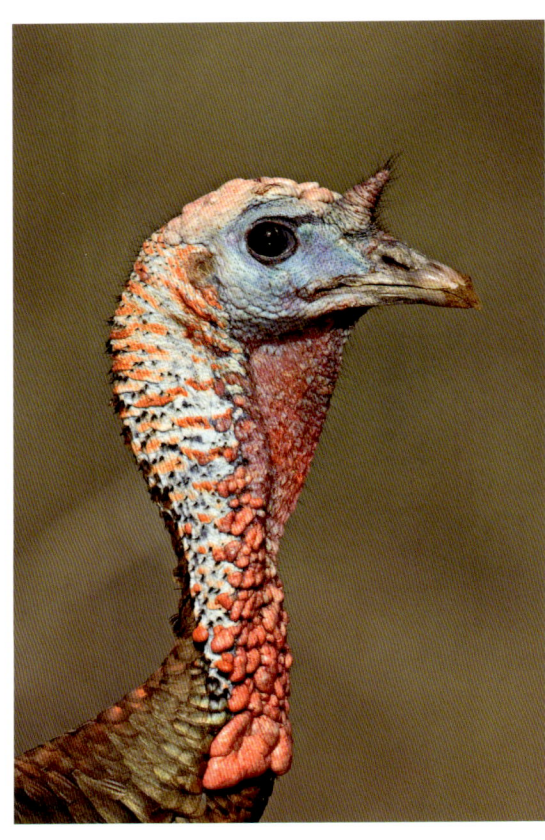

The head of a **Wild Turkey** is a complicated pattern of red and blue skin and feathers. This turkey was near a South Texas water hole in Hidalgo County, and it kept an eye on me as I followed its movements with a telephoto lens from a blind.

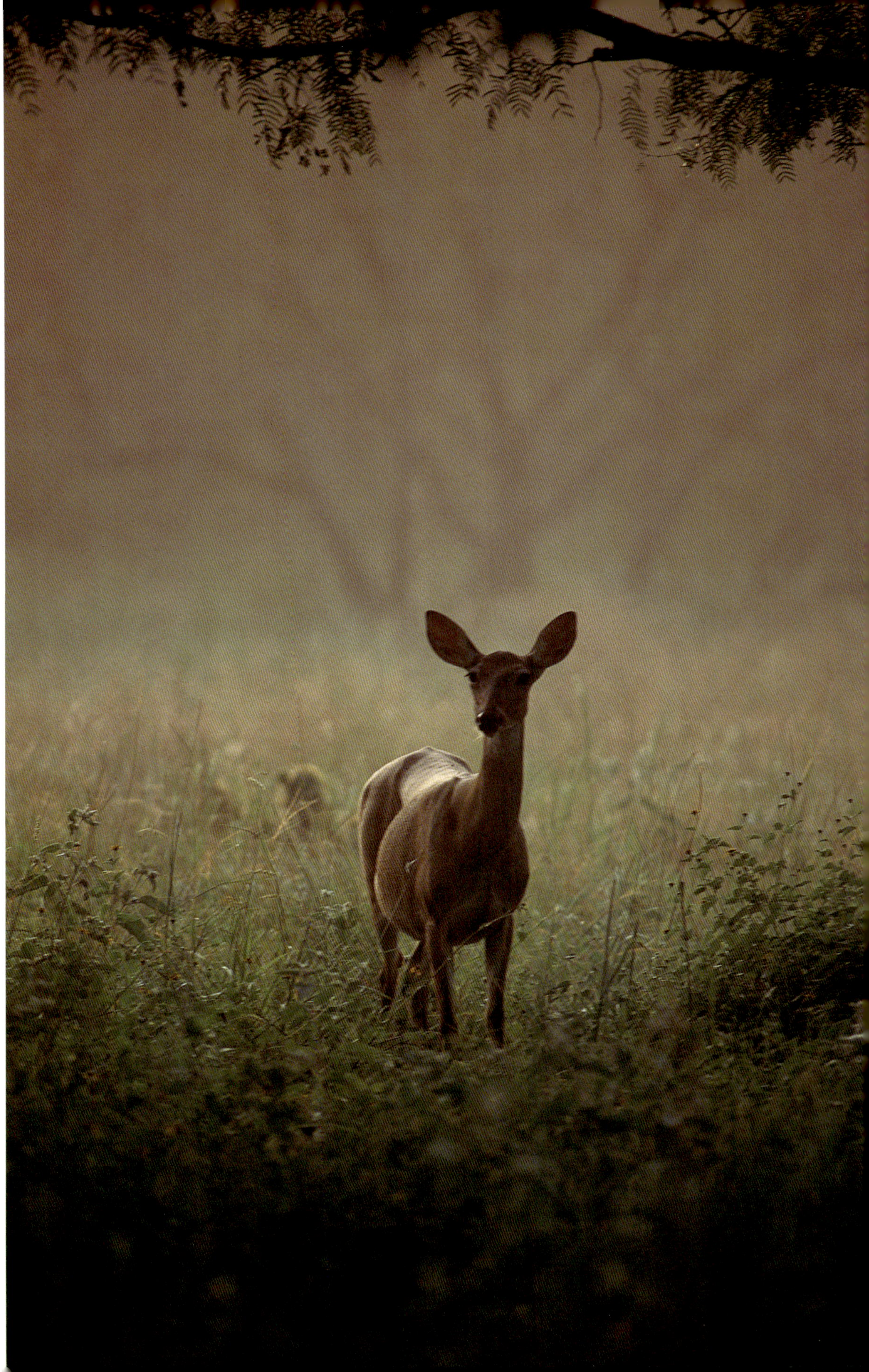

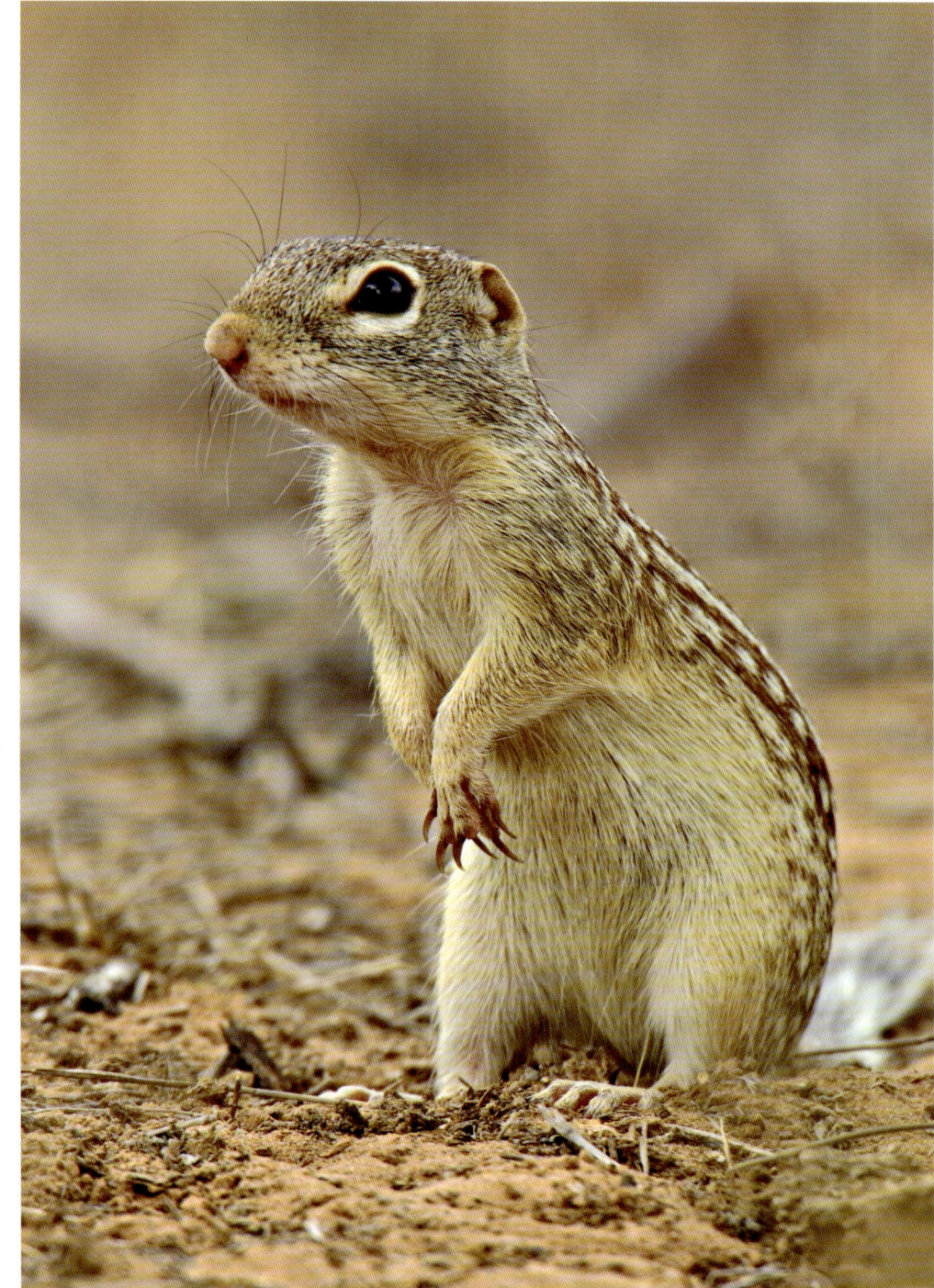

Right:
I was sitting in a blind in Hidalgo County in South Texas one spring morning, waiting for some birds to show up at a small water hole. A quick motion suddenly caught my eye as this **Mexican Ground Squirrel** *scurried out to investigate the surroundings. Over the next day or so, a pair of these small rodents visited me often and allowed me to take many images. They are incredibly alert animals, but then, they are considered prey by every hawk and snake in the neighborhood, so such vigilance is quite warranted!*

Opposite:
White-tailed Deer *occur all across Texas in many habitats. The hunting of these animals is big business in Texas, but many people enjoy just watching them. Books and magazines are full of images of majestic buck whitetails with incredible antlers, which would be a prize for any hunter. The image here of a fat doe on a hazy September morning in Kenedy County is certainly not your typical hunter oriented shot, but I have always liked it.*

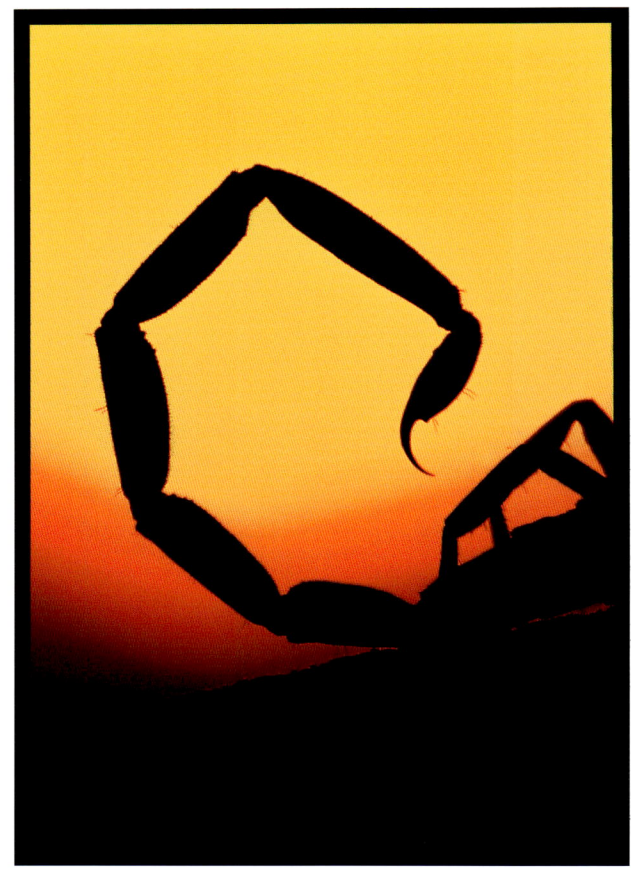

If you spend much time in the Texas outdoors, you are bound to come across a **Scorpion** *now and then. They can have a painful sting that should be avoided, but despite their somewhat nasty reputation, I have found them to be interesting photography subjects on several occasions. A tight shot with a macro lens allowed me to get an interesting image of this one against a summer sunset in Kenedy County.*

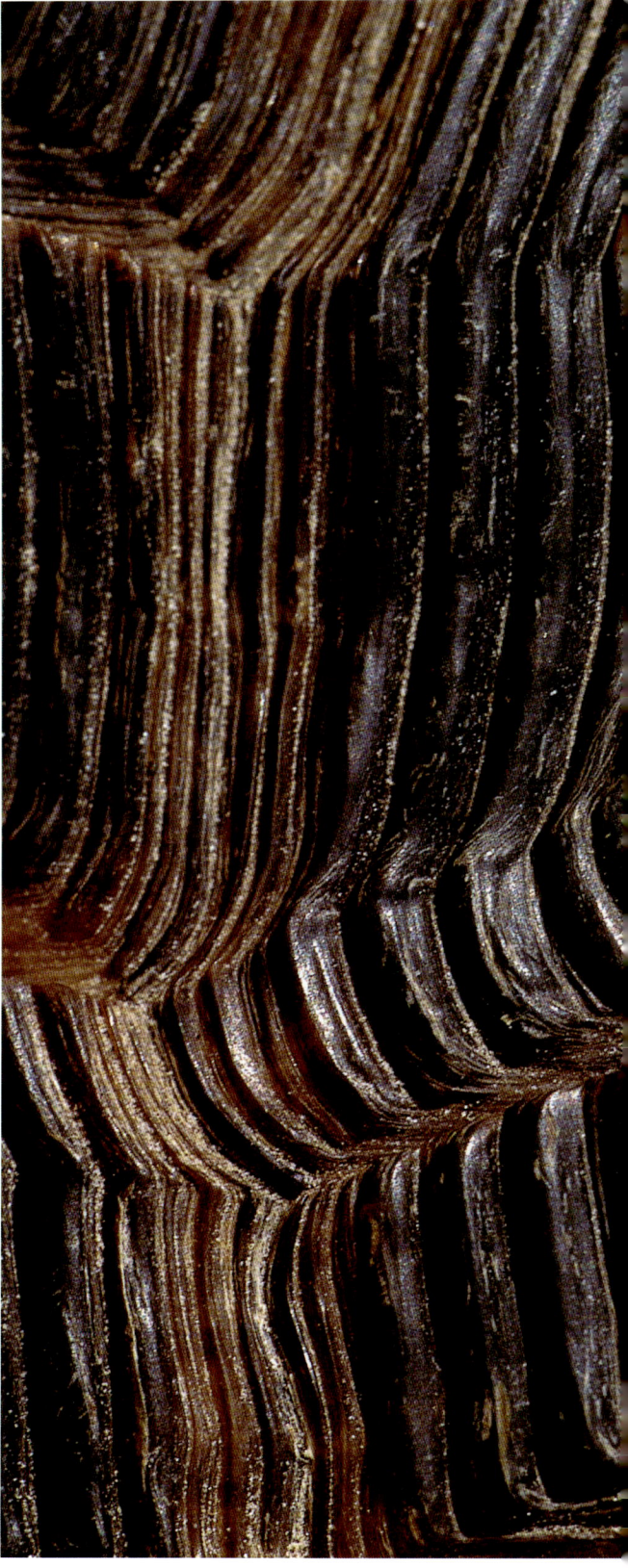

The **Texas Tortoise** *is a state endangered species that only occurs in sandy soils of far South Texas. This tortoise burrows into the soft sand to make its home and feeds on a variety of vegetation, including the fruits of prickly pear cactus. I have always marveled at its shell, so one day after coming across a tortoise crossing a sandy ranch road in Brooks County, I simply took a series of shots looking straight down on the back of one of these animals. The result is a strange mosaic of lines and textures that is difficult to describe.*

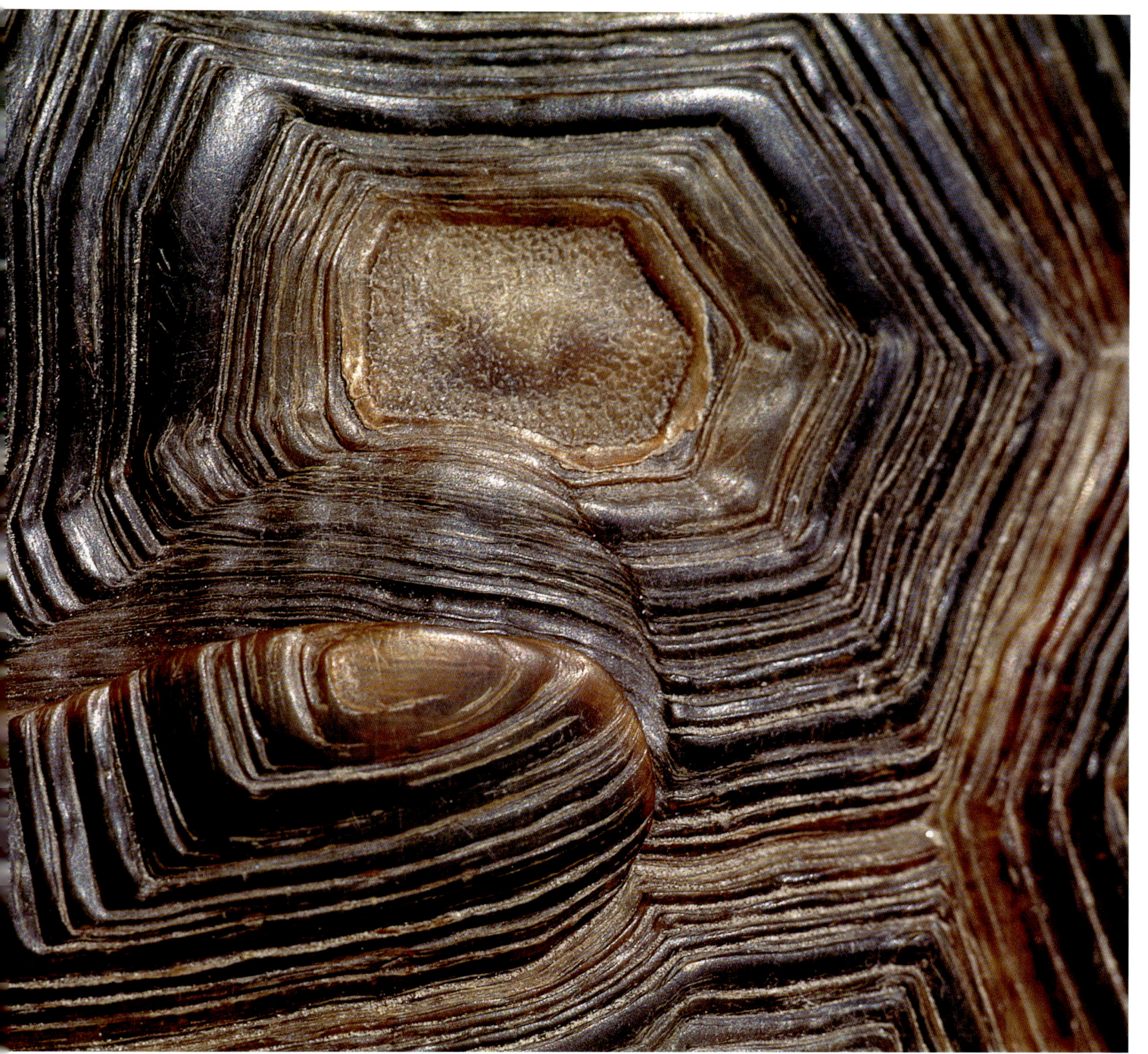

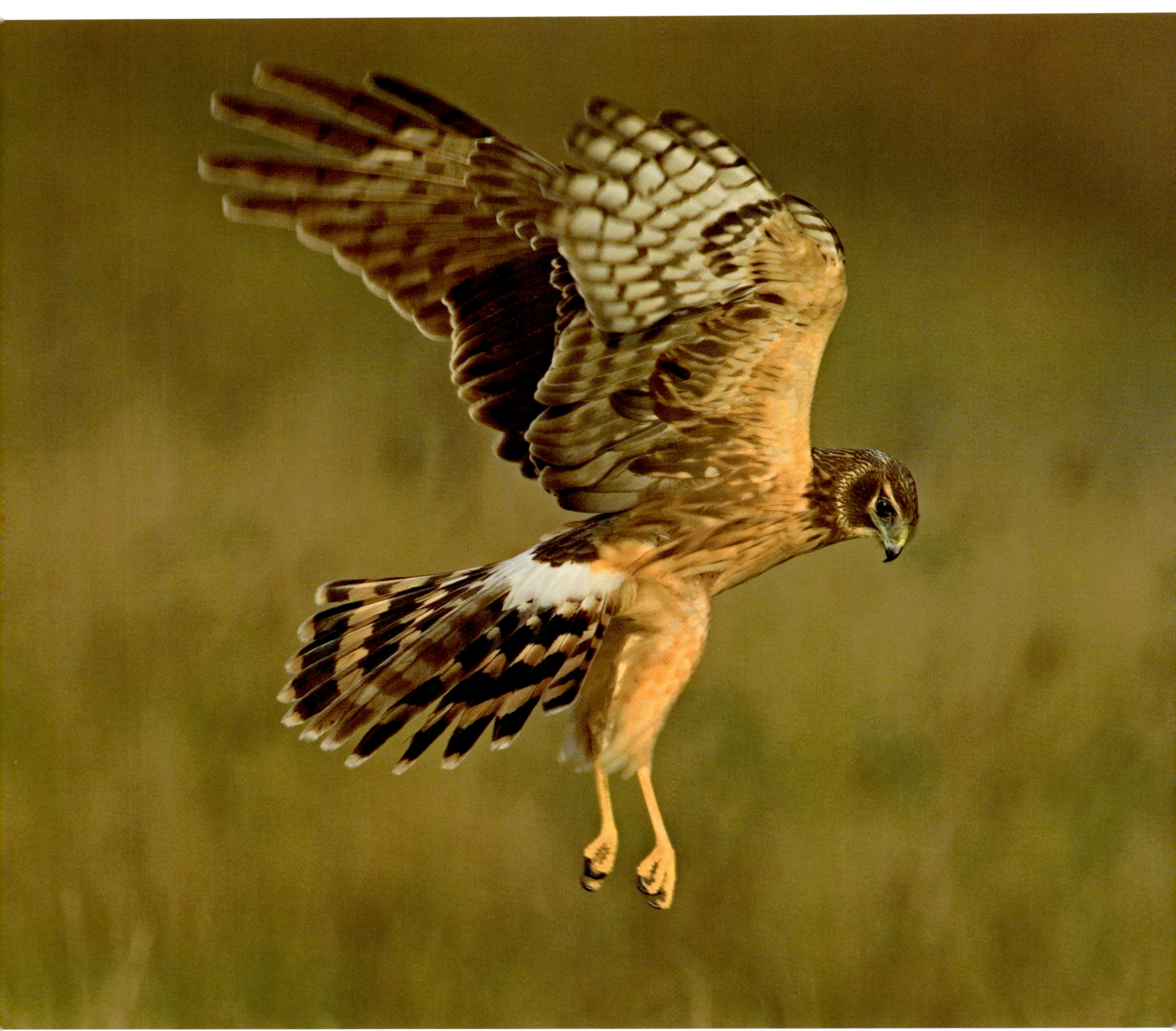

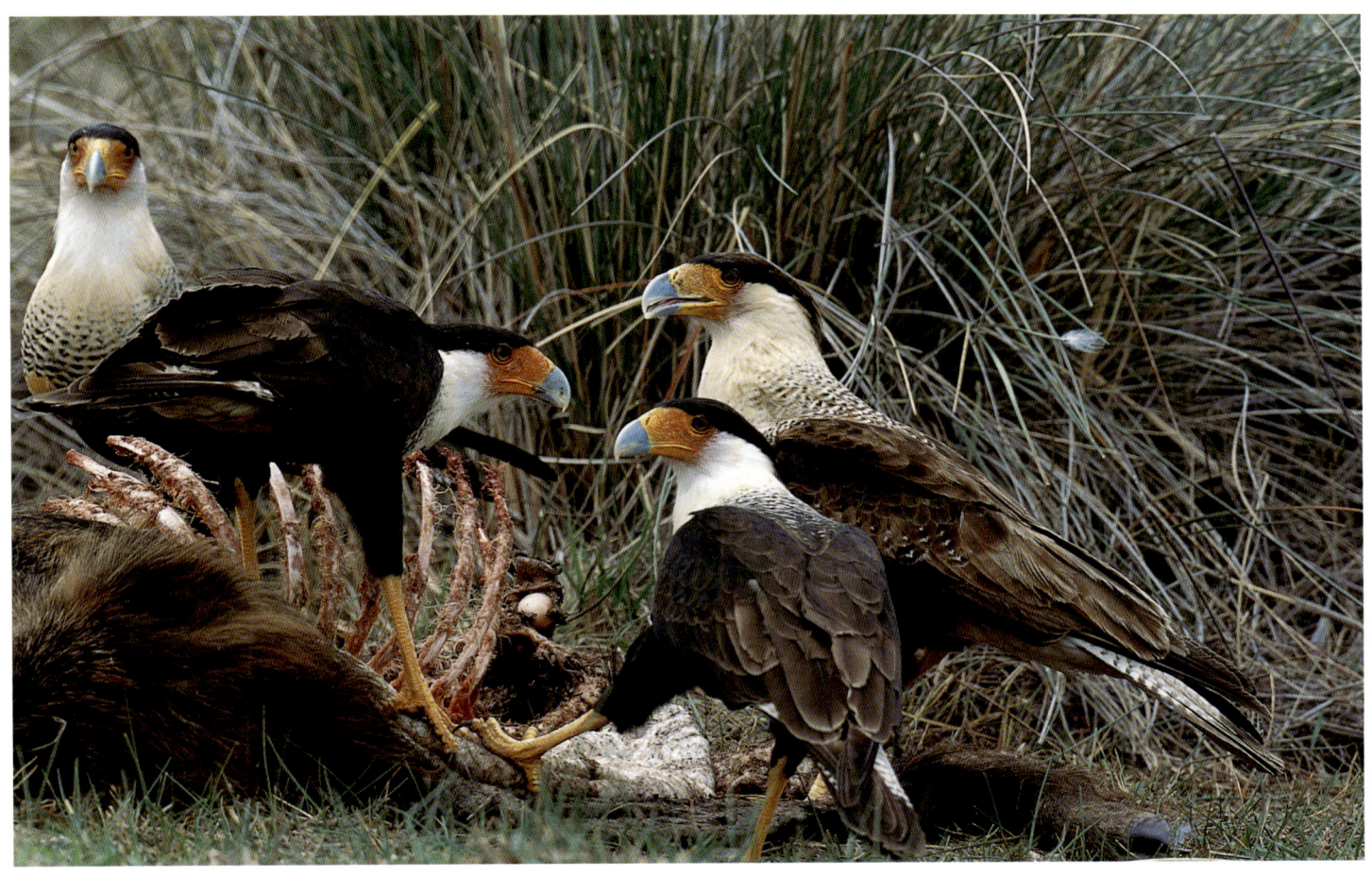

Within Texas, **Northern Harriers** *may occasionally nest in the northern Panhandle, but most of these birds nest farther north on the Great Plains and in Canada. They are fairly common in Texas all winter, however, and often may be seen coursing low over grasslands or marshes hunting for rodents. I was parked alongside a marsh on the Peach Point Wildlife Management Area on the upper Texas coast in Brazoria County, watching some ducks, when I saw a Northern Harrier approaching me, seemingly intent on hunting. As the bird made a pass within about a hundred feet of me, I was able to get a few quick shots.*

Crested Caracaras *are largely scavengers, and they do a wonderful job of cleaning up roadkill or other carcasses. This group of caracaras was busy feeding on the carcass of a feral hog in South Texas in Kenedy County. Immature caracaras, such as the bird on the right, are more brownish than the darker adults.*

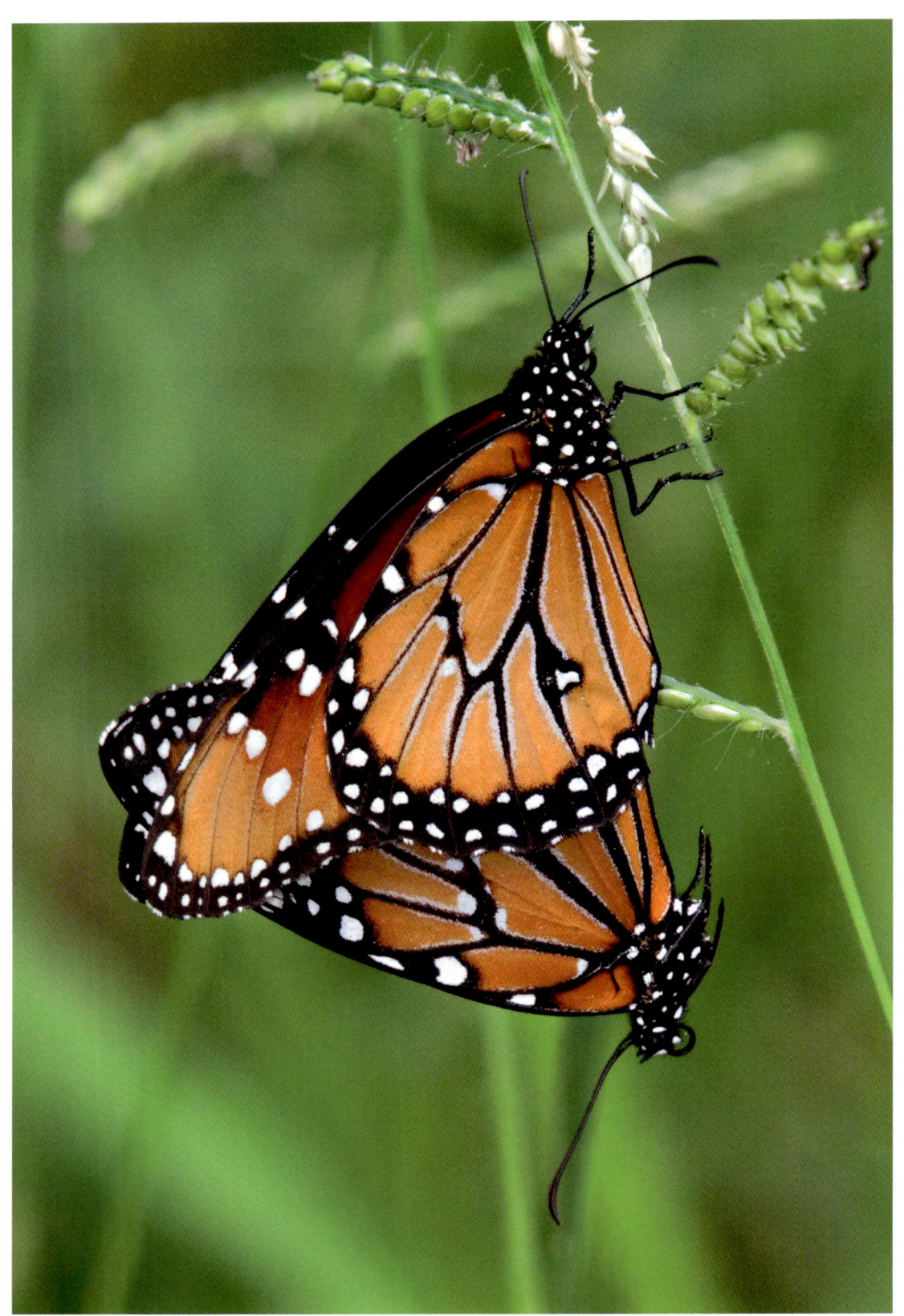

The miracle of life can be seen all around us if we but take the time to look. The **Queen** butterfly is widespread and commonly encountered across Texas. This mating pair used a weed stem to perch on in Kleberg County near Kingsville.

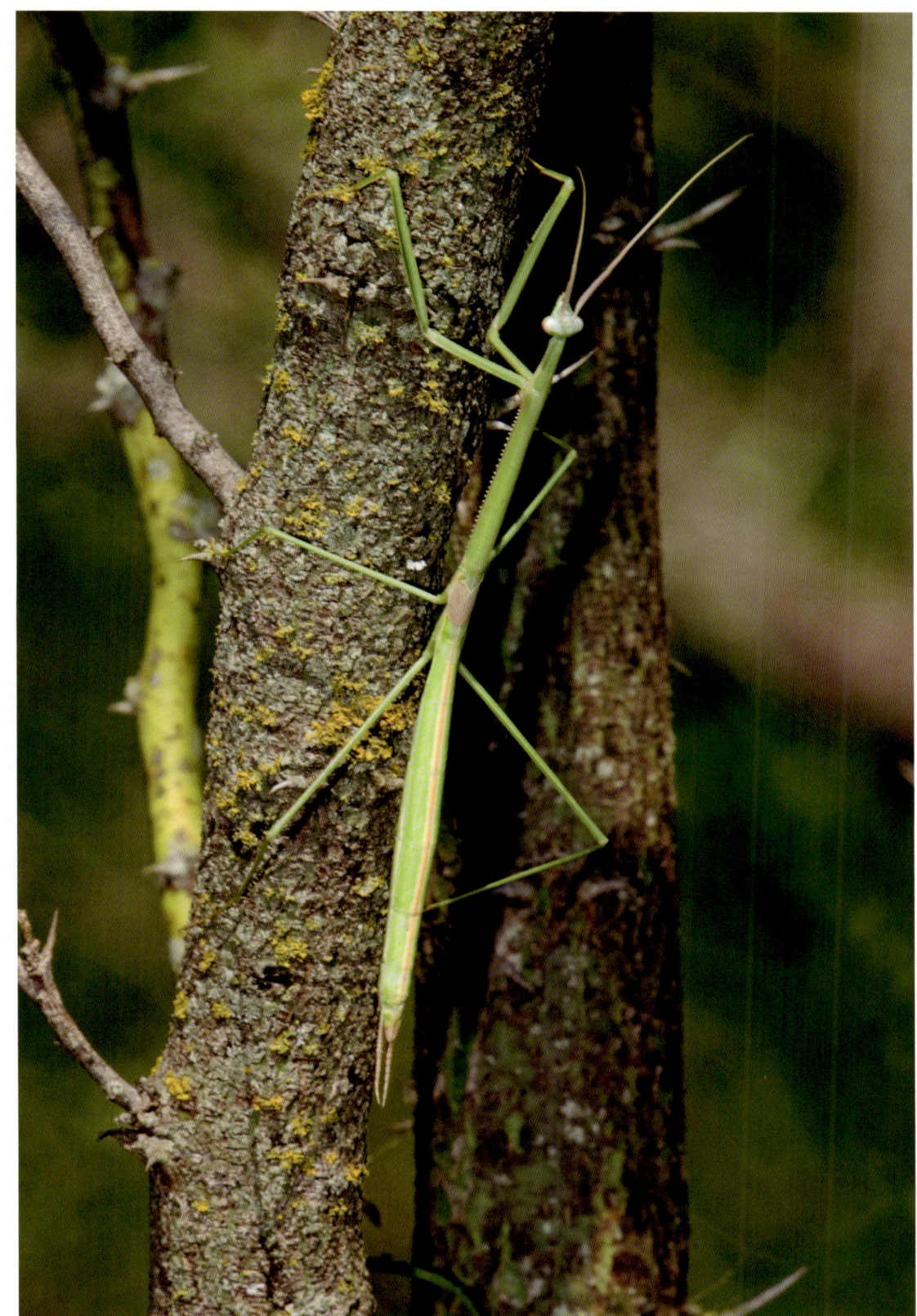

The **Brunner's Mantis** looks much like an insect called a Walking Stick, but it is a true mantid. It is sometimes called American Stick Mantis. This mantis can be extremely difficult to locate as it moves along green leaves and twigs, but when out in the open, such as this one, they are quite visible. Interestingly, males are unknown for this species, and reproduction is by means of parthenogenesis, which means that the female is able to produce eggs that can develop without fertilization. This Brunner's Mantis was in Travis County near Austin.

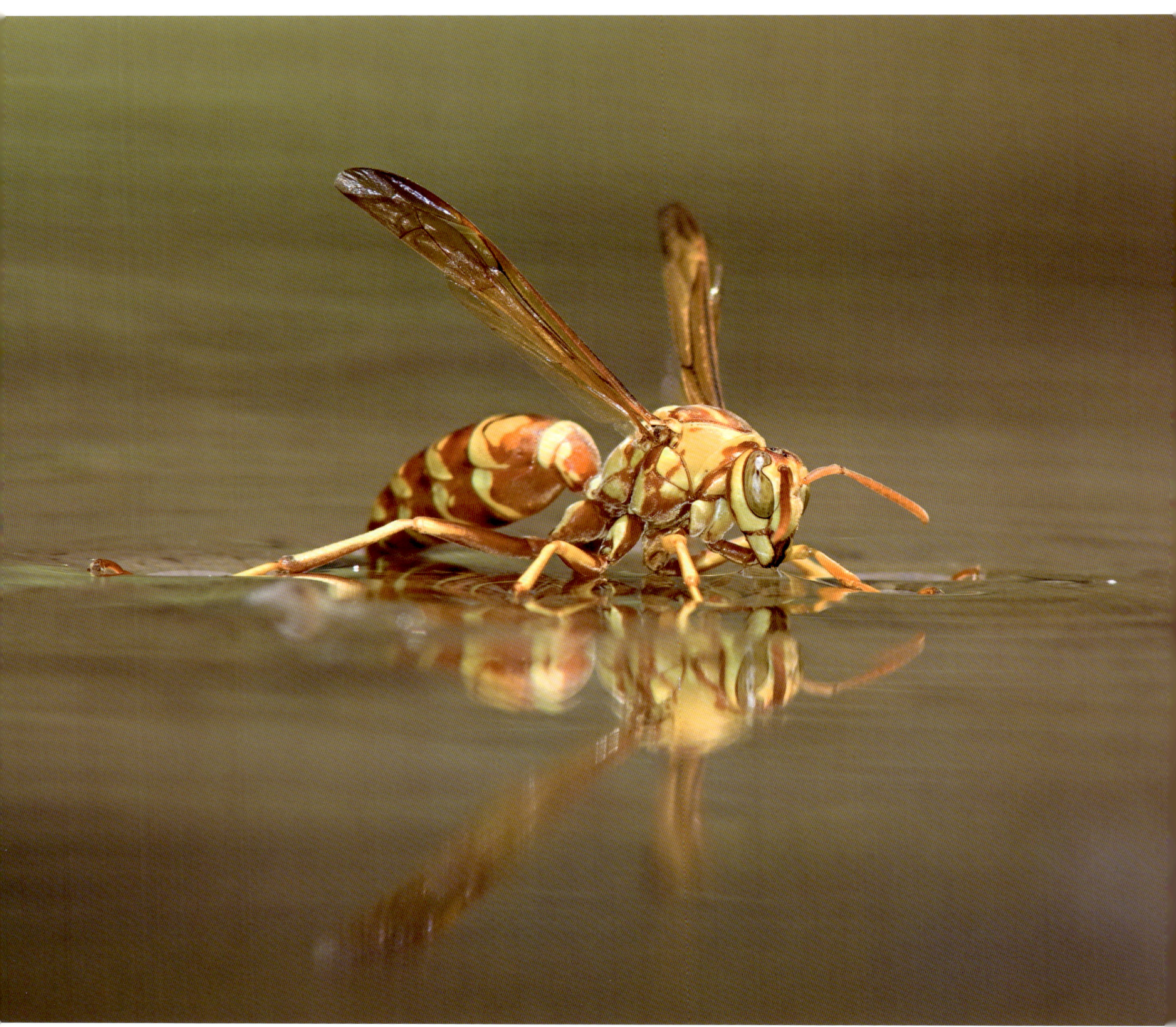

Opposite: On hot summer days, **Paper Wasps** *will often land on the surface of a pond or water hole to drink and collect water. Due to their light weight, water-repellant waxy coating, and the surface tension of the water, these wasps are able to float along with ease. The legs of a wasp depress the water's surface slightly, as can be seen in this shot. I was lying on the ground near this floating wasp, a species in the genus* Polistes, *to get this eye-level shot on a South Texas ranch in Hidlago County.*

Right: Dragonflies are aerial predators, but there are also many things that prey upon dragonflies, including birds and even other insects. The **Robber Fly** *in this image has no common name, but its scientific name is* Promachus hinei. *The robber had captured a dragonfly known as Eastern Pondhawk and flown to the top of a grass clump to eat its prey. This shot was taken on a tract of the Balcones Canyonlands National Wildlife Refuge in Burnet County.*

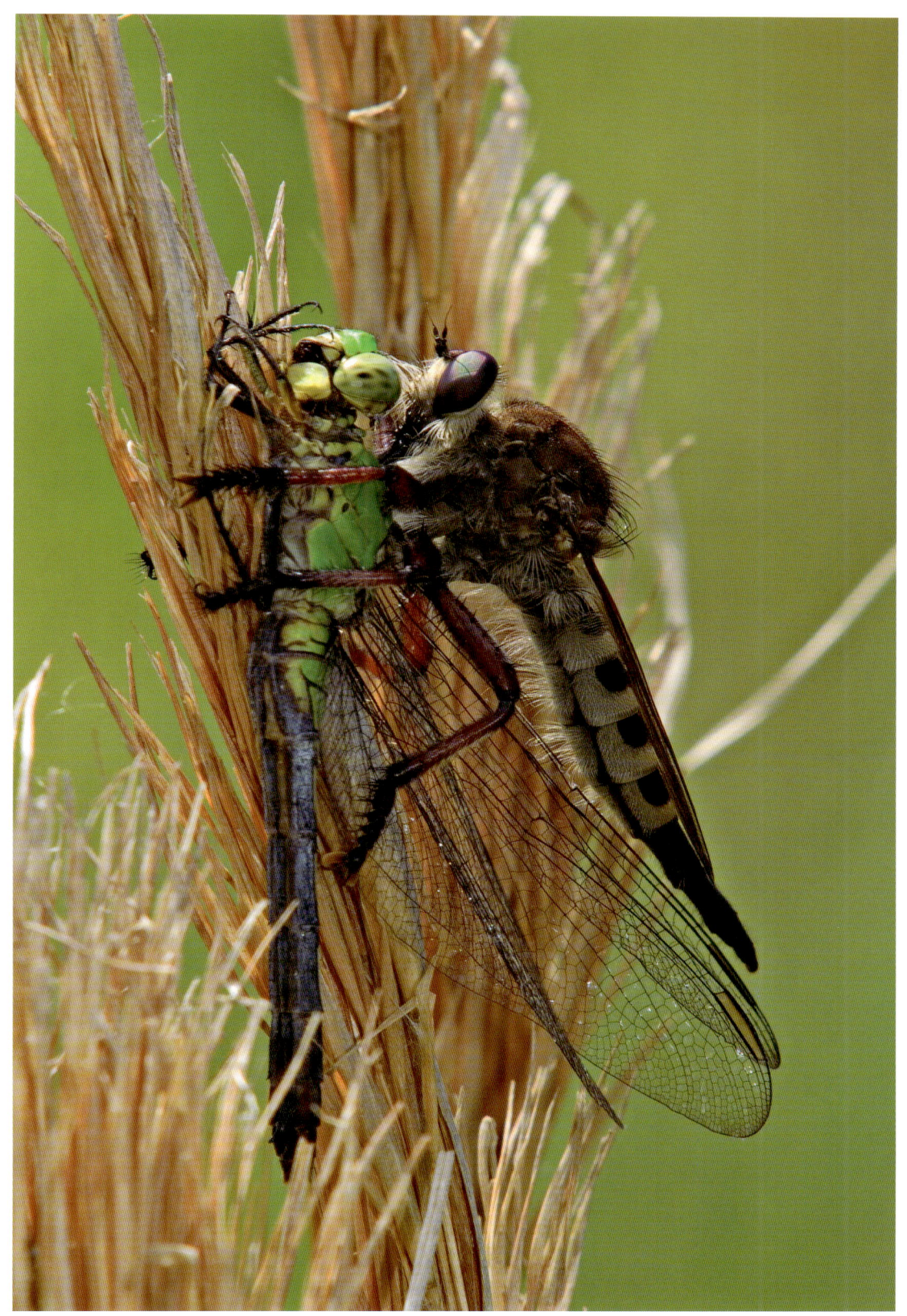

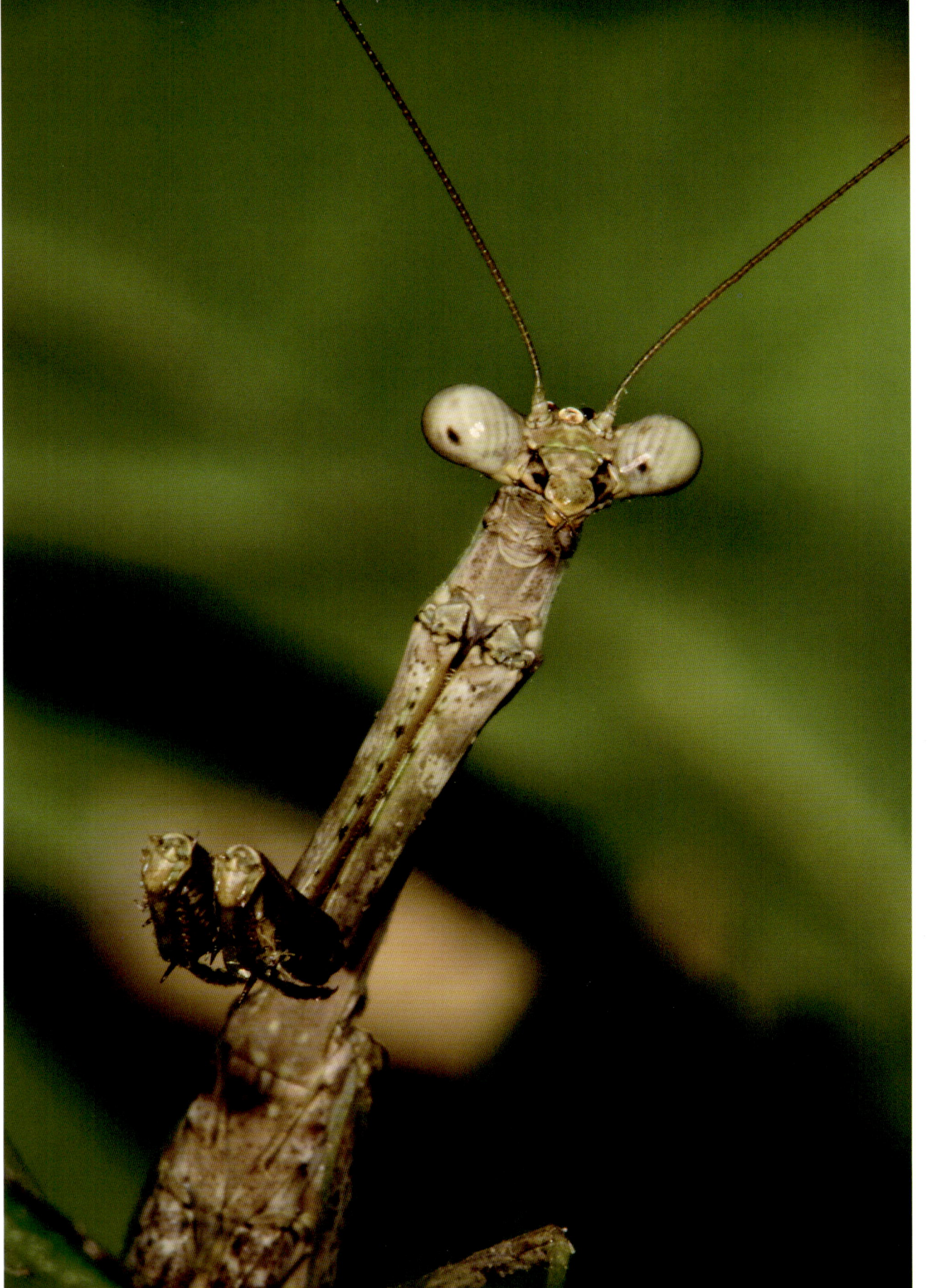

The most familiar member of the mantid family is the **Praying Mantis,** so called because of its "prayerlike" posture of holding its front legs out in front of its body. The common name is applied to a number of similar species, but all are carnivorous insects that feed primarily upon other insects. They have a triangular shaped head and large eyes. The Praying Mantis in this shot, probably the species Stagmomantis carolina, watched me as I moved around it trying out various camera angles. Looking through a macro lens at this creature made me happy that they are not six feet tall, or we would all be in trouble. This shot was taken in South Texas in Hidalgo County.

It is surprising to see the wide variety of insects that may collect around a light at night. While visiting a ranch in Hidalgo County near Edinburg, I occasionally left an outside light on when there was no wind. In the morning, I often found many different moths, beetles, and other insects gathered on the nearby vegetation. These two **Blister Beetles,** *of the genus Pyrota, were attracted in this way. There are many species of Blister Beetles, so called because their bodies contain a chemical called cantharidin, which may cause blisters on human skin. It is not a good idea to handle these insects, due to the possible chemical reaction, but they are very interesting to watch. Blister Beetles feed on a variety of plants.*

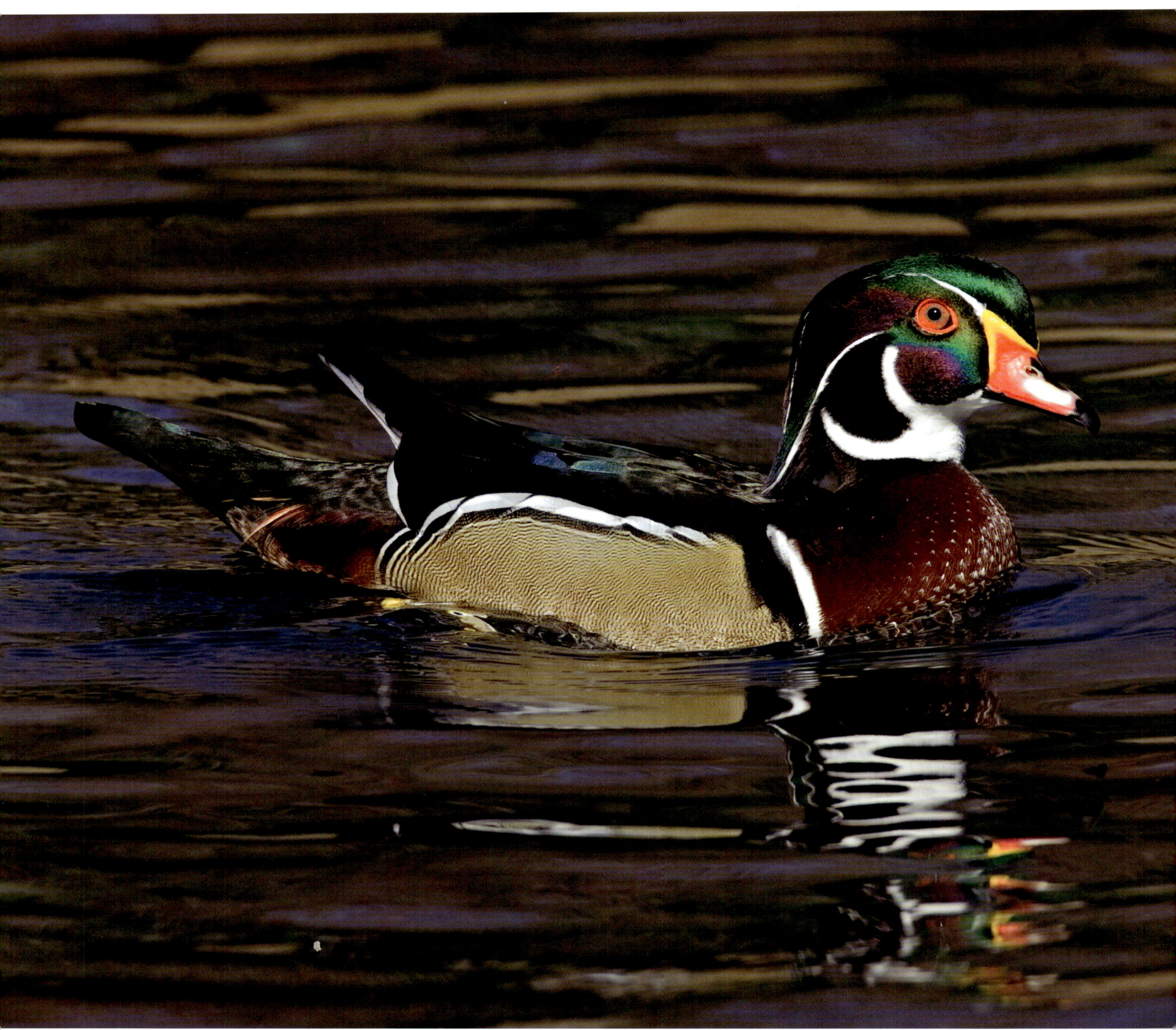

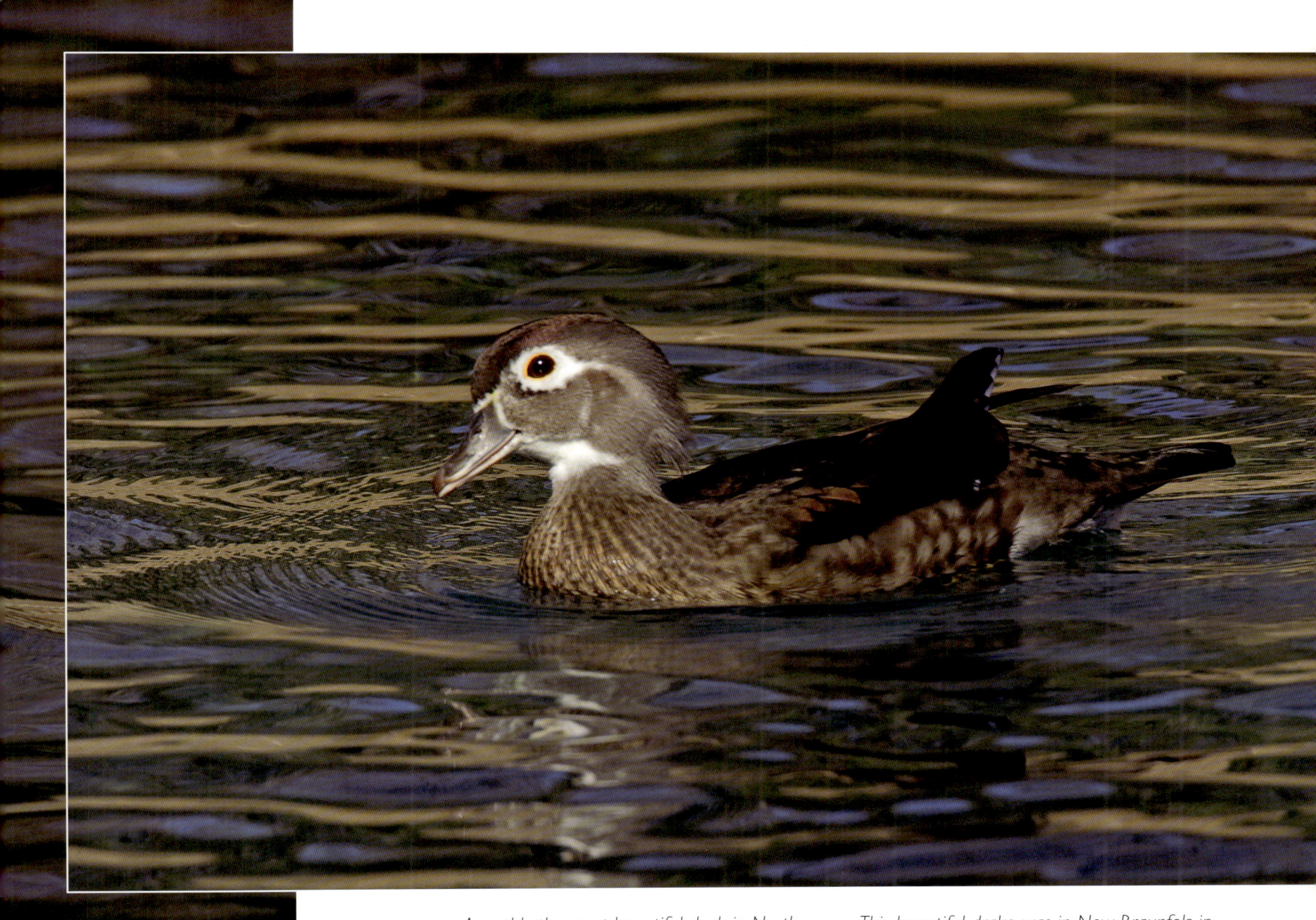

Arguably the most beautiful duck in North America is the drake **Wood Duck.** *The species is a cavity nester, which means it nests in hollow tree trunks or even in artificial duck boxes. It can be common in parts of the eastern half of Texas and is found locally in a few spots in the western parts of our state. It is often fairly tame when seen in city parks.*

This beautiful drake was in New Braunfels in Comal County in Central Texas.

The female Wood Duck (above) is more subtly plumaged than the male, but the bold white patch around the eye and the distinctive head shape are characteristic of the bird.

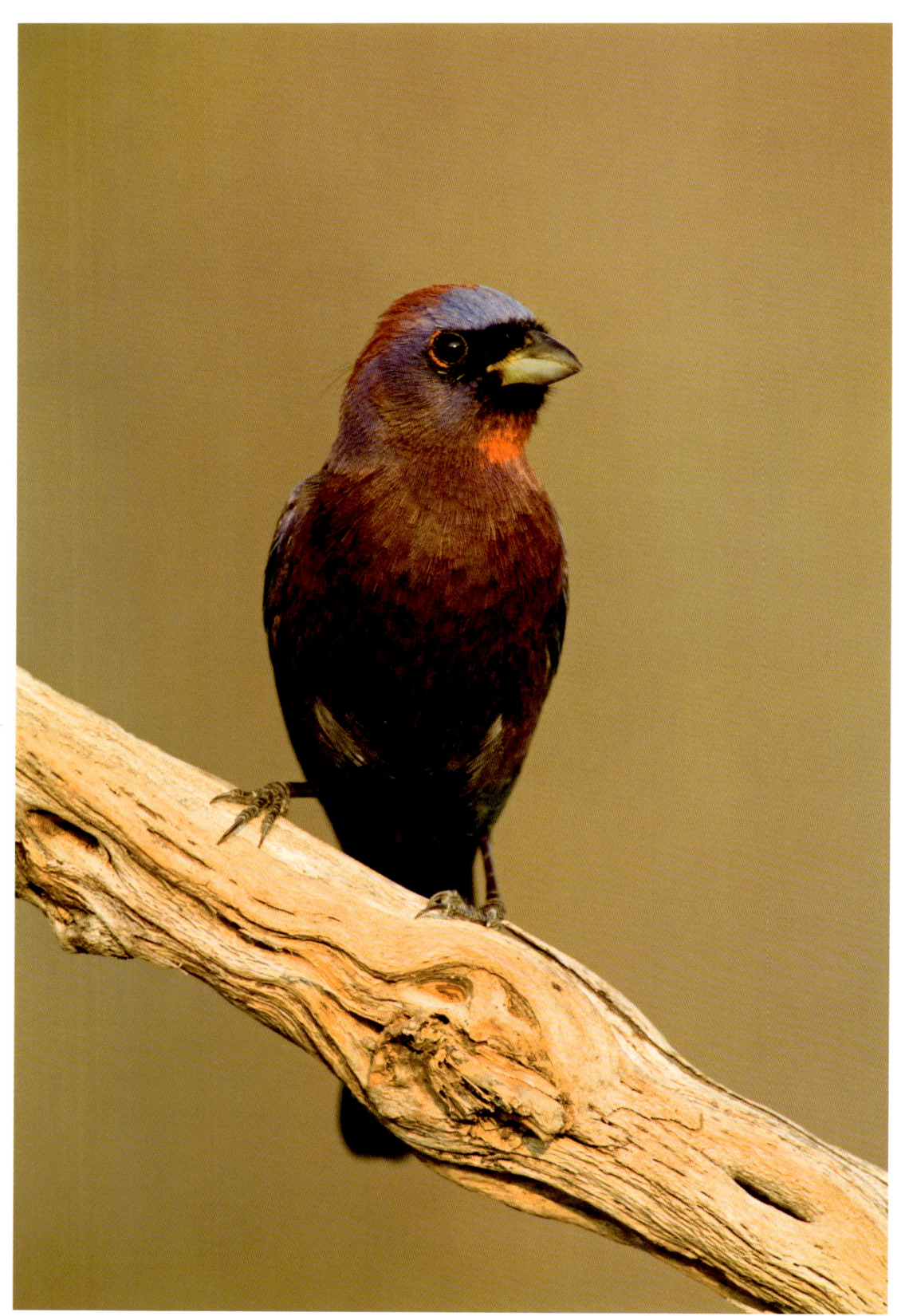

The **Varied Bunting** *is typically found in parts of southwestern Texas, often west of the Pecos River. Sometimes it appears in unexpected locations. This bright male spent much of an entire spring on a ranch in Hidalgo County in the Lower Rio Grande Valley. The blue, purple, and black plumage of this bird is quite distinctive, and it can rival the Painted Bunting in beauty if seen in good light. This bird was near a water hole, waiting to drink.*

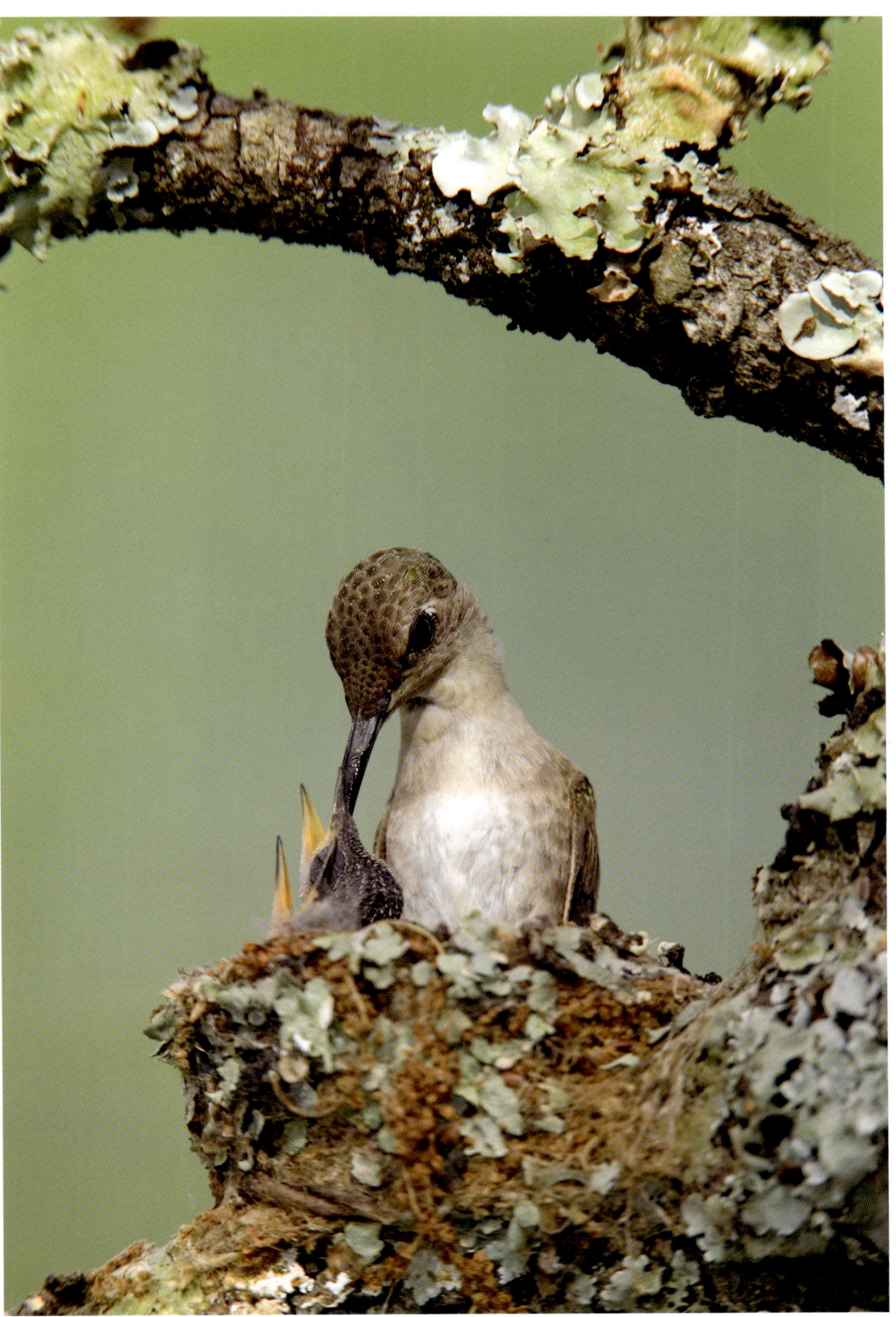

Black-chinned Hummingbirds *can be found across the western half of Texas during the warmer months. The female Black-chinned Hummingbird builds the nest and raises the young by herself. The nest is only about as large as the diameter of a half-dollar coin. This female was feeding two hungry youngsters in a delicate nest made of lichen and other plant material near Bee Cave in Travis County. It may seem as though she might puncture the throat or stomach of the babies with her bill, but I assure you, she knows what she is doing and the young do not suffer any injury.*

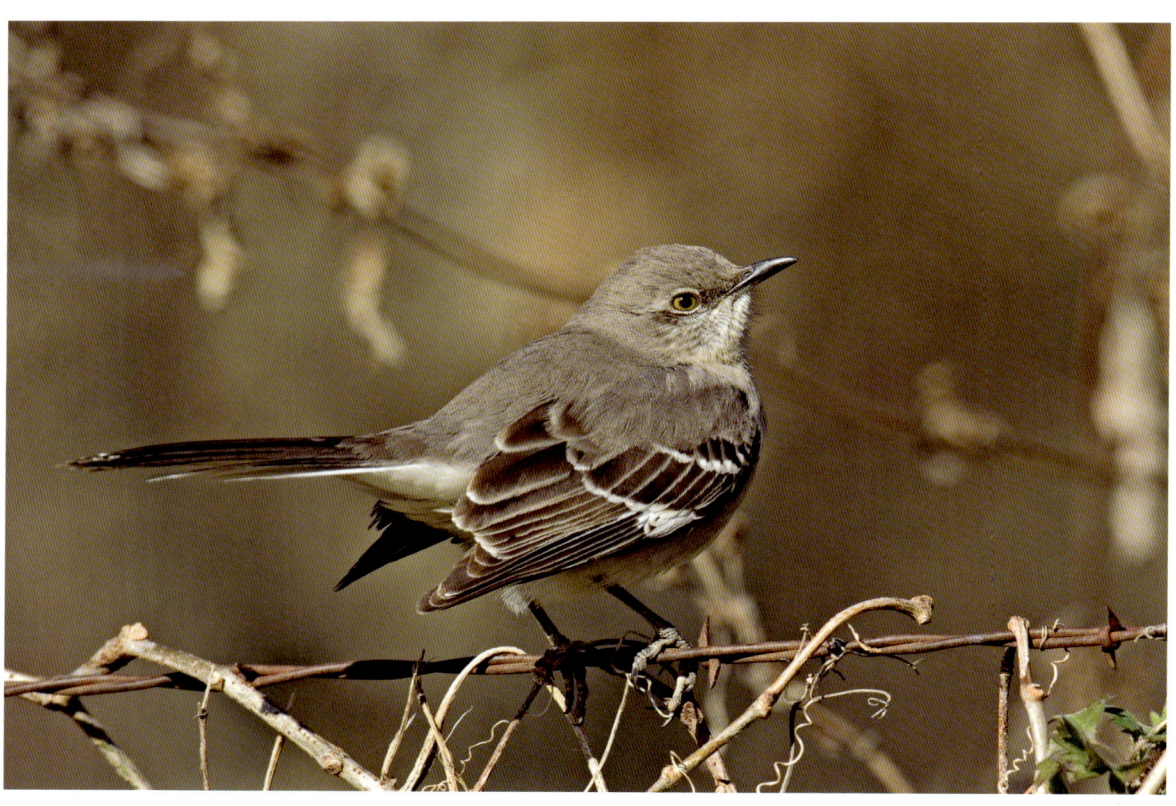

The **Northern Mockingbird** is the official state bird of Texas, so I thought a shot of one must be included in this particular collection of images. The species is common all over the state in many habitats. This is the way people often see a mockingbird, perched on a barbed wire fence. This particular mockingbird was in our state's capital city of Austin.

Opposite: **Aplomado Falcons** *were residents of South and West Texas until the early 1900s when a number of factors combined to make the species extremely rare within the United States. Beginning in the 1980s, the species was reintroduced into the state, and it may now be encountered in a number of areas. This juvenile bird was near one of the release sites on a West Texas ranch in Jeff Davis County. The bird had gone after a sparrow, which it missed, and was returning to an agave stalk to perch when I was able to get a few shots as it passed by me, wings and tail spread wide.*

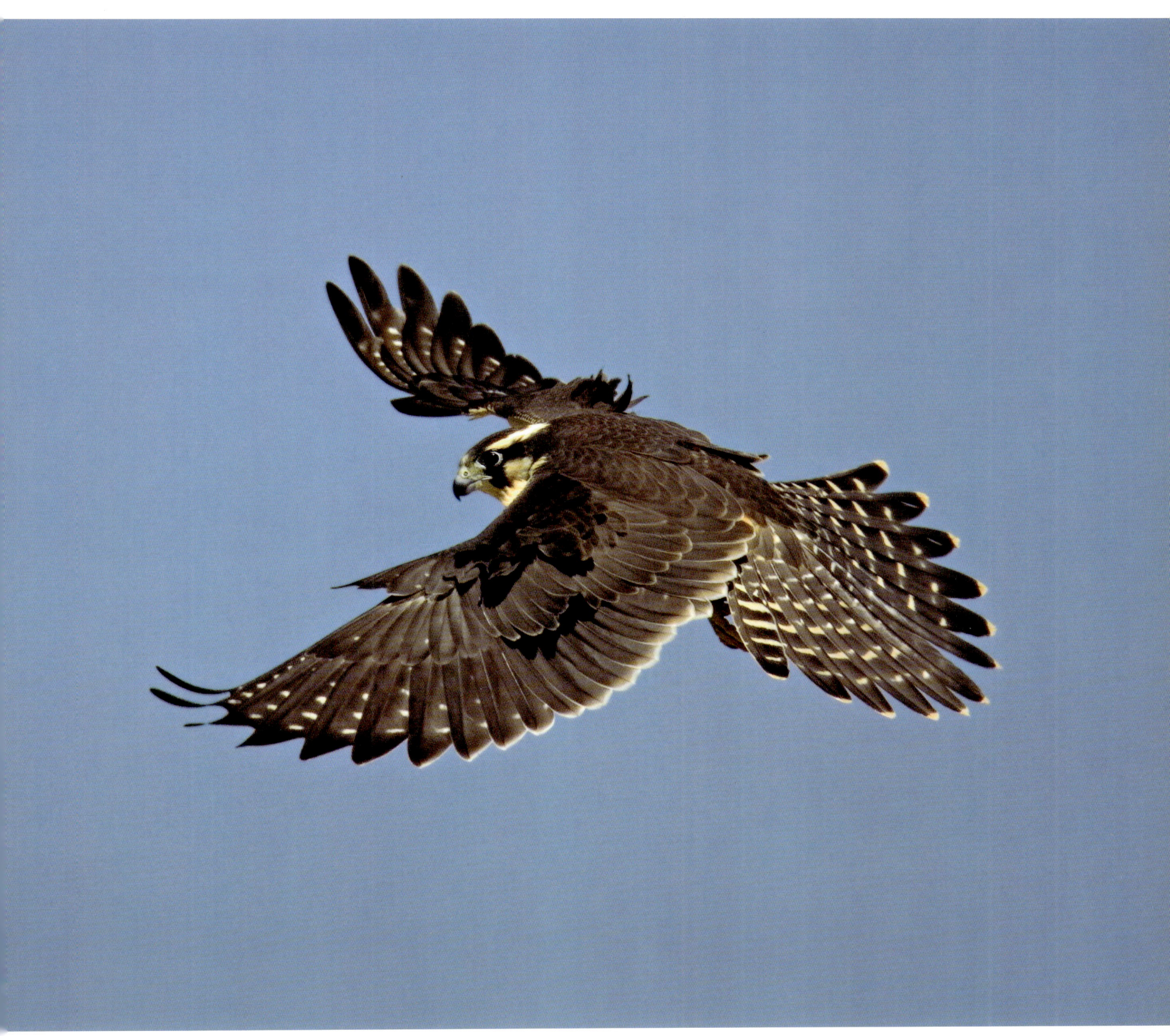

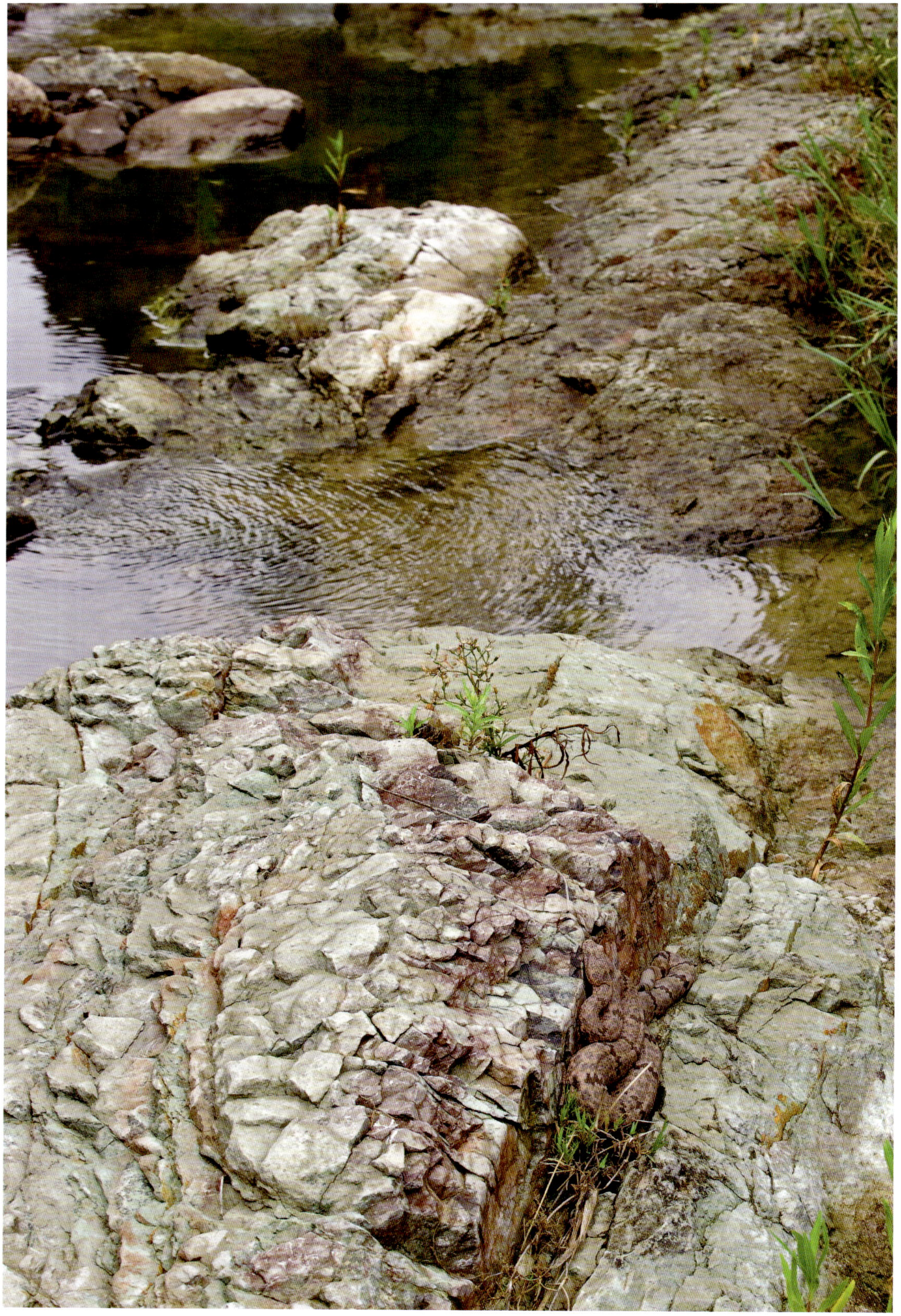

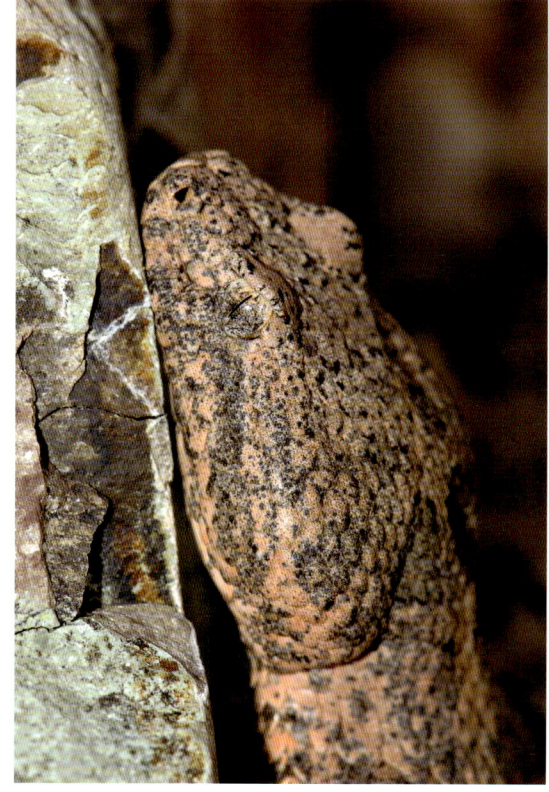

Left: I was hiking along a stream on a Presidio County ranch on a cool September morning, looking for dragonflies, when I came across the scene you see here. This beautiful **Rock Rattlesnake** was nestled in a rock crevice in such a way as to expose as much of its body as possible to the rays of the sun in an effort to warm up. Rock Rattlesnakes, despite the fact that they are venomous, are typically quite inoffensive. They may be found in portions of the Texas Hill Country as well as the Trans-Pecos region. It is amazing how the pinkish coloration of the snake blends in with the pinkish rocks, a fine example of protective coloration. After taking a number of shots of this snake, including many close-ups, I continued my trek up the canyon. Two hours later on my return past this spot, the snake was still in virtually the same place.

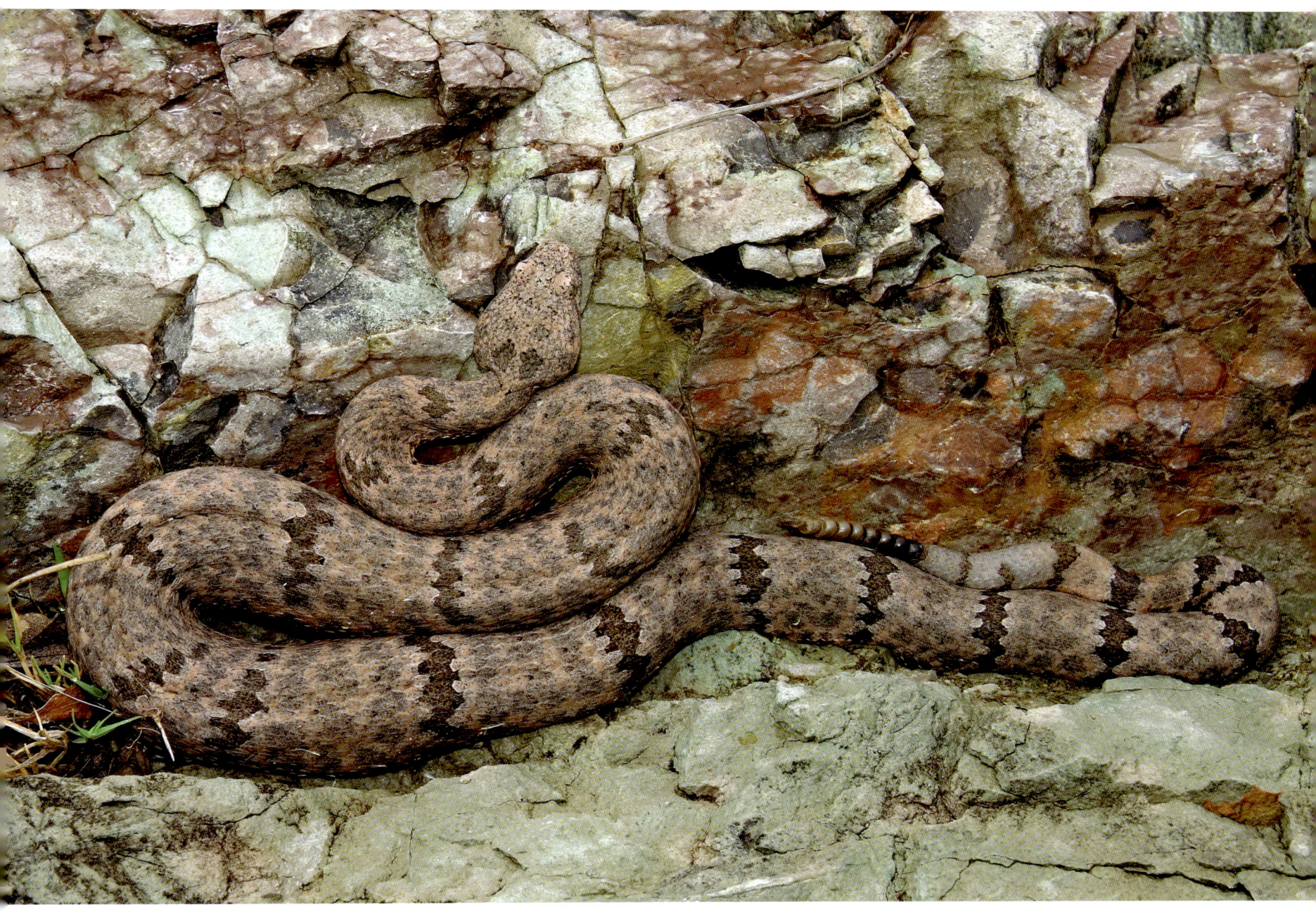

Opposite, right:
A close-up shot of the head of the Rock Rattlesnake shows its elliptical pupil and the mottled pattern of its pink and gray coloration.

Rock Rattlesnakes *can vary in overall coloration depending upon where they are found. I have seen individuals that are quite gray overall, while others, such as this one, have a distinct pinkish coloration. I love the way the snake blends into its background in this shot, and I marvel at how close some of the colors of the snake match the colors of the rocks.*

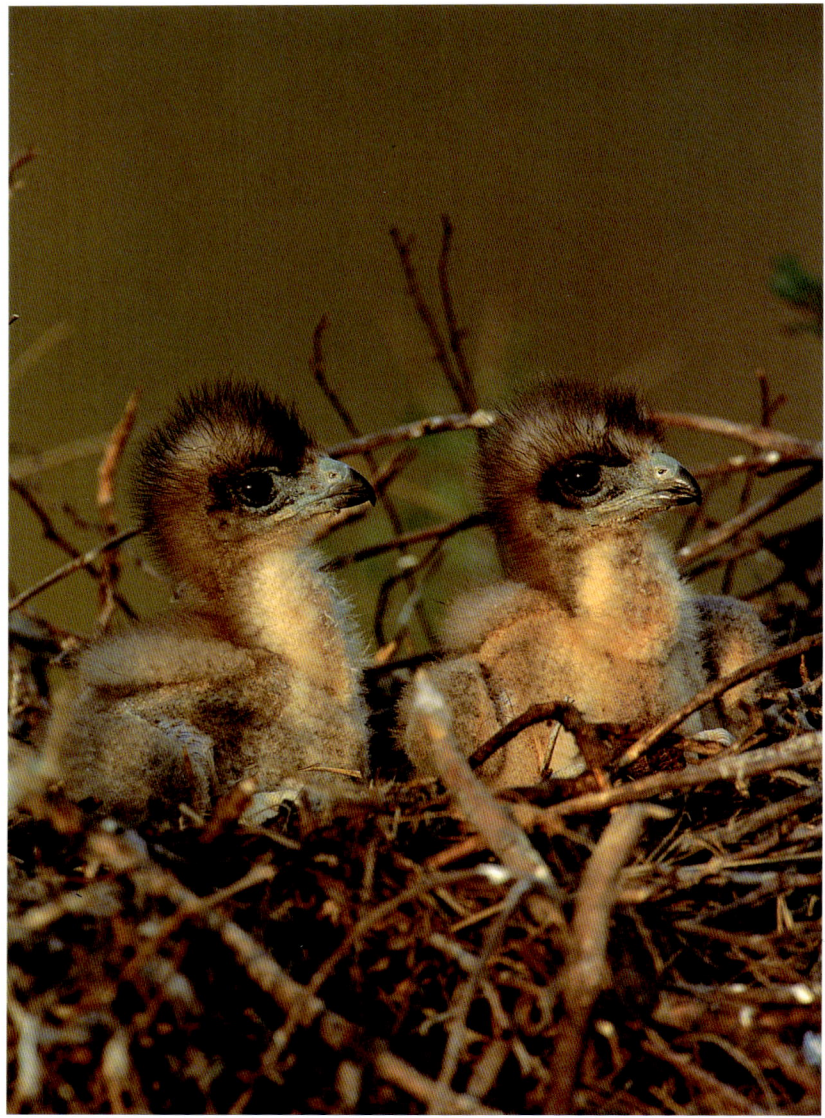

White-tailed Hawks *live in the grassland habitat of the coastal prairies of South Texas. They usually nest in the top of a thick shrub or small tree surrounded by mostly open space. In this way, a hawk on the nest can keep a clear watch in all directions for food as well as potential problems. I was able to spend some time in a blind set up near a White-tailed Hawk nest in Kenedy County in late spring several years ago. The two youngsters here were photographed from that blind as they waited for the adult to bring in a meal.*

Within the United States, the **White-tailed Hawk** *only occurs in South Texas. This distinctive hawk preys on rodents and other small mammals as well as insects and reptiles. The adult in this shot was soaring over grassland in Hidalgo County.*

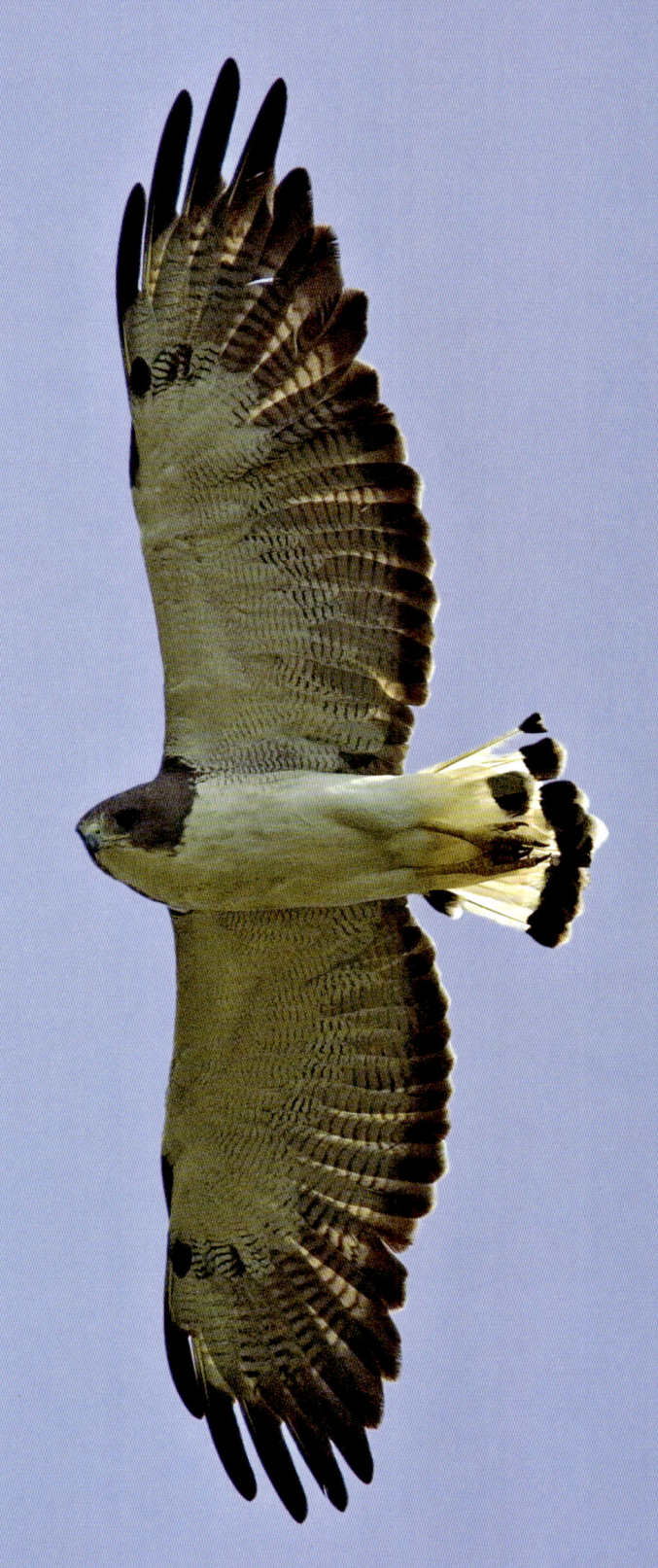

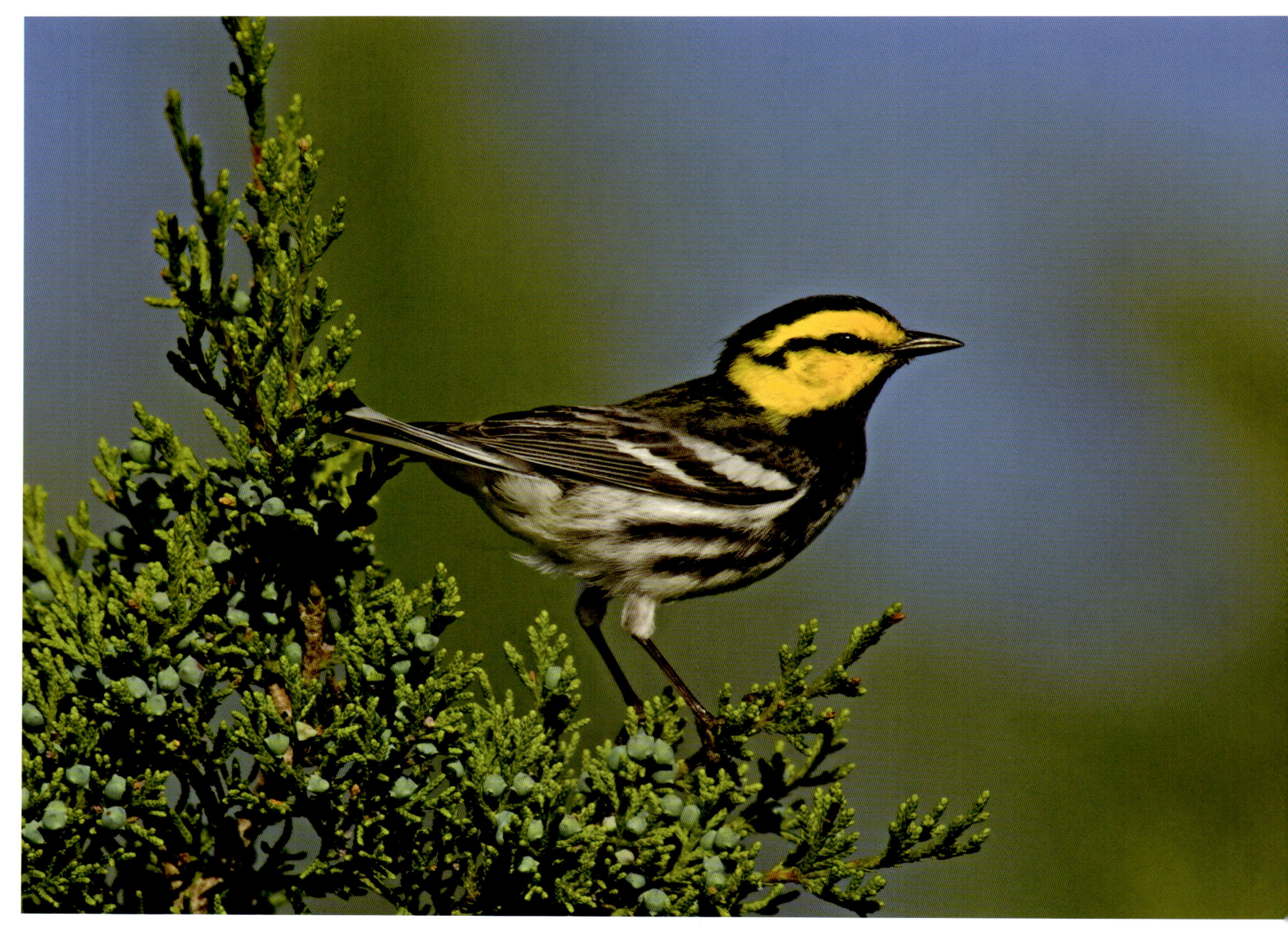

The **Golden-cheeked Warbler** is the only species of bird that nests exclusively in Texas. This endangered species may be found during spring and early summer in oak and juniper woodlands along the Edwards Plateau of Central Texas. Golden-cheeks are true Texas natives, and bird-watchers from all over the world come to Texas hoping to see this bird. The male bird in this photo is probably about two years old, judging from the olive coloration of part of the back. Mature birds have entirely black backs. This young male, perched in an Ashe juniper, was on his nesting territory in Travis County near Austin.

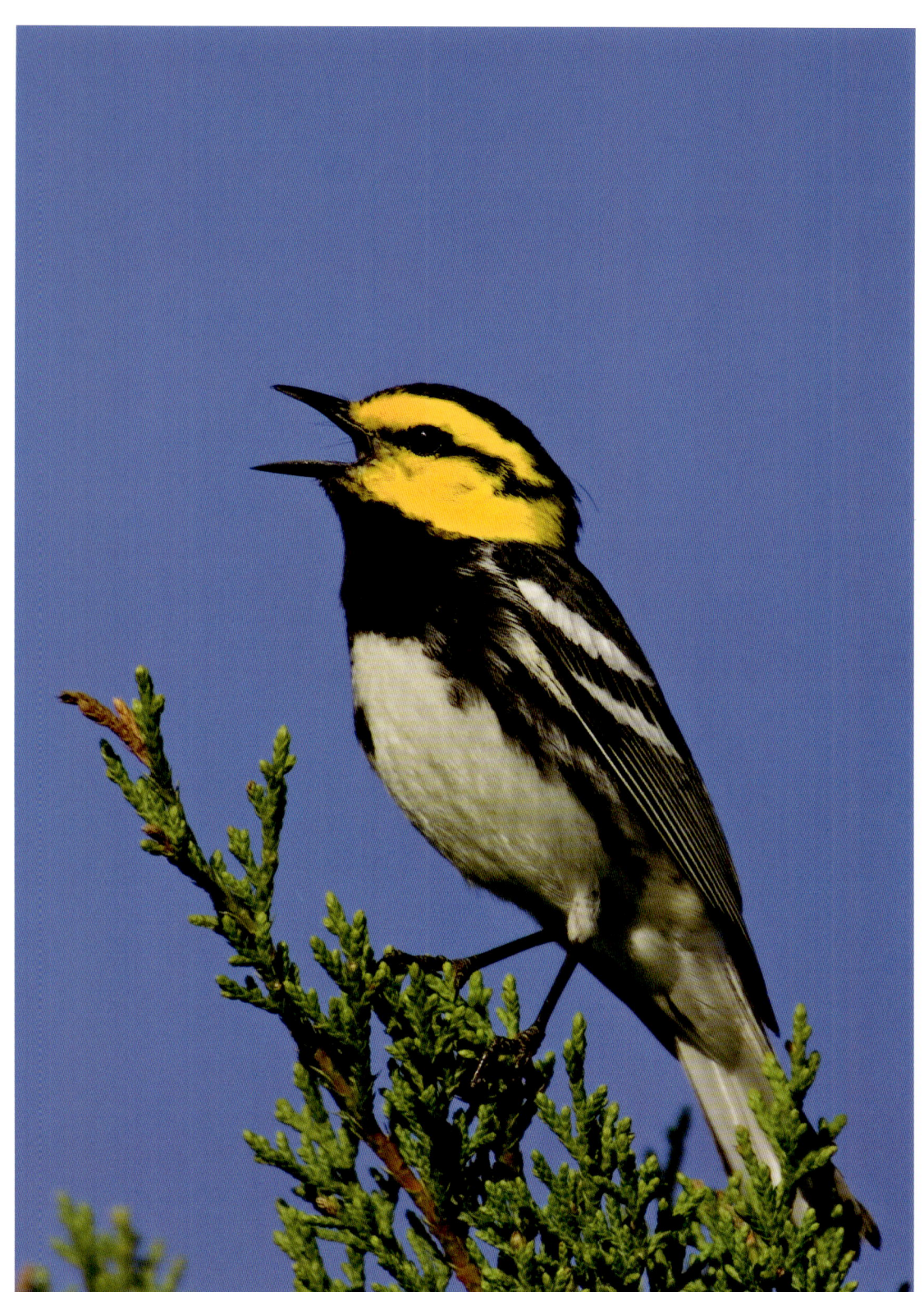

The male **Golden-cheeked Warbler** *in this photo was singing from the top of an Ashe juniper tree in Travis County near Austin.*

Following page: I was sitting in a blind near a small water hole on a Hidalgo County ranch, photographing small birds as they came in for a drink. Since I was after small birds, I was armed with a large telephoto lens mounted on my camera and tripod. When a **Wild Turkey** *came strutting up to the water hole, all I was able to get in the frame were shots of its plumage. The feathers on the bird's side as the sun reflected off of them created a beautiful pattern of bronze, black, and gold.*

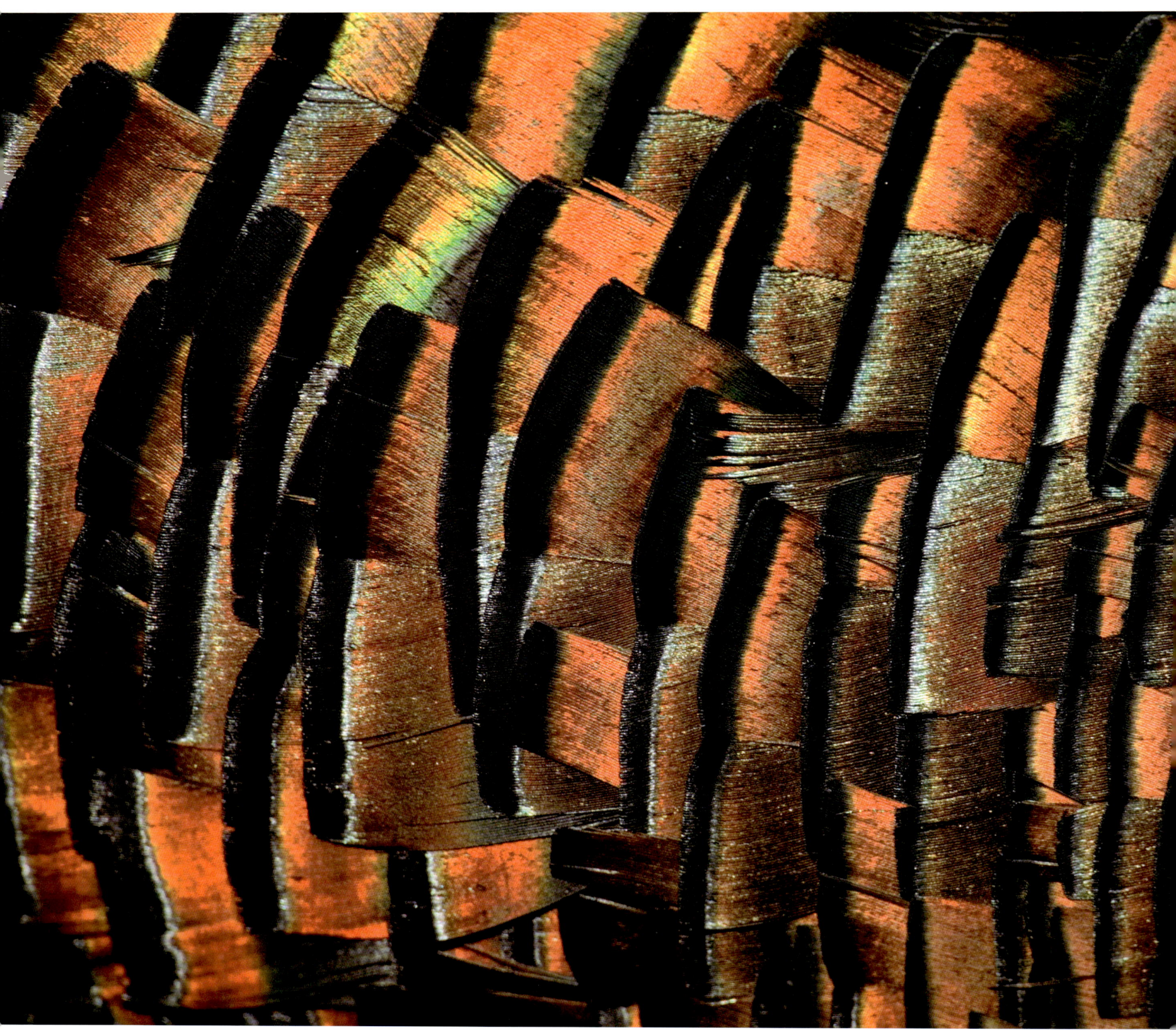

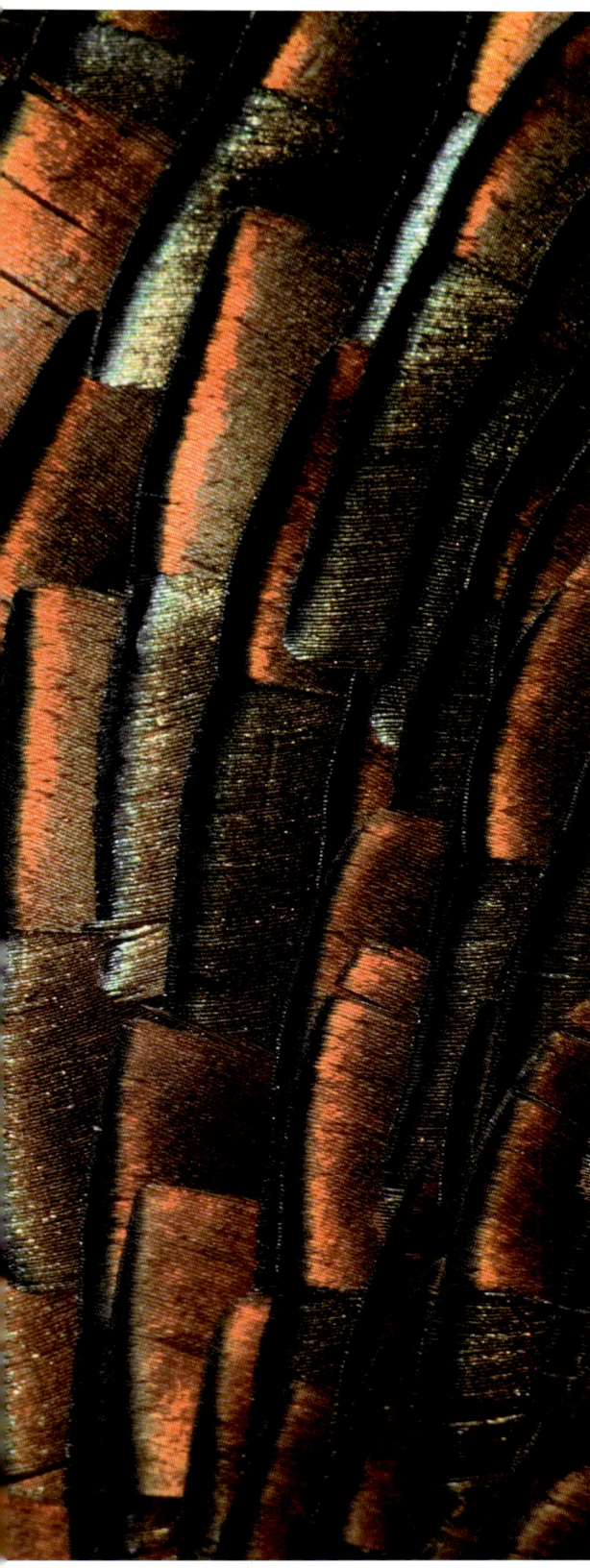

Acknowledgments

ANY BOOK, even a book of photographs, would not be possible without colleagues, friends, mentors, and others who have shared their time, knowledge, and experience over many years. This book is no exception. I have explored the wilds of Texas for more than thirty years, looking at and photographing nature and wildlife wherever I found it. I have been in all 254 counties of this state and have taken photos in many of them. I have waded in East Texas swamps looking for snakes, sweated in the heat of the Rio Grande Valley in August photographing dragonflies, frozen my feet trying to get shots of hawks in a Panhandle snow storm, and stood in the highest mountains of West Texas while a rare Red-faced Warbler paid me a visit. On the majority of my jaunts across Texas, I have benefited from the companionship and help of fellow photographers, biologists, birders and other naturalists. Thirty years of tramping across Texas brings back memories far too numerous to list here, but I certainly must acknowledge some of the photographers and other field companions, from Texas and elsewhere, who have taught me so much along the way. My sincere thanks and appreciation go to John Abbott, Mark Adams, Red and Marjorie Adams, Kevin Anderson, Keith Arnold, John Arvin, Giff Beaton, Bob Behrstock, Tony Bennett, Steve Bentsen, Nora and Rick Bowers, Kelly Bryan, Kathy and Gary Clark, Scarlet Colley, Arlie and Mel Cooksey, Don Connell, Dave and Jan Dauphin, Paul Deman, Larry Ditto, Kim Eckert, Carol Edwards, Mark Elwonger, Victor Emanuel, Ted Eubanks, Mike and Rose Farmer, Dave and Linda Ferry, Mark Flippo, Brush Freeman, Tony Gallucci, John Gee, Carl Haynie, Linda and David Hedges, Petra Hockey, John Ingram, Eric Isley, Cheryl Johnson, John Karges, Richard Kinney, Jane Kittleman, Ed Kutac, Paul and Georgean Kyle, Mark Lockwood, Brad McKinney, Laura Elaine Moore, Jim Morgan, Arthur Morris, John Muldrow, Mike Murphy, Nicholas Murphy, Derek Muschalek, June Osborne, Mike Overton, Paul Palmer, Jim Paton, Dwight Peake, Jim Peterson, Fr. Tom Pincelli, Rebecca Plunkett, Mike Quinn, Martin Reid, John and Barbara Ribble, Sid and Shirley Rucker, Peter Scott, Willie Sekula, Chuck Sexton, Ken Seyffert, Cliff Shackelford, Bob Thomas, John and Gloria Tveten, Tom Urban, Roland Wauer, Fred and Marie Webster, Dave Welling, Matt White, Bret Whitney, David and Mimi Wolf, Alan Wormington, and Barry Zimmer. The days, weeks, and, in some cases, months that I have spent in the field in Texas with these people over the years have all had a part in whatever success I have gained as a student of Texas wildlife and as a wildlife photographer.

Unlike some other western states, the majority of land in Texas is privately owned. Most Texas landowners are conscientious stewards of the land and take great pride in their property, and it shows. While many of the images in this book were taken in parks and other public places, many were taken on private ranches and preserves. I would like to thank the following kind folks who have allowed me to photograph on their land, whether or not any of those images appear in this particular book: Pat and Sharon Barber, Steve Bentsen, Monica and Ray Burdette, Don and Ann Connell, Paul and Bettye Rae Davis, Clay and Jody Miller, Mike and Julie Murphy, James McAllen and family, Lowry, Jessica, and Isaac McAllen, Robert and Margaret McAllen, Bud and Jimmy Payne, and Judy and Tom Taylor. It has always been a privilege for me to spend time with these gracious people on their property.

Lastly, I thank Shannon Davies, editor at Texas A&M University Press, for twenty years of patience as she waited for me to write the book she saw in my images. Largely because of her enduring enthusiasm and encouragement, this is in your hands.

Wildlife Photo Index

with technical data for each image

American Alligator *Alligator mississippiensis*
p. 37: Canon EOS 1D Mark II digital camera body and an EF 70–200mm f/2.8 L IS lens shot at 1/320 s at f/14.0 at 400 ISO
p. 62: Canon EOS 3 camera body and an EF 500mm f/4 L IS lens and Fuji Velvia film; unknown shutter speed and aperture

American Bittern *Botaurus lentiginosus*
p. 31: Canon EOS 3 camera body and an EF 500mm f/4 L IS lens and Fuji Velvia film; unknown shutter speed and aperture

American Oystercatcher *Haematopus palliates*
p. 15: Canon EOS 1D Mark II digital camera body and an EF 600mm f/4 L IS lens and 2X teleconverter shot at 1/800 s at f/9.0 at 400 ISO

American Snout *Libytheana carinenta*
p. 70: Canon EOS 1D Mark II digital camera body and an EF 300mm f/4 L IS lens and 2X teleconverter shot at 1/160 s at f/32.0 at 400 ISO with flash

American White Pelican *Pelecanus erythrorhynchos*
p. 6: Canon EOS 1D Mark II digital camera body and an EF 600mm f/4 L IS lens and 2X teleconverter shot at 1/1000 s at f/10.0 at 400 ISO

Aplomado Falcon *Falco femoralis*
p. 115: Canon EOS 1D Mark II digital camera body and an EF 600mm f/4 L IS lens and 1.4X teleconverter shot at 1/6400 s at f/5.6 at 400 ISO

Banded Pennant *Celithemis fasciata*
p. 42: Canon EOS 10D digital camera body and an EF 70–200mm f/2.8 L IS lens and 2X teleconverter shot at 1/160 s at f/18.0 at 400 ISO with flash

Barn Swallow *Hirundo rustica*
p. 16: Canon EOS 1D Mark II digital camera body and an EF 300mm f/4 L IS lens and 2X teleconverter shot at 1/250 s at f/8.0 at 400 ISO

Bewick's Wren *Thryomanes bewickii*
p. 94: Canon EOS 1D Mark II digital camera body and an EF 600mm f/4 L IS lens and 1.4X teleconverter shot at 1/1250 s at f/7.1 at 400 ISO

Black Saddlebags *Tramea lacerata*
p. 75: Canon EOS D60 digital camera body and an EF 180mm f/3.5 macro lens and 1.4X teleconverter shot at 1/100 s at f/20.0 at 400 ISO

Black-bellied Whistling-Duck *Dendrocygna autumna*
p. 65: Canon EOS 1D Mark II digital camera body and an EF 600mm f/4 L IS lens and 1.4X teleconverter shot at 1/200 s at f/14.0 at 400 ISO

Black-capped Vireo *Vireo atricapilla*
p. 56: Canon EOS 1D Mark II digital camera body and an EF 600mm f/4 L IS lens and 2X teleconverter shot at 1/125 s at f/8.0 at 400 ISO

Black-chinned Hummingbird *Archilochus alexandri*
p. 113: Canon EOS 1D Mark II digital camera body and an EF 600mm f/4 L IS lens and 1.4X teleconverter shot at 1/160 s at f/10.0 at 400 ISO

Black-tailed Gull *Larus crassirostris*
p. 9: Canon T90 camera body and an FD 600mm f/4 L lens shot on Fuji Sensia 100 film; unknown shutter speed and aperture

Black-tailed Jackrabbit *Lepus californicus*
p. 34: Canon EOS 1N camera body and an EF 600mm f/4 L lens and Fuji Velvia film; unknown shutter speed and aperture

Blackpoll Warbler *Dendroica striata*
p. 95: Canon EOS 1D Mark II digital camera body and an EF 500mm f/4 L IS lens and 2X teleconverter shot at 1/400 s at f/8.0 at 500 ISO

Blister Beetle *Pyrota* sp.
p. 109: Canon EOS 1D Mark II digital camera body and EF 180mm f/3.5 macro lens and 2X teleconverter shot at 1/80 s at f/32.0 at 400 ISO with flash

Blue Dasher *Pachydiplax longipennis*
p. 69: Canon EOS 1D Mark III digital camera body and an EF 300mm f/4 L IS lens and 2X teleconverter shot at 1/60 s at 500 ISO

Blue-faced Ringtail *Erpetogomphus eutainia*
p. 44: Canon EOS 10D digital camera body and an EF 70–200mm f/2.8 L IS lens and 2X teleconverter shot at 1/200 s at f/18.0 at 400 ISO with flash

Botteri's Sparrow *Aimophila botterii*
p. 12: Canon EOS 1N camera body and an EF 600mm f/4 L lens and 2X teleconverter and Fuji Velvia film; unknown shutter speed and aperture

Bronzed Cowbird *Molothrus aeneus*
p. 55: Canon EOS 1D Mark II digital camera body and an EF 500mm f/4 L IS lens and 1.4X teleconverter shot at 1/320 s at f/6.3 at 400 ISO

Brown Pelican *Pelecanus occidentalis*
p. 60: Canon EOS 1N camera body and an EF 600mm f/4 L lens and Fuji Velvia film; unknown shutter speed and aperture

Brown-crested Flycatcher *Myiarchus tyrannulus*
p. 87: Canon EOS 1D Mark II digital camera body and an EF 600mm f/4 L IS lens and 2X teleconverter shot at 1/1000 s at f/9.0 at 400 ISO

Brunner's Mantis *Brunneria borealis*
p. 105: Canon EOS 10D digital camera body and EF 70–200mm f/2.8 L IS lens and 2X teleconverter shot at 1/160 s at f/20.0 at 400 ISO

Buff-bellied Hummingbird *Amazilia yucatanensis*
p. 59: Canon EOS 3 camera body and an EF 300mm f/2.8 L lens and 2X teleconverter and Fuji Velvia film; unknown shutter speed and aperture

Burrowing Owl *Athene cunicularia*
p. 50, top left: Canon EOS 1D Mark III digital camera body and an EF 600mm f/4 L IS lens and 1.4X teleconverter shot at 1/640 s at f/10.0 at 400 ISO
p. 50, top right: Canon EOS 1D Mark III digital camera body and an EF 600mm f/4 L IS lens and 1.4X teleconverter shot at 1/1000 s at f/7.1 at 400 ISO
p. 50, bottom: Canon EOS 1D Mark III digital camera body and an EF 600mm f/4 L IS lens shot at 1/400 s at f/9.0 at 400 ISO
p. 51: Canon EOS 1D Mark III digital camera body and an EF 600mm f/4 L IS lens and 2X teleconverter shot at 1/320 s at f/14.0 at 400 ISO

Cactus Bee *Diadasia* sp.
p. 74, top: Canon EOS 1D Mark II digital camera body and an EF 180mm f/3.5 macro lens and 2X teleconverter shot at 1/200 s at f/32.0 at 400 ISO with flash

Cattle Egret *Bubulcus ibis*
p. 53: Canon EOS 1D Mark II digital camera body and an EF 300mm f/4 L IS lens and 2X teleconverter shot at 1/125 s at f/10.0 at 400 ISO

Common Yellowthroat *Geothlypis trichas*
p. 86: Canon EOS 10D digital camera body and an EF 600mm f/4 L IS lens and 1.4X teleconverter shot at 1/640 s at f/8.0 at 400 ISO

Coyote *Canis latrans*
p. 35: Canon EOS 1V camera body and an EF 600mm f/4 L lens and Fuji Velvia film; unknown shutter speed and aperture

Crested Caracara *Caracara cheriway*
pp. 24–25: Canon EOS 3 camera body and an EF 500mm f/4 L lens and Fuji Velvia film; unknown shutter speed and aperture
p. 26: Canon EOS 1D Mark II digital camera body and an EF 600mm f/4 L IS lens and 2X teleconverter shot at 1/500 s at f/11.0 at 400 ISO
p. 103: Canon EOS 3 camera body and an EF 600mm f/4 L lens and Fuji Velvia film; unknown shutter speed and aperture

Eastern Ringtail *Erpetogomphus designatus*
p. 45: Canon EOS 10D digital camera body and an EF 70–200mm f/2.8 L IS lens and 2X teleconverter shot at 1/200 s at f/14.0 at 400 ISO with flash

Eastern Screech-Owl *Otus asio*
p. 21: Canon EOS 1D Mark II digital camera body and an EF 600mm f/4 L IS lens and 2X teleconverter shot at 1/160 s at f/8.0 at 400 ISO

Ebony Jewelwing *Calopteryx maculata*
p. 43: Canon EOS 10D digital camera body and an EF 70–200mm f/2.8 L IS lens and 2X teleconverter shot at 1/160 s at f/18.0 at 400 ISO with flash

Ferruginous Pygmy-Owl *Glaucidium brasilianum*
p. 57: Canon EOS 1N camera body and an EF 300mm f/2.8 L lens and 2X teleconverter and Fuji Velvia film with flash; unknown shutter speed and aperture

Fishing Spider *Dolomedes* sp.
p. 67: Canon EOS 1D Mark II digital camera body and an EF 300mm f/4 L IS lens and 2X teleconverter shot at 1/200 s at f/16.0 at 400 ISO with flash

Flame Skimmer *Libellula saturata*
p. 68, top: Canon EOS 10D digital camera body and an EF 70–200mm f/2.8 L IS lens and 2X teleconverter shot at 1/200 s at f/18.0 at 400 ISO with flash

Forster's Tern *Sterna forsteri*
p. 64: Canon EOS 1D Mark II digital camera body and an EF 600mm f/4 L IS lens and 1.4X teleconverter shot at 1/3200 s at f/5.6 at 400 ISO

Golden-cheeked Warbler *Dendroica chrysoparia*
p. 11: Minolta X570 camera body and Vivitar 400mm lens shot on Kodachrome 200 film; unknown shutter speed and aperture
p. 120: Canon EOS 1D Mark II digital camera body and an EF 600mm f/4 L IS lens and 2X teleconverter shot at 1/1250 s at f/8.0 at 400 ISO
p. 121: Canon EOS 1D Mark II digital camera body and an EF 600mm f/4 L IS lens and 2X teleconverter shot at 1/2000 s at f/8.0 at 400 ISO

Great Kiskadee *Pitangus sulphuratus*
p. 91: Canon EOS 1D Mark II digital camera body and an EF 500mm f/4 L IS lens and 2X teleconverter shot at 1/500 s at f/16.0 at 400 ISO

Gulf Fritillary *Agraulis vanillae*
p. 71, top: Canon EOS 1Ds Mark II digital camera body and an EF 300mm f/4 L IS lens and 2X teleconverter shot at 1/200 s at f/14.0 at 400 ISO with flash

Halloween Pennant *Celithemis eponina*
p. 40: Canon EOS 10D digital camera body and an EF 70–200mm f/2.8 L IS lens and 2X teleconverter shot at 1/400 s at f/13.0 at 400 ISO with flash

Harris's Hawk *Parabuteo unicinctus*
p. 38: Canon EOS 1D Mark II digital camera body and an EF 500mm f/4 L IS lens shot at 1/5000 s at f/5.0 at 400 ISO

Hill Country
endpapers: Canon EOS 1V camera body and an EF 70–200mm f/2.8 L IS lens and Fuji Velvia film; unknown shutter speed and aperture

Hispid Cotton Rat *Sigmodon hispidus*
p. 4: Canon EOS 1D Mark II digital camera body and an EF 600mm f/4 L IS lens and 1.4X teleconverter shot at 1/125 s at f/6.3 at 400 ISO

Horse Lubber Grasshopper *Taeniopoda eques*
p. 78: Canon EOS 1D Mark II digital camera body and an EF 180mm f/3.5 macro lens and 2X teleconverter shot at 1/160 s at f/20.0 at 400 ISO with flash

House Finch *Carpodacus mexicanus*
p. 89: Canon EOS 1D Mark II digital camera body and an EF 600mm f/4 L IS lens and 2X teleconverter shot at 1/800 s at f/9.0 at 400 ISO

Inca Dove *Columbina inca*
p. 88: Canon EOS 1D Mark II digital camera body and an EF 500mm f/4 L IS lens and 1.4X teleconverter shot at 1/100 s at f/14.0 at 400 ISO

Laughing Gull *Larus atricilla*
pp. 2–3: Canon EOS 1N camera body and an EF 17–35mm f/2.8 L lens and Fuji Velvia film; unknown shutter speed and aperture

Least Bittern *Ixobrychus exilis*
p. 52: Canon EOS 3 camera body and an EF 300mm f/2.8 L lens and 2X teleconverter on Fuji Velvia film; unknown shutter speed and aperture

Least Grebe *Tachybaptus dominicus*
p. 82: Canon EOS 1D Mark II digital camera body and an EF 60mm f/4 L IS lens and 2X teleconverter shot at 1/125 s at f/8.0 at 400 ISO
p. 83: Canon EOS 3 camera body and an EF 300mm f/2.8 L lens and 2X teleconverter on Fuji Velvia film; unknown shutter speed and aperture

Lesser Prairie-Chicken *Tympanuchus pallidicinctus*
p. 80: Canon EOS 1D Mark II digital camera body and an EF 600mm f/4 L IS and 2X teleconverter shot at 1/640 s at f/8.0 at 400 ISO

p. 81, left: Canon EOS 1D Mark II digital camera body and an EF 500mm f/4 L IS lens shot at 1/3200 s at f/5.0 at 400 ISO

p. 81, right: Canon EOS 1D Mark II digital camera body and EF 500mm f/4 L IS lens shot at 1/250 s at f/4.0 at 400 ISO

Long-jawed Spider *Tetragnatha* sp.
p. 66: Canon EOS 1D Mark II digital camera body and an EF 300mm f/4 L IS lens and 2X teleconverter shot at 1/200 s at f/14.0 at 400 ISO with flash

Longhorn Beetle *Plinthocelium* sp.
p. 49: Canon EOS 1D Mark II digital camera body and an EF 180mm f/3.5 macro lens shot at 1/160 s at f/22.0 at 400 ISO with flash

Luna Moth *Actias luna*
p. 77, bottom: Canon EOS 10D digital camera body and an EF 70–200mm f/2.8 L IS lens shot at 1/160 s at f/18.0 at 400 ISO with flash

Masked Duck *Nomonyx dominica*
p. 9: Canon T90 camera body and Sigma 500mm f/4.5 lens and 1.4X teleconverter shot on Fuji Sensia 100 film; unknown shutter speed and aperture

Masked Tityra *Tityra semifasciata*
p. 9: Minolta X570 camera body and Vivitar 400mm lens shot on Kodachrome 200 film; unknown shutter speed and aperture

Mayan Setwing *Dythemis maya*
p. 5: Canon EOS 1D Mark II digital camera body and an EF 300mm f/4 L IS lens and 2X teleconverter shot at 1/200 s at f/14.0 at 400 ISO with flash

Mexican Ground Squirrel *Spermophilus mexicanus*
p. 99: Canon EOS 1D Mark II digital camera body and an EF 600mm f/4 L IS lens and 2X teleconverter shot at 1/250 s at f/9.0 at 400 ISO

Nine-banded Armadillo *Dasypus novemcinctus*
p. 23: Canon EOS 1D Mark II digital camera body and an EF 600mm f/4 L IS lens and 2X teleconverter shot at 1/640 s at f/11.0 at 400 ISO

Northern Cardinal *Cardinalis cardinalis*
p. 58: Canon EOS 1D Mark II digital camera body and an EF 500mm f/4 L IS lens and 2X teleconverter shot at 1/320 s at f/10.0 at 400 ISO

Northern Cat-eyed Snake *Leptodeira septentrionalis*
p. 47: Canon EOS 1D Mark II digital camera body and an EF 180mm f/3.5 macro lens shot at 1/80 s at f/22.0 at 400 ISO with flash

Northern Harrier *Circus cyaneus*
p. 102: Canon EOS 1D Mark II digital camera body and an EF 500mm f/4 L IS lens and 2X teleconverter shot at 1/800 s at f/8.0 at 400 ISO

Northern Mockingbird *Mimus polyglottos*
p. 114: Canon EOS 1D Mark II digital camera body and an EF 600mm f/4 L IS lens shot at 1/1000 s at f/8.0 at 400 ISO

Painted Bunting *Passerina ciris*
p. 18: Canon EOS 1D Mark II digital camera body and an EF 600mm f/4 L IS lens and 2X teleconverter shot at 1/500 s at f/9.0 at 400 ISO

p. 19: Canon EOS 1D Mark II digital camera body and EF 600mm f/4 L IS lens and 2X teleconverter shot at 1/1000 s at f/11.0 at 400 ISO

p. 19, right: Canon EOS 1D Mark II digital camera body and EF 600mm f/4 L IS lens and 2X teleconverter shot at 1/640 s at f/11.0 at 400 ISO

Painted Damsel *Hesperagrion heteroduxum*
p. 73: Canon EOS 1D Mark II digital camera body and an EF 180mm f/3.5 macro lens and 1.4X teleconverter shot at 1/160 s at f/18.0 at 400 ISO with flash

Pallid Bat *Antrozous pallidus*
p. 34: Canon EOS 1D Mark II digital camera body and an EF 300mm f/4 L IS lens and 2X teleconverter shot at 1/160 s at f/16.0 at 400 ISO with flash

Paper Wasp *Polistes* sp.
p. 106: Canon EOS 1D Mark II digital camera body and an EF 300mm f/4 L IS lens and 2X teleconverter shot at 1/250 s at f/16.0 at 400 ISO with flash

Plains Clubtail *Gomphus externus*
p. 72: Canon EOS 10D digital camera body and an EF 70–200mm f/2.8 L IS lens and 2X teleconverter shot at 1/160 s at f/18.0 at 400 ISO with flash

Prairie Warbler *Dendroica discolor*
p. 93: Canon EOS 10D digital camera body and an EF 600mm f/4 L IS lens and 1.4X teleconverter shot at 1/800 s at f/5.6 at 400 ISO

Praying Mantis *Stagmomantis* sp.
p. 108: Canon EOS 1D Mark II digital camera body and EF 180mm f/3.5 macro lens and 2X teleconverter shot at 1/80 s at f/32.0 at 400 ISO with flash

Prothonotary Warbler *Protonotaria citrea*
p. 54: Canon EOS 10D digital camera body and an EF 600mm f/4 L IS lens and 1.4X teleconverter shot at 1/125 s at f/10.0 at 400 ISO with flash

Pyrrhuloxia *Cardinalis sinuatus*
p. 90: Canon EOS 1D Mark II digital camera body and an EF 600mm f/4 L IS lens and 1.4X teleconverter shot at 1/200 s at f/8.0 at 400 ISO

Queen *Danaus gilippus*
p. 104: Canon EOS 10D digital camera body and an EF 70–200mm f/2.8 L IS lens and 2X teleconverter shot at 1/200 s at f/16.0 at 400 ISO with flash

Red-eared Slider *Pseudemys scripta*
p. 30: Canon EOS 3 camera body and an EF 180mm f/3.5 macro lens shot at 1/90 s at f/22.0 on Fuji Velvia film pushed one stop

Red-tailed Pennant *Brachymesia furcata*
p. 40: Canon EOS 1D Mark II digital camera body and an EF 180mm f/3.5 macro lens shot at 1/100 s at f/29.0 at 400 ISO with flash

p. 41: Canon EOS 1D Mark II digital camera body and an EF 180mm f/3.5 macro lens shot at 1/100 s at f/29.0 at 400 ISO with flash

Redhead *Aythya americana*
p. 65: Canon EOS 1D Mark II digital camera body and an EF 500mm f/4 L IS lens and 2X teleconverter shot at 1/1600 s at f/8.0 at 400 ISO

Robber Fly (no common name) *Eccritosia zamon*
p. 74, bottom: Canon EOS 1D Mark II digital camera body and an EF 300mm f/4 L IS lens and 2X teleconverter shot at 1/160 s at f/18.0 at 400 ISO with flash

Robber Fly (no common name) *Promachus hinei*
p. 107: Canon EOS 10D digital camera body and an EF 70-200mm f/2.8 L IS lens and 2X teleconverter shot at 1/160 s at f/18.0 at 400 ISO with flash

Rock Rattlesnake *Crotalus lepidus*
p. 116, left: Canon EOS 1D Mark II digital camera body and EF 70-200mm f/2.8 L IS lens shot at 1/200 s at f/14.0 at 400 ISO

p. 116, right: Canon EOS 1D Mark II digital camera body and EF 180mm f/3.5 macro lens and 2X teleconverter shot at 1/200 s at f/16.0 at 400 ISO with flash

p. 117: Canon EOS 1D Mark II digital camera body and EF 70–200mm f/2.8 L IS lens shot at 1/200 s at f/14.0 at 400 ISO with flash

Roseate Skimmer *Orthemis ferruginea*
p. 68, bottom: Canon EOS 1D Mark II digital camera body and an EF 300mm f/4 L IS lens and 2X teleconverter shot at 1/200 s at f/16.0 at 400 ISO with flash

Roseate Spoonbill *Ajaia ajaja*
p. 61: Canon EOS 10D digital camera body and an EF 600mm f/4 L IS lens and 1.4X teleconverter shot at 1/800 s at f/8.0 at 200 ISO

Sanderling *Calidris alba*
p. 13: Canon EOS 1N camera body and an EF 600mm f/4 L lens and a 1.4X teleconverter and Fuji Provia film; unknown shutter speed and aperture

Scorpion *Centruroides vittatus*
p. 100: Canon EOS 3 camera body and an EF 180mm f/3.5 macro lens on Fuji Velvia film pushed one stop; unknown shutter speed and aperture

Spider Web (unknown genus and species)
p. 32–33: Canon EOS 3 camera body and an EF 180mm f/3.5 macro lens on Fuji Velvia film pushed one stop; unknown shutter speed and aperture

Springwater Dancer *Argia plana*
p.17: Canon EOS 1D Mark II digital camera body and an EF 300mm f/4 L IS lens and 2X teleconverter shot at 1/200 s at f/20.0 at 400 ISO with flash

Texas Horned Lizard *Phrynosoma cornutum*
p. 48: Canon EOS 1D Mark II digital camera body and an EF 180mm f/3.5 macro lens shot at 1/1250 s at f/13.0 at 400 ISO

Texas Indigo Snake *Drymarchon corais erebennus*
p. 47: Canon EOS 1D Mark II digital camera body and an EF 500mm f/4 L IS lens shot at 1/250 s at f/8.0 at 400 ISO

Texas Spiny Lizard *Sceloporus olivaceus*
p. 36: Canon EOS 1D Mark II digital camera body and an EF 300mm f/4 L IS lens and 2X teleconverter shot at 1/200 s at f/18.0 at 400 ISO with flash

Texas Tortoise *Gopherus berlandieri*
p. 100–101: Canon EOS 3 camera body and an EF 180mm f/3.5 macro lens on Fuji Velvia film pushed one stop; unknown shutter speed and aperture

Thornbush Dasher *Micrathyria hagenii*
p.16: Canon EOS 1D Mark II digital camera body and an EF 300mm f/4 L IS lens and 2X teleconverter shot at 1/250 s at f/18.0 at 400 ISO with flash

Toothpick Grasshopper *Achurum sumichrasti*
p. 79: Canon EOS 10D digital camera body and an EF 70–200mm f/2.8 L IS lens and 2X teleconverter shot at 1/125 s at f/18.0 at 400 ISO with flash

Tufted Flycatcher *Mitrephanes phaeocercus*
p.9: Canon T90 camera body and Canon FD 400mm f/4.5 lens shot on Kodachrome 200 film; unknown shutter speed and aperture

Turkey Vulture *Cathartes aura*
p. 63: Canon EOS 10D digital camera body and an EF 600mm f/4 L IS lens shot at 1/640 s at f/11.0 at 400 ISO

Varied Bunting *Passerina versicolor*
p. 112: Canon EOS 1D Mark II digital camera body and EF 500mm f/4 L IS lens and 2X teleconverter shot at 1/200 s at f/8.0 at 400 ISO

Variegated Fritillary *Euptoieta claudia*
p.22: Canon EOS 10D digital camera body and an EF 70–200mm f/2.8 L IS lens and 2X teleconverter shot at 1/200 s at f/22.0 at 400 ISO with flash

Verdin *Auriparus flaviceps*
p. 92: Canon EOS 1D Mark II digital camera body and an EF 600mm f/4 L IS lens and 2X teleconverter shot at 1/1250 s at f/8.0 at 400 ISO

Vine Sphinx *Eumorpha vitis*
p. 76: Canon EOS 1D Mark II digital camera body and an EF 300mm f/4 L IS lens and 2X teleconverter shot at 1/125 s at f/13.0 at 400 ISO with flash

Western Diamond-backed Rattlesnake *Crotalus atrox*
p.20: Canon EOS 1D Mark II digital camera body and an EF 70–200mm f/2.8 L IS lens and 1.4X teleconverter shot at 1/125 s at f/22.0 at 400 ISO with flash

p. 46: Canon EOS 1D Mark II digital camera body and EF 70–200mm f/2.8 L IS lens and 2X teleconverter shot at 1/125 s at f/13.0 at 400 ISO with flash

White Moths (no common name) *Anacamptodes* sp. and *Idaea* sp.
p. 77, top: Canon EOS 1D Mark II digital camera body and an EF 180mm f/3.5 macro lens shot at 1/200 s at f/32.0 at 400 ISO with flash

White-crowned Sparrow *Zonotrichia leucophrys*
p. 54: Canon EOS 1D Mark II digital camera body and an EF 600mm f/4 L IS lens and 2X teleconverter shot at 1/1600 s at f/8.0 at 400 ISO

White-striped Longtail *Chiodes catillus*
p. 71, bottom: Canon EOS 1D Mark II digital camera body and an EF 300mm f/4 L IS lens and 2X teleconverter shot at 1/250 s at f/20.0 at 400 ISO with flash

White-tailed Deer *Odocoileus virginianus*
p. 98, right: Canon T-90 camera body and Sigma 500mm f/4.5 lens on Fuji Sensia film; unknown shutter speed and aperture

White-tailed Hawk *Buteo albicaudatus*
p. 118: Canon EOS 3 camera body and an EF 600mm f/4 lens and 2X teleconverter on Fuji Velvia film pushed one stop; unknown shutter speed and aperture

pp. 118–19: Canon EOS 1D Mark II digital camera body and an EF 500mm f/4 L IS lens and 1.4X teleconverter shot at 1/4000 s at f/5.6 at 400 ISO

Wild Turkey *Meleagris gallopavo*
p. 98, left: Canon EOS 1D Mark II digital camera body and an EF 600mm f/4 L IS lens shot at 1/1600 s at f/8.0 at 400 ISO

p. 122: Canon EOS 1D Mark II digital camera body and an EF 500mm f/4 L IS lens and 2X teleconverter shot at 1/500 s at f/13.0 at 400 ISO

Wolf Spider Family Lycosidae (unknown genus or species)
p. 96: Canon EOS 1D Mark III digital camera body and an EF 300mm f/4 L IS lens and 2X teleconverter shot at 1/160 s at f/22.0 and 320 ISO with flash

p. 97: Canon EOS 1D Mark III digital camera body and an EF 180mm f/3.5 macro lens and 2X teleconverter shot at 1/100 s at f/32.0 at 320 ISO with flash

Wood Duck *Aix sponsa*
p. 110: Canon EOS 1D Mark II digital camera body and EF 500mm f/4 L IS lens and 1.4X teleconverter shot at 1/640 s at f/11.0 at 400 ISO

p. 111: Canon EOS 1D Mark II digital camera body and EF 500mm f/4 L IS lens and 1.4X teleconverter shot at 1/640 s at f/11.0 at 400 ISO

Yellow Warbler *Dendroica petechia*
p. 85: Canon EOS 1D Mark II digital camera body and an EF 500mm f/4 L IS lens and 2X teleconverter shot at 1/250 s at f/8.0 at 400 ISO

Yellow-throated Warbler *Dendroica dominica*
p. 84: Canon EOS 1D Mark II digital camera body and an EF 600mm f/4 L IS lens and 1.4X teleconverter shot at 1/200 s at f/8.0 at 400 ISO

Index

acknowledgments, 123
Alligator, American, 34, 37, 63–64
American Birds, 10, 28
Armadillo, Nine-banded, 23
Arnold, Keith, 10
Arvin, John, 10
Austin Police Department, 11, 28

Bat, Pallid, 34, 36
Bee, Cactus, 74
Beetle: Blister, 109; Longhorn, 49
Birder's Guide to Texas (Kutac), 11
Bird Records Committee (American Birding Association), 10–11
Bittern: American, 30, 31; Least, 52
Bunting: Painted, 18–19, 112; Varied, 112

Caracara, Crested, 14, 24–26, 103
Cardinal, Northern, 58
Clark, Kathy Adams, 14, 16, 22
Clubtail, Plains, 72
Cowbird, Bronzed, 55
Coyote, 34, 35

Damsel, Painted, 73
Dancer: Dusky, 66; Springwater, 17, 20
Dasher: Blue, 69; Thornbush, 16, 17
Deer, White-tailed, 98, 99
Ditto, Larry, 12, 13, 14, 29–30
Dove, Inca, 88–89
Duck: Masked, 8–9; Wood, 110–11

Egret, Cattle, 53
Emanuel, Victor, 10, 28
Eubanks, Ted, 10

Falcon, Aplomado, 114–15
Finch, House, 89
Fly, Robber, 22, 74, 107
Flycatcher: Brown-crested, 87; Tufted, 8–9
Focus on the Wild (Valley Land Fund), 12, 14
Fritillary: Gulf, 71; Variegated, 22

Grasshopper: Horse Lubber, 78; Toothpick, 79
Grebe, Least, 82–83
Ground Squirrel, Mexican, 99
Gull: Black-tailed, 8–9; Laughing, 2–3, 4

Harrier, Northern, 102–03
Hawk: Harris's, 36, 38–39; White-tailed, 118–19
Hummingbird: Black-chinned, 59, 113; Buff-bellied, 59; Ruby-throated, 59

Jackrabbit, Black-tailed, 30, 34
Jewelwing, Ebony, 42–43

Kiskadee, Great, 91
Kutac, Ed, 11

Lasley, Greg: acknowledgments by, 123; comments by, 27–30, 32, 34, 36, 39; introduction to work of, 7–22; wildlife photo information, 124–27
Lizard: Texas Horned, 48; Texas Spiny, 36
Longtail, White-striped, 71

Mallard, 65
Mantis: Brunner's, 105; Praying, 108
Mockingbird, Northern, 114
Morgan, Jim, 10
Moth, Luna, 77

North American Birds, 10

Owl, Burrowing, 50–51
Oystercatcher, American, 14, 15

Pelican: American White, 6–7, 14; Brown, 60
Pennant: Banded, 42; Halloween, 40; Red-tailed, 40–41
Peterson, Roger Tory, 10
Philmont Scout Ranch, 27
Prairie-Chicken, Lesser, 80–81
Pulich, Warren, 10
Pygmy-Owl, Ferruginous, 57
Pyrrhuloxia, 90

Queen, 104

Rat, Hispid Cotton, 4
Rattlesnake: Canebrake, 27; Rock, 36, 116–17; Western Diamond-backed, 20, 21, 46
Redhead, 65
Ringtail: Blue-faced, 44; Eastern, 45

Saddlebags, Black, 74–75
Sanderling, 13, 14

Scorpion, 100
Screech-Owl, Eastern, 21
Setwing, Mayan, 5, 20, 36
Sexton, Chuck, 10
Skimmer: Flame, 68; Roseate, 68
Slider, Red-eared, 30
Snake: Northern Cat-eyed, 47; Texas Indigo, 47
Snout, American, 70
Sparrow: Botteri's, 12; White-crowned, 54
Sphinx, Vine, 76
Spider: Fishing, 67; Long-jawed, 66; Wolf, 96–97
spider web, 32
Spoonbill, Roseate, 61
Swallow, Barn, 14, 16

Tern, Forster's, 64
Texas Bird Records Committee (Texas Ornithological Society), 10
Texas Highways Magazine, 28
Texas Parks and Wildlife Magazine, 28
Tityra, Masked, 8–9
Tortoise, Texas, 100–102
Tucker, Jim, 10
Turkey, Wild, 98, 121, 122
Tveten, John & Gloria, 7–22

U.S. Air Force, 28

Valley Land Fund Wildlife Photo Contest, 7, 12, 29–30
Verdin, 92
Victor Emanuel Nature Tours, 11, 28–29
Vireo, Black-capped, 56
Vulture, Turkey, 63

Warbler: Blackpoll, 95; Golden-cheeked, 11, 12, 28, 32, 120–21; Mangrove, 85; Prairie, 93; Prothonotary, 54; Red-faced, 123; Yellow-throated, 84–85; Yellow, 85
Wasp, Paper, 106, 107
Whistling-Duck, Black-bellied, 65
Wildlife Conservation, 28
wildlife photo index, 22, 124–27
Wren, Bewick's, 94

Yellowthroat, Common, 86

ISBN-13: 978-1-60344-057-8
ISBN-10: 1-60344-057-7

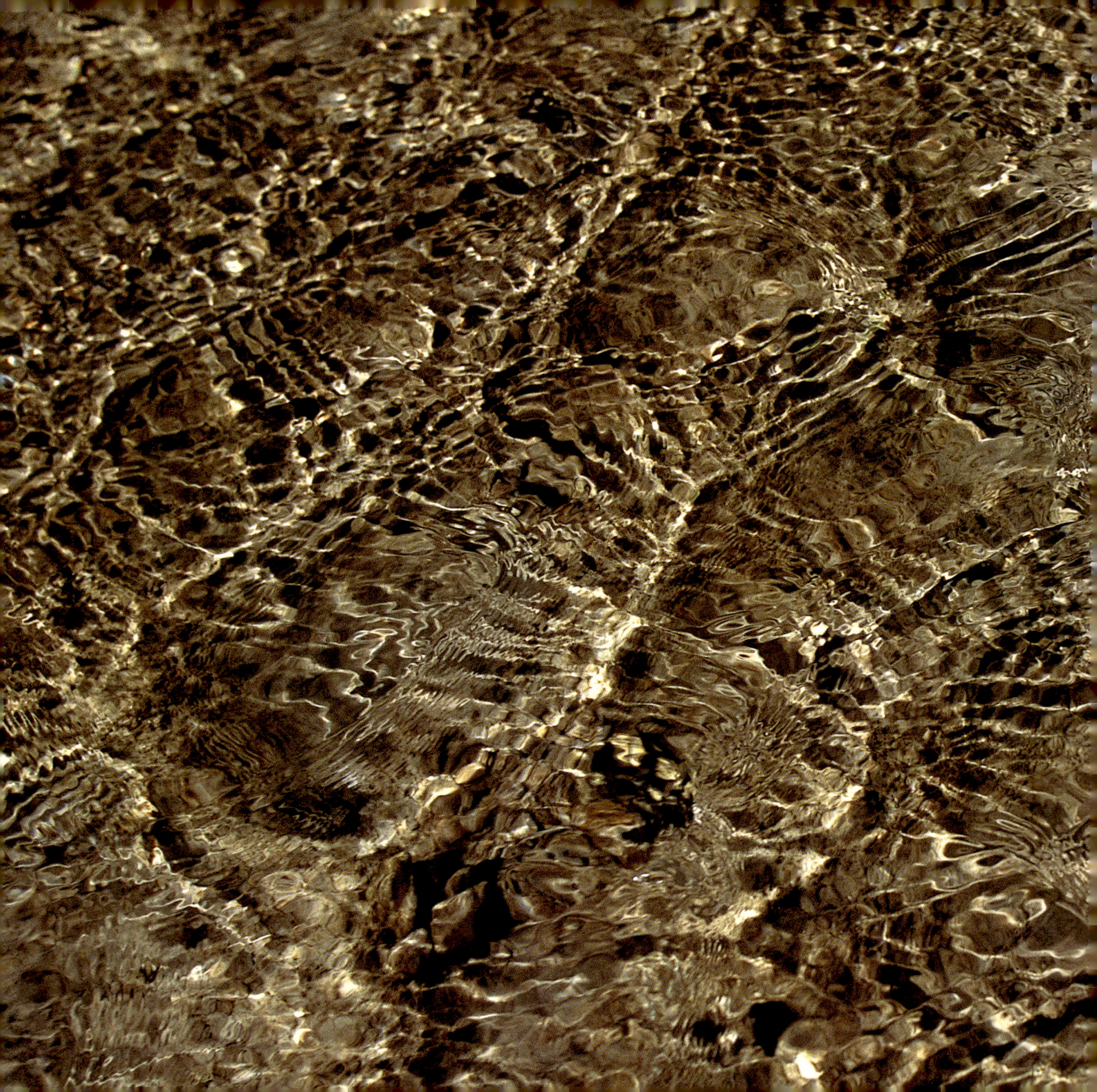